WORFIELD

The History of a Shropshire Parish from Earliest Times

Jane Smith

Share Our Past Ltd 2017

Bob Parton and Bonnie at Tasley. Bob later farmed at Hartlebury in Worfield Parish and became well known as a sheep shearer and hedge layer.

ISBN 978-0-9573505-2-6

Copyright © Share Our Past Ltd. 2017

All rights reserved. No part of the book may be reproduced without the author's written permission

Share Our Past Ltd, Perton, Staffordshire, WV6 7UE

Contents

Introduction	1
Chapter 1 Early History	3
chapter 2 Early Medieval	17
chapter 3 Sixteenth Century	40
chapter 4 Seventeenth century	52
chapter 5 Eighteenth century	78
chapter 6 Nineteenth century	100
chapter 7 Twentieth Century	139
chapter 8 Walks	174

Appendix 1 Inhabitants

1327 Lay Subsidy	182
1524 Lay Subsidy	182&183
1573 Forest of Morfe return	184
1583 List of Tenants	185
1600 Hundred of Brimstree return	186
1672 Hearth Tax	187
1788 Owners and Occupiers of land	188

Appendix 2 Maps

Ewke	194
The Forest of Morfe 1582	195
Roughton & Barnley 1613	196
Rudge Heath	197
Barnley 1613	198
Burcott, Swancott & Hoccom 1613	199
Bromley 1613	200
Rudge Heath (part) & Crows Heath	201
East of the Parish drawn 1839	202
Newton, Nineteenth Century	203

Illustrations

The Miller, G. A. Catford. Front Cover
The River Worfe and Worfield Church. Back Cover
Bob Parton at Tasley, courtesy of Geoff Parton
Worfield Parish map
Worfield Main Street 1
River Worfe at Rindleford 3
Flints 5
The Walls map 6
The Walls Hillfort 7
Iron Age cosmetic mortar 7
Ramparts at Chesterton 8
Steps from Littlegain 8
Roman brooch 9
Saxon artefacts -sceatta, strap end & pinhead 10
Saxon Placenames map 12
Hallon Castle map 13
Worfield Church and Castle Hill from the Sonde 14
Cave by St Peter's Well 15
Roman Brooch and coin 16
Sheep were a key factor in the wealth of Worfield in medieval times 17
Seal attached to the Worfield Charter 19
The Old Grammar School & Court House 24
The Old Rectory (Lower Hall) and the New Parsonage 25
Stone coffin 26
Worfield Picture Doors 27
Worfield and Swedish Picture Doors 28
The Worfield Chest 29
The Old Lodge map 30
Harness pendant 32
Edward I silver penny 32
Seal 32
Papal Bulla 32
Worfield Church exterior prior to its Restoration. Copyright: Lichfield Cathedral 39
Worfield Church interior prior to its Restoration. Copyright: Lichfield Cathedral 39
Tombstone of Sir John Lye 40
John Talbot vervel 44
Hallon Hall, the home of the Bromley family 45

Sir George and Dame Jane Bromley tomb 45
Baker's Cottage, Bromley 46
Spindle Whorl 49
Lead tokens 49
Lower Hall, Tailors Platform 51
Crossed Swords at Hayes Bank, Stableford, courtesy of Peter Hollingsworth 54
William Pendrill and the Boscobel Oak, courtesy of Roger Pendrill 60
Weight 67
Commonwealth coin 67
Cloth seal 68
Charles I coin 68
Bradney Farm 77
Main Street Worfield 1906, courtesy of Eileen Tracey 78
Enclosures map 83
Crows Heath Enclosure map 85
Davenport House, courtesy of Eileen Tracey 87
Davenport House interior 90
Crotal Bell 91
Pattens 91
Barn at Lower Burcote 99
Birthplace of William Hardwicke at Allscott 100
New Farmhouse at Allscott 101
Worfield Mill 102
Chesterton mill map 103
Worfield mill map 104
Rindleford Mill 105
Rindleford Mill 106
Rindleford Bridge, courtesy of Eileen Tracey 106
Burcote Bridge & Burcote Cottages 107
Worfield Workhouse 110
Toll House by the Worfe Bridge 113
Toll House by the Wheel Inn postmarked 1907, courtesy of Eileen Tracey 113
Map of part of the Stourbridge Turnpike Road 115
B4176, The Rabbit Run before widening, courtesy of Bruce Gilson 116
The Broad Bridge at Stableford 117
Road to the ferry map 119
Cave Holloway 120
Bosun's Whistle 120
Worfield School 121

Church and Worfield School Staff 1887 123
Roughton Cottage Sale Particulars 1879 125
Worfield Grammar School Advertisement 126
The Rev T. W. Turner 127
Roughton Grammar School as a private house 127
Crucifixes 130
Valentine Vickers ox horn 130
Derelict Building at the Batch 137
Worfield Village circa 1850 map 138
The Old Blacksmith's Shop in Hallon, courtesy of Eileen Tracey 139
Wheel Inn, Worfield, courtesy of Eileen Tracey 140
Albrighton Hounds at the Wheel, 1909 courtesy of Bob Adams 140
Walter Bishop, courtesy of Geoff Tomlinson 142
Jeremiah Mapp, courtesy of the Mapp family 142
Sibell Corbett, courtesy of Val and Peter Williams & Sue Riches 145
Interior of Recreation Room 1915, courtesy of the late Jeff Hughes 148
Nursing Staff at Worfield VAD Hospital, courtesy of the late Jeff Hughes 149
Wyken House car taking patients for an outing, courtesy of the late Jeff Hughes 150
Harvesting at Wyken Farm, courtesy of the late Jeff Hughes 151
Frank and Rebecca Turner, courtesy of Joe Turner 153
Worfruna Garage, Wyken, courtesy of Eileen Tracey 154
Wyken and Wyken Garage 155
The Botley Family at Hartlebury Farm, courtesy of Geoff Parton and Ian Botley 156
RAF Bridgnorth Memorial 157
General Patton and Margaret Davenport at Tabley 159
Ackleton 1905 and 1910, courtesy of Chippine Breeze & Eileen Tracey 160
Worfield Home Guard, courtesy of Gail Tudor 162
Margaret and Oliver Leese cutting their wedding cake 164
Worfield Mill and Mrs Robinson's house 165
Sir Oliver Leese at home at Lower Hall 169
Rookery Cottages, Wyken, courtesy of Eileen Tracey 173
St John's Chapel Chesterton, copyright Shropshire Archives 174
Hilton looking towards the Bridge, courtesy of Bob Adams 193

Acknowledgments

So many people have helped me over the ten years it has taken me to gather the material for this book that if I begin to name everyone I am sure to miss someone out and there would be no way of making amends for such an omission. It seems like ducking the issue, which it is, but I hope you will forgive me. I am so grateful to all of you and in truth this is your book in more senses than one. I would like to thank you:

- for the photographs and information you have shared and for trusting me with your personal stories and family histories.
- for correcting me when I got things wrong and your patience when I struggled to understand.
- for encouraging me when I have flagged a little.
- for showing me round your homes and farms which I would never otherwise have seen nor understood.
- for walking round the parish with me in all weathers to try to understand the history on the ground.
- for the specialists in their field who have helped me understand artefacts and documents.

Thank you so much for all your help.

The book is dedicated to the lovely Evie, who, from her vantage point on the sofa, almost saw this project through to the end.

Preface

The Farmer
By W.D. Ehrhart

Each day I go into the fields
to see what is growing
and what remains to be done.
It is always the same thing: nothing
is growing, everything needs to be done.
Plow, harrow, disc, water, pray
till my bones ache and hands rub
blood-raw with honest labor-
all that grows is the slow
intransigent intensity of need.
I have sown my seed on soil
guaranteed by poverty to fail.
But I don't complain - except
to passersby who ask me why
I work such barren earth.
They would not understand me
if I stooped to lift a rock
and hold it like a child, or laughed,
or told them it is their poverty
I labour to relieve. For them,
I complain. A farmer of dreams
knows how to pretend. A farmer of dreams
knows what it means to be patient.
Each day I go into the fields

"The Farmer" is reprinted from *Beautiful Wreckage* by W.D. Ehrhart, Adastra Press, 1999, by kind permission of the author.

Preface

In 2007 I left Gainsborough Farm which had been my home on and off for forty years. A farm is an irreplaceable way of life, both a home and a business, and this was a dark time. Before I left my home on that day at the beginning of November, the new owners were already moving in the equipment of their business - diggers, dumpers, earthmoving equipment of all sorts. Unwittingly the property had been sold to someone who would transform the landscape by dumping vast amount of 'material.' Valleys were filled in and ancient woodland destroyed. An area which not long before had been designated by the Council as of ecological importance was now allowed to be destroyed by the same authority. Such is history and the fickleness of man.

The question was how to move forward and fill a very large hole in my life. Suddenly I had time to do what I wanted, and after a few false starts I returned to my early love of history. As an undergraduate I was introduced to the book, 'Worfield and its Townships,' by John Randall. This is an excellent book but left me feeling that there was much more to be told about Worfield. A degree in historical geography taught me the importance of landscape, primary sources and oral history in understanding the past. A spark had been lit, but in reality I knew nothing.

After a lapse of forty years I took a course in family history. This opened my mind to sources of information which I never knew existed but family history was not for me. At the same time I started a website where people could upload and share their history. Most historical material is in private hands and I thought the digital solution to sharing data would be welcomed. Unfortunately, mass enthusiasm was not the response. Individuals, groups and societies now put photographs on Facebook without a thought but in those early days of the twenty-first century the idea seemed a very alien proposition.

So it was a very despondent Jane Smith who arrived one day at the door of a little cottage near Worfield, the home of Frank Taylor. I had been told that Frank had been metal detecting in the area for many years and arguably knew more about the history of Worfield than anyone else. I suppose this made me doubly shy of meeting him but I had no reason to worry. No-one could have had a better teacher. Frank patiently displayed before me a collection of locally found artefacts, such as flints, Roman brooches, medieval coins and tokens. It was so exciting to be literally touching and feeling history. Frank died in 2013, but other excellent metal detectorists in Worfield continue to add to our understanding of the past.

While Frank was helping me to understand prehistoric Worfield I was aware that his sister was working with a group led by Sylvia Watts translating manor court rolls from Latin to English. My aim, of course, was to translate the Worfield court rolls. What I didn't know was that Worfield has an almost complete run of these documents for four hundred years. We have started early in the fourteenth century and, at the time of writing this book, about 150 rolls have been translated. Again, I was fortunate in having a great teacher. Sadly, Sylvia died in 2014 but a small group of us meet each week to carry on the work. I am truly grateful for their dedication.

All the above approaches have played their part in piecing together the history of Worfield and I hope you enjoy the book.

Preface

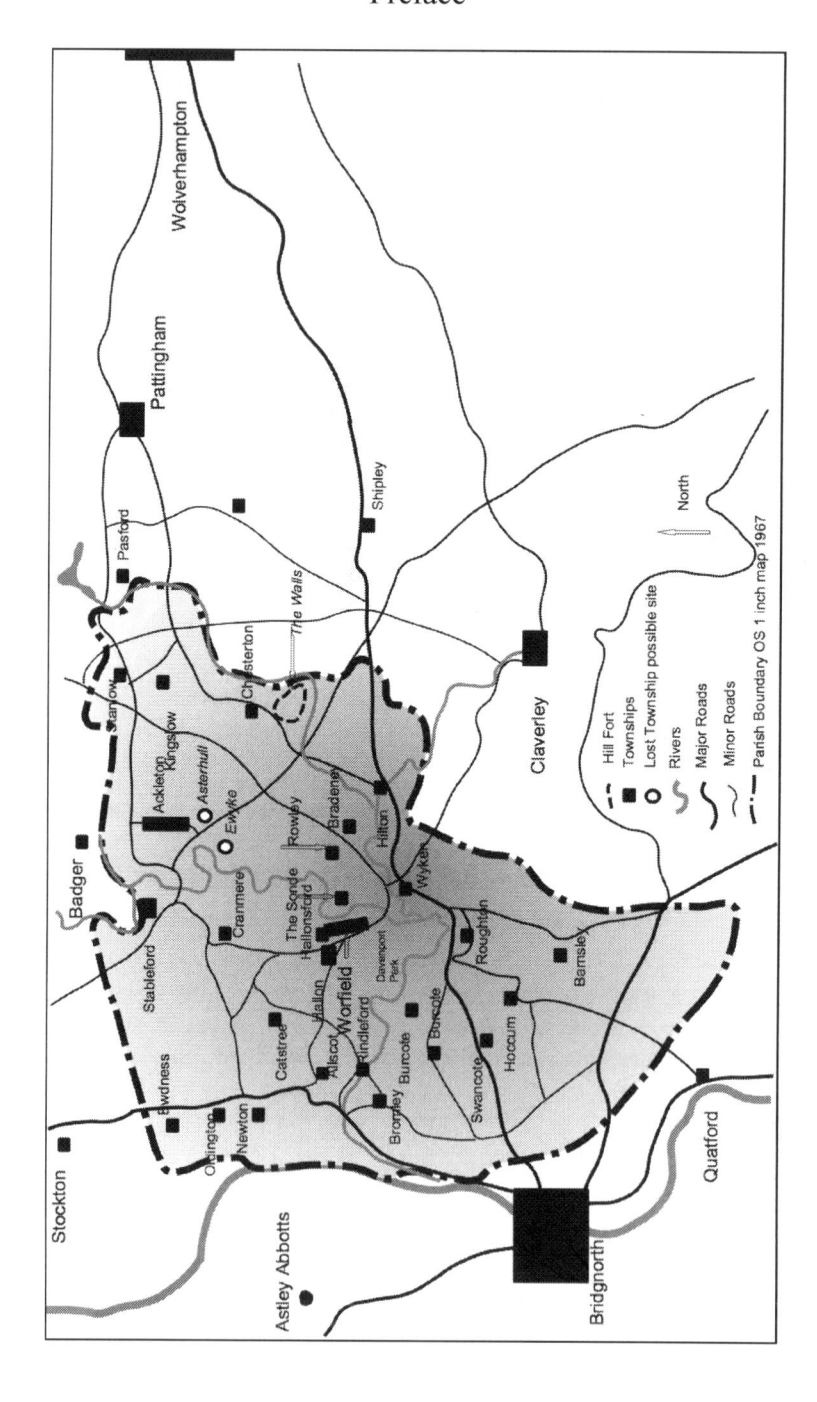

Worfield Parish. Scale: half an inch to 1 mile

Introduction

Main Street, Worfield mid twentieth century

Location of Worfield, pronunciation and spelling.
I don't imagine that many of you outside the locality will have heard of Worfield. Even those who live just a few miles away may struggle to place it. Many people will know exactly where Claverley is, but Worfield is just one of those places whose identity is much more fuzzy. Most people believe that the village of Worfield is where the Wheel Inn is situated, on the A454 from Wolverhampton to Bridgnorth. This is a logical mistake to make since the Wheel is known as the Wheel of Worfield or as it used to be known, The Wheel of Worvill. The Wheel Inn is, in fact, in the village of Wyken, not the village of Worfield. To find the village of Worfield one needs to take a turn off the main road, opposite The Wheel, at a wooden signpost. Then bear left and take the first turn right which is opposite an entrance to Davenport Park. If you are visiting outside school hours you may park your car opposite the Dog Inn. You are now in Worfield which must be one of the prettiest villages in the country and one of the least known. You may be forgiven for thinking that it is the sort of place where nothing of note happened. In a sense you may be right; ordinary people have lived their lives here, generation after generation, untouched by what was happening in the wider world.

Fascinating as the village of Worfield is, the scope of this book is wider than this, being a history of the parish of Worfield. It has been said that Worfield Parish was the second largest parish in England. I don't know whether that is true or not, but it is very large, extending to about thirty

Introduction

square miles, from Bridgnorth and the River Severn on the west to Rudge, Shipley and Claverley on the east, and from Pattingham on the north east to Quatford in the south. At the time of the Domesday Book, Worfield was in Seison Hundred in Staffordshire but then became part of Brimstree Hundred in Shropshire. The parish was in Lichfield Diocese until 1905 when it was transferred to the Diocese of Hereford. Worfield always seems to be on the edge - on the eastern boundary of Shropshire and at the extremity of whichever diocese it was in. Not least this leads to the inconvenience of chasing across different archives to find information.

Just a word on pronunciation. The first syllable of Worfield is pronounced as in work and Worksop and not as the Mor in Morville. Just to confuse matters Morville was referred to in medieval times as Morveld. The first syllable of Roughton has become generally pronounced row as in an argument but should more properly be pronounced row as in a row of seats. Sonde was sometimes written Sound or Sund so may have pronounced Sund in the same way as Cound is pronounced Cund. Woundale is similarly pronounced Wundle and not Woundale as in a wound (it was written in medieval times as Woundwall). Would that we had a clear idea of how Shrewsbury was pronounced but the spellings seems to reflect the two different ways of pronouncing the name that we have today, for example, Shrosbry and Shroughsbury. Ewyke is an odd one. Initially I tried two syllables - E-Wyke but that never seemed right. Then on old maps and in old documents I found that it was sometimes written as Yewke, Yoke or even York and so concluded that it was pronounced Yewke as in a ewe with a k on the end. A leasowe, is pronounced 'lezur' but apart from that pronunciation is pretty straightforward.

Spelling is often phonetic and so can give an indication of how people spoke. The Hermitage may be written Armitage, Oldington as Woldington, Worfield as Worvill, horses are 'osses'. 'A leaven' caused me some grief until I said it aloud and realised it was eleven. 'Whom' was another difficult word until I realised that it was home. In the Black Country home is still often pronounced 'wum' so I asume that is how Worfield people would have said it. People's names are also variable. Lee might be spelt Lea or Leigh, Haynes might be Haines or Hains, and so on. I have left the spellings as they were in the original documents rather than standardising them in the spellings of today. I felt that something would be lost in this process.

Chapter 1   Early History

The River Worfe at Rindleford

Introduction

The period before written records began is called by the rather odd name of 'prehistory,' as though there was no history before something was written down. Archaeologists, of course, know differently. In the 1960s W. G. Hoskins wrote a series of books for local historians, most notably, 'The Making of the English Landscape,' which pointed out that landscape, too, can provide evidence for man's work over the centuries. Technology has helped and hindered in this regard. The archaeological tools now at man's disposal, as well as aerial photography and sophisticated metal detectors, have helped us to understand a great deal more than our predecessors could ever have imagined. On the other hand, increasingly efficient machinery can change the surface structure of the soil, and remove traces of the past, in the blink of an eye. I have already mentioned personal experience of this at Littlegain where valleys were filled in and ancient woodlands destroyed, all with full permission from the authorities. The guilt I feel is no compensation for the landscape I unwittingly helped to destroy.

This is perhaps an appropriate point to say something about finds; artefacts such as coins, jewellery, flints and pottery. Local historians in the past tended to ignore casual finds and much information was in consequence lost to history, locked away in private collections. Thankfully that has now changed. In 1996 a new Treasure Act was passed to recognise the historical importance of all finds and not just those classed as treasure trove. A scheme called the Portable Antiquities Scheme was set up to record artefacts and the location in which they were found and to make the

Chapter 1   Early History

finds available online. All finds more than three hundred years old should be recorded in this way. By putting an artefact into a place not only can we can understand more about the local history but another dimension is added to our relationship with our ancestors. Holding a Roman brooch and admiring the workmanship is very different from reading about this in a book. Knowing that the person who made or wore such an item once walked the very same footpaths we walk today sends a tingle down the spine.

To understand the landscape of Worfield before man's intervention we need to go back to the end of the last Ice Age. As the ice retreated, the effects of glaciation would have remained. Deep, steep sided valleys, had been cut through the sandstone and piles of moraine dumped here and there. Today this gives the landscape a lumpy appearance seen very clearly at Burcote and Swancote. The meltwater created a large expanse of water, Lake Lapworth, and as the water level fell, rivers and streams flowed across the land. Much reduced in size, these streams now look out of proportion in the glaciated valleys they flow through. The initially bleak and desolate landscape was gradually clothed in vegetation and temperatures warmed. Climate had a direct effect on the growth of population. From 6,000 - 3,000 BC it was warmer than today and the rainfall may have been heavier but after 1,000 BC temperatures fell and from around AD 80 to 1200-1300 the world warmed again and civilisation prospered.

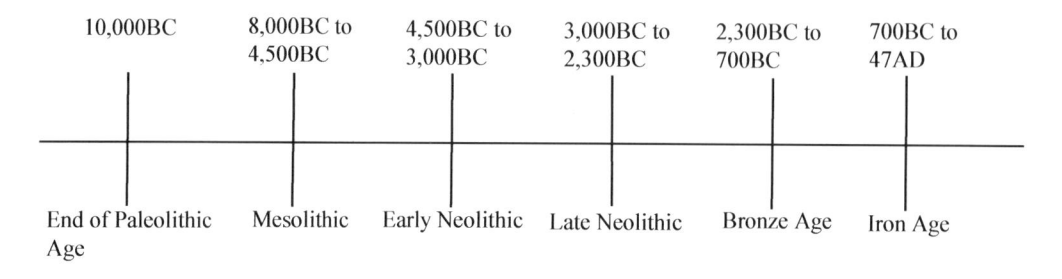

10,000BC	8,000BC to 4,500BC	4,500BC to 3,000BC	3,000BC to 2,300BC	2,300BC to 700BC	700BC to 47AD
End of Paleolithic Age	Mesolithic	Early Neolithic	Late Neolithic	Bronze Age	Iron Age

Mesolithic and Neolithic

By 6,500BC, the Mesolithic period, we have the first indication of people in Worfield. They left evidence in the form of flints, whose enduring quality makes it a good marker as regards to dates. It is found in isolated finds, in small scatters across the whole parish and in much larger agglomerations. In one such collection, in the Civil Parish of Worfield and Rudge, Frank Taylor found 400 flints in all stages of being worked into tools, such as blades, awls, scrapers, and arrowheads[1].

We have yet to fully understand these mesolithic and neolithic settlements but from the flints found we can see an extensive coverage across the Parish. The early settlers may have come from the east or south east and have been nomadic, visiting Worfield at certain times of the year. Which

Chapter 1   Early History

areas of Worfield they favoured it is hard to be definitive about. We have find locations but of course we can't be certain that people were not also in areas where no finds have been made.

In the Neolithic Period, 4,000BC to 2,500BC, farming began to replace a hunter-gatherer lifestyle. Crude tools and semi-domesticated pigs were used to turn over the soil and slowly the landscape would have changed. Aerial photographs indicate man's work in Worfield at these very early times in the form of enclosures and pit alignments and show a continuity of settlement from the Mesolithic age through the Neolithic period, the Bronze Age, and into the Iron Age

A variety of flint tools, arrowheads, scrapers, awls and blades

Iron Age
Flints provides glimpses of prehistory but the hill fort at Chesterton is a visible reminder of early settlement in Worfield. Chesterton is now a hamlet, but once it was a hill fort of over 20 acres lying just to the south of where the village now stands. Hill forts were fortified enclosures located, unsurprisingly, on hill tops, and circumscribed by one or more lines of defensive earthworks. Large enough to support permanent occupation, The Walls is a rarity amongst hill forts and has been designated of national importance, yet we know very little about it. There have been no

Chapter 1　　　　　　　　　　Early History

archaeological digs and very few finds, all from the Roman period, rather than the Iron Age. The status of scheduled monument confers some restrictions. Metal detecting and digging are not permitted, nor the removal of surface finds.

The people who lived at The Walls between 600BC and 47 AD were part of the Cornovii, a Celtic tribe whose name may have meant people of the horn. The tribe lived in North Staffordshire, Shropshire and Cheshire. Their economy was mainly based on agriculture and they bred and traded cattle. They also controlled the south Cheshire salt-making industry which gave them considerable wealth. The Walls was on the south eastern edge of Cornovii territory and part of a network of hillforts in Shropshire which included Titterstone Clee, the Wrekin, Oswestry and Weston under Redcastle. The strategic significance of the location is not clear but the advantages of the site are obvious. Flat land and light soil made for easy cultivation and the site was perfect for settlement. Streams and springs provided a constant water supply and naturally steep slopes on three sides made the area easy to defend. Although there is now no trace of the houses the Cornovii lived in, other hill forts have shown that people lived in oval or circular houses which were often clustered along streets. The streets were probably paved and there may also have been raised granaries, fences, hearths and ovens. We know that the Cornovii were skilled weavers and proud of their appearance. They applied powder, which they had ground, to their faces and loved bright colours. The women wore their hair in two plaits. At the Manor House Museum in Ilkley there is a tombstone on which is carved the image of a 30 year old Cornovian woman called Verdica.

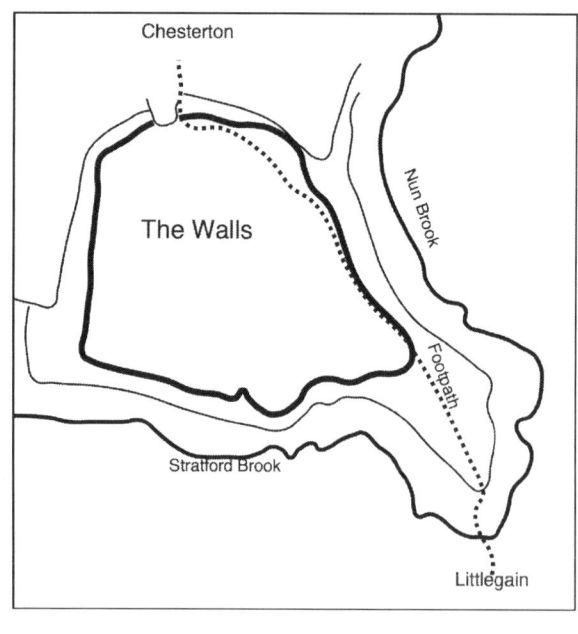

Scale 1 inch to 250 yards

Chapter 1   Early History

Why 'The Walls,' you may ask, since as you look around there are no walls visible? In the nineteenth century, a Victorian antiquarian, J. B. Blakeway, noted that there was a wall which was partly embanked around the hillfort. In width this created a barrier some 2.5-3.5 metres in width and almost a metre in height. The core of the wall was river pebbles and this was faced with sandstone blocks. The rampart was topped with similar stone material.

Approaching from either Chesterton or Littlegain you will be using one of the original entrances. From Littlegain the approach is via steps believed to have been used during the construction of the hillfort. Climbing up these steps you get a very good idea of how steeply the land drops away from the flat interior and how easily defended it would have been. The entrance from Littlegain gave access to a flat area of land which was an annexe to the hill fort itself. The Chesterton entrance was the main entrance. When approaching from this direction you may feel rather underwhelmed at the expanse of flat land in front of you which reveals nothing of the bustling iron age town this would once have been. Gone are the people, their huts and roads, invisible is the smoke which would have risen from the fires and silent are the sheep and cattle which would have grazed here. The banks and ditches which would have been such a striking feature, have softened over time, banks eroded and ditches infilled, and both are now covered with vegetation. We must recreate the picture of life from the landscape itself and a few Iron Age finds from nearby, such as cosmetic pestles and mortars and clothes fastenings. We long for more.

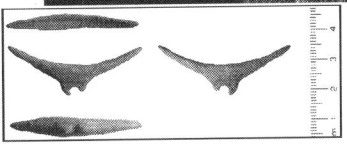

The extent of the hill fort as seen from the Chesterton entrance. Trees indicate the boundary 2014.

Cosmetic mortar, sometimes known as a woad grinder, found in the parish of Rudge. This is half of a pestle & mortar. 300BC-AD200. (HESH-ED9F96.)
Image courtesy of Portable Antiquities Scheme

Chapter 1   Early History

Right: Steps from Littlegain to The Walls 2014.
Above: Mason's marks 2016

Ramparts near the main entrance which have become softened over the years

Chapter 1   Early History

Iron Age occupation of Worfield was not restricted to the Walls. Aerial photographs have revealed enclosures near Ewdness, and at Stanmore, the Hermitage Farm and Cranmere.

Roman Worfield
In AD47 the Romans invaded Britain and marched westward to the Cornovian capital, Viroconium. From the Greensforge camps, near Swindon in Staffordshire, they would have gone along what is now the B4176 and past The Walls which they may have used as a temporary marching camp. At one time there was a certainty that the Romans used The Walls as a marching camp but more recently this has been toned down to a probability. The reason for this is that the finds, a few coins and a gold ring with an inset stone, are not thought conclusive evidence of Roman occupation. Mary Foster nee Bradburn, whose family still farm in Chesterton, remembers that a number of broken fibulae were found in the Nun Brook (see page 6), once called Wall Brook, when the stream was straightened in the mid twentieth century, but even this may not be proof of Roman occupation. Having said that, there has been no attempt to find out more by any archaeological digs, and much evidence has probably now been lost by ploughing and stone removal.

The Romans were in England for around 350 years and one can imagine that they would have intermarried amongst the native population. Many would have stayed after the Roman armies left. The sheer number of coins and other artefacts found across the parish are testimony to a Roman presence but the legacy on the ground is not easy to see. Romans are associated with road building and the B4176 from Upper Ludstone towards Stableford was certainly a route used by the Romans as their armies marched from Greensforge. Another Roman route is thought to have gone through Roughton and Swancote and on towards Bridgnorth but whether the Romans built these roads, or improved what was already there, it is hard to say. Some roads may date from as far back as Neolithic times.

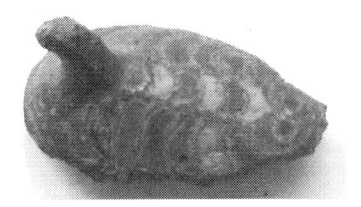

Roman zoomorphic duck brooch. Cast copper alloy, enamelled. The brooch is in vibrant colours and measures 7.88mm by 5.1mm. Estd date AD100-200
Portable Antiquities Scheme number: HESH-ED64C4
Finder Frank Taylor. Found in the parish of Pattingham and Patshull

Chapter 1   Early History

The Dark Ages

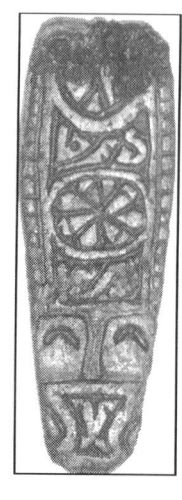

Silver sceatta AD680-710
HESH-110A96
Found by Frank Taylor.

These images are reproduced courtesy of the Portable Antiquities Scheme

Copper alloy strap end, partly silvered
AD 800-900
WMID-DFCCD4

Cast copper alloy pinhead
42.6mm by 34mm AD700-900
HESH-543615
Found by Frank Taylor

    The Dark Ages are a confusing period of about 600 years when there was an assimilation of Germanic (Saxon) people from the East, and then of Nordic people from the North. The variety of art forms shown in the metal detected finds above indicates different cultural influences. The sceatta, a coin from the Dorestad area in Lower Saxony is a rare find in Shropshire. The pin head is from the Hiberno-Norse people who may have come up the River Severn.

    There is one find which has been lost but may well have dated from this period. Hardwicke describes it as follows[2]. It was found when some drains were being dug in about 1787, *8ft down, on a field at Rowley and contiguous to Wolpheresford, near Hallonsford*

It resembled the skin of an animal as a thong with small round pieces of gold attached, with a variety of hieroglyphics eg sun, moon, battle axes, chariot wheels, depicted. It was found by a man employed digging drains and the man gave it to the vicar, the Rev Henry Bromwich who didn't know what it was and gave it back to the man. It was years after that Bromwich found out that the sun was the year, the moon the month. The vicar tried to get it back but the man, thinking it to be of no value, gave it to some children of the hayens to play with and that was that ...it was called a memory belt.

Chapter 1 — Early History

At first glance we might despair that the Dark Ages tell us little about the history of Worfield but there is more evidence than we might at first think. We know from the Anglo Saxon Chronicles that in 896 the Danes came to Quatford and over-wintered there before they moved on. The English must have been very relieved when they eventually left the area. The Chronicle account, according to Horovitz, records that, *By the mercy of God, the army had not utterly crushed the English people* [who] *were much more seriously afflicted in those three years by the mortality of cattle and men, and most of all in that many of the best king's thegns* [elite warriors] *who were in the land died in those three years*[3].

The Saxon legacy is also evident in field and place names and a settlement pattern of isolated farmsteads which became small villages. Margaret Gelling's[4] guidance on the Saxon origins of many of Worfield's place names is used in the map overleaf. One can never be certain of the origins of place names and I am sure as we learn more we may come to some different conclusions. Catstree may have been significant in Saxon times as an assembly place, Catt being a person's name and trēow. The latter could be translated tree but it could also mean an agreement hence the place where an agreement or pledge is made. The same form is seen in Oswestry and Brimstree. This would certainly fit in with Catstree's central location within the Manor of Worfield.

Ewdness is another odd name with two very different possibilities. The first is that it came from Anglo Saxon ēow meaning sheep, it could also be your or yew, and ness meaning a cliff or ridge. An alternative possibility is that it is from the Welsh. Gelling doesn't favour the Celtic, dinas, a fortified settlement, but as late as the fifteenth century Ewdness was written Eudinas in the manor court rolls, so it seems a possible derivation. Ewyke, now lost, and not to be confused with Wyken, could have taken its name from the Anglo Saxon, wīc, for a dwelling or it could have been occupational. The Hwicce, who lived along the banks of the River Severn near Worcester, wove rushes and reeds. Is it a coincidence that rushes still grow on the marshy area alongside the Worfe at Ewyke?

Worfield's name, Saxon in origin, is thought to come from the Worfe's wandering nature, frequently flooding and wandering onto land on either side of its normal course. On the other hand there is a Worfelden in Germany which does not have a meandering river as far as I can see. One suggestion is that it comes from wor meaning marshy and feld or veld meaning open land. In fourteenth century court rolls Worfield is written Worfeld. The first syllable may have been ur and a w put in front of the vowel as it often was, for example, Oldington being written Woldington. The description may therefore be of the place, marshy land, which then gave its name to the river, rather than the other way round. We see this elsewhere in the parish. Stratford, for example, the place where the stream crosses the road, gives its name to the brook itself, Stratford Brook.

Chapter 1   Early History

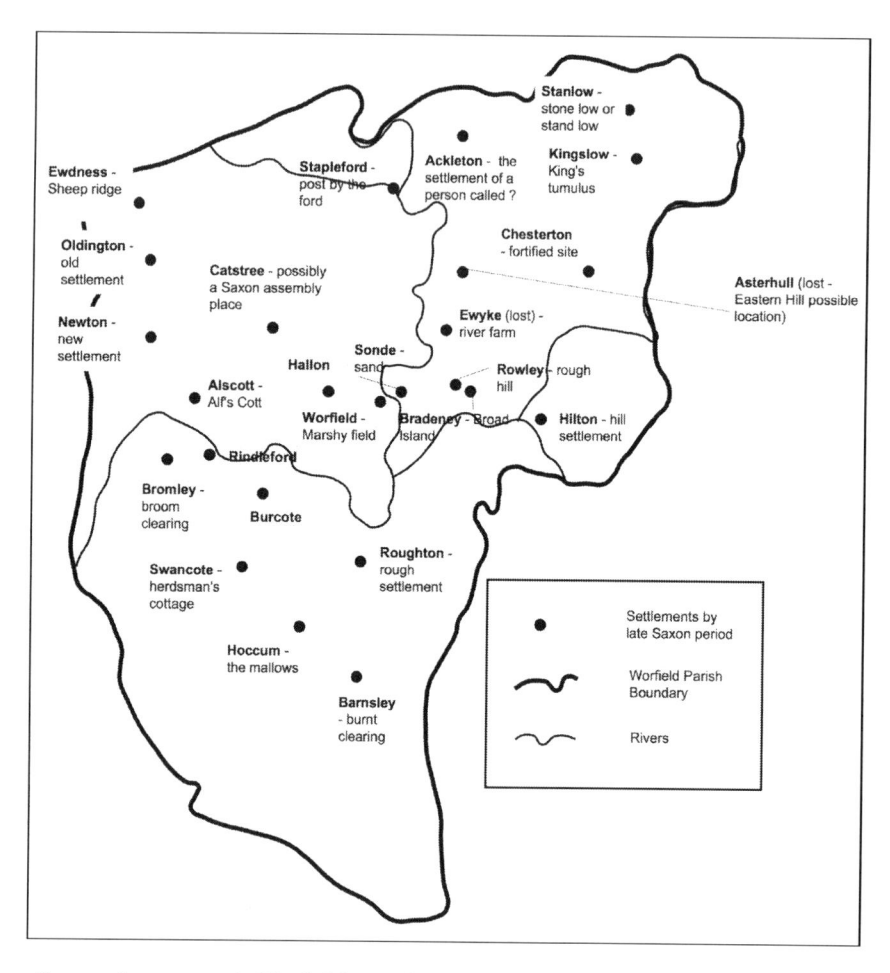

Saxon place names in Worfield Parish

Perhaps the most tantalising of Worfield's Saxon history is the prospect that there was a castle at Hallon, on the hill near Hallonsford. Hardwicke believed that Queen Ethelflaed (who died in 918) stayed at Hallon while the fortification on Panpudding Hill was being built. Whether that was so, or not, it would make sense for a fortification to be built here in Hallon as the site has good views to the north, the direction from which the enemy was likely to approach. Hardwicke, born in 1772, further believed that a castle was built by Wulfric Spot (died 1004) to protect a crossing point of the Worfe at Wolferesford (Hallonsford). This was nearly a hundred years after Queen Ethelflaed. It would be lovely to know where Hardwicke's evidence came from but sadly he doesn't quote his sources.

Chapter 1   Early History

- *On Castle Hill. several small strips were granted to the lower peasantry. It continued to be mentioned up to the time of the first court rolls in the reign of Edward III* [1328]
- *1329 Matilda of the castle died seized of a cottage here.*
- *1334 Robert New was presented to the court for unjustly throwing up a certain ditch at the castle in Hale for which he was fined by the jury*
- *1337 Thomas de Rowlowe was admitted to a pleck of land on castle hill 40 ft long and 30 ft wide.*
- *In (1341) John de Wynneswanstone and Alice his wife surrendered a cottage and curtilage in a place called hale on the castel hul [hill] to the use of Simon de Whiteby.*
- *1 Henry 4 (1399/1400) Dawkeyn de Oken and Ann his wife surrendered 2 cottages in Hallon near to the fortification (the castle thus being noticed) to the use of Roger Jones and Edith his wife.*

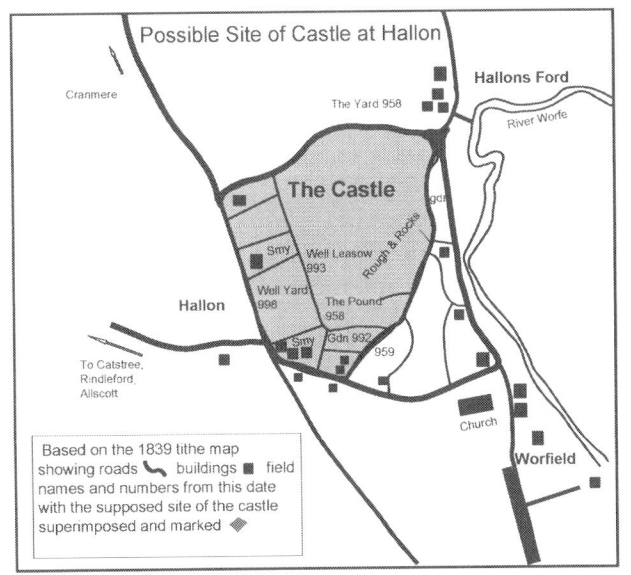

Scale: 200 yards to 1 inch

Hardwicke bemoans the fact that all evidence of a castle has now been lost, having been replaced by the parish pound which according to the Constables' Accounts was built between 1600 and 1650.

Long has its solitary site been enclosed with a rugged and pitiful stone wall, after the repeated and unheeded outrages and expoliations of ignorance and apathy had been committed upon it, being now consigned to the ignoble, debased and brutal purpose of the parish pinfold. A circumscribed enclosure, to secure such animals which had been trespassing upon their neighbours' lands, or found upon the public roads, all trace and discovery among the community, of the interesting and traditionary details of former times, occurrences and events, having been sunk and lost in oblivion.

Chapter 1　　　　　　　　Early History

Castle Hill

Looking towards Worfield Church and Castle Hill from The Sonde

When we think of a castle today we usually visualise a castellated stone fortification. It is possible that this area, which can be approached down Pound Lane, may have been the site of the original settlement at Hallon, although we have no definite evidence. Nor do we know exactly what the castle might have looked like. The Anglo Saxon word 'Castel,' has a variety of meanings, apart from what we would understand as a castle today, including a village, a fortified house and a walled enclosure.

Writing of the nearby area of Masserdine (erdine being an early clearance and Maz/Mass, a maple tree, perhaps) Hardwicke again sees a Saxon connection in the name of a ford near Hallonsford, Wolpheresford. It is very useful to have a record of these old names which have now been forgotten but whether Hardwicke is correct in connecting the name to Wulfhere is not certain.

To the ancient word Masserdine at which we are struck by its singularity, the Saxon intruders added feld or veld, ...now written Masserdine field. This is to the south of Hallon and adjoining *to the NE the castle hill and its opposite ford called Wolpheresford, the name taken from Wolpher (now called Wulfhere), King of Mercia who began his reign in 659, died 675, a reign of extermination, bloodshed and robbery in conflict with the Britons.*

St Peter's Church, Worfield, is believed to have been founded by Earl Leofric, husband of Lady Godiva. The first church may have been wooden and replaced by the current sandstone building. The location of the Church may strike you as odd. Built in a valley, St Peter's was hidden away and at a later date a huge spire was added to make the church visible from a distance. The reason for the choice of location may lie in the proximity to St Peter's Well. Some have thought that the Well was within the Churchyard but it is more likely to have been a short distance from the Church, at a

Chapter 1   Early History

place called Wolstone or Walstone. If you walk from the Church away from the village of Worfield, shortly after the junction of a road on your left, you will find exposed sandstone rock and a number of caves, once inhabited, (caves^ occur throughout the Parish) and what is thought to be St Peter's Well.

Cave by St Peter's Well.
From Worfield on the Worfe by S. B. James (Bemrose & Sons 1873)

Chapter 1   Early History

Lost and Found

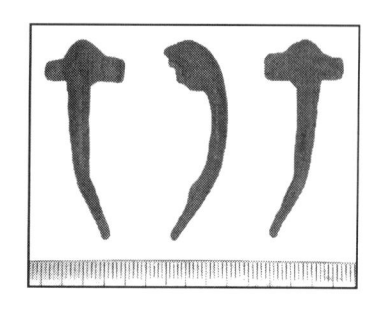

Roman Brooch AD 43-200.
WMID-9363B2

Nummus of Constantine I struck in London
AD 307-318 HESH-1145E3
Images courtesy of Portable Antiquities Scheme

References
1. Taylor, F. and Smith, J., A Life's Work (Share Our Past Ltd 2012) ISBN 978 0 9573505 0 2
2. Collections for a History of Worfield by William Hardwicke. (held at the William Salt Library 351/40). See also Hardwicke of Co. Stafford, 1878.
3. Horovitz, D., The Battle of Tettenhall 910 AD and Other Researches (David Horovitz 2010) ISBN 978-0-9550309-1-8
4. Gelling, M. (in collaboration with the late H.D.G. Foxall), The Place Names of Shropshire Part 6 (Nottingham English Place Name Society) ISBN-10:0 904889 83 1
5. Worfield Court Roll 5586/1/240. (Shropshire Archives)

Notes
A In 1809, John Bell Hardwick of Burcott was removing some soil covering an overhanging rock above a meadow and uncovered a cave with the bones of several people, including a child, a sheep and a pig. There were three human skulls on a ledge at the back of the cave and from the state of the teeth they were thought to be the skulls of young adults. Unfortunately the bones have not been kept, as far as we know, and the exact location of the cave is unknown.

Chapter 2   Chapter 2 Early Medieval

Sheep were the mainstay of the Worfield economy in the medieval period. Photo taken in 2017

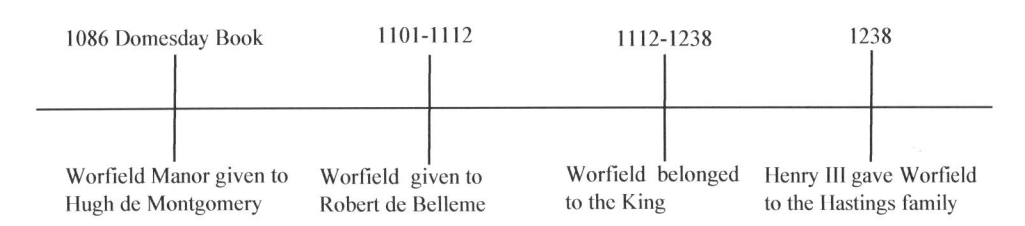

1086 Domesday Book	1101-1112	1112-1238	1238
Worfield Manor given to Hugh de Montgomery	Worfield given to Robert de Belleme	Worfield belonged to the King	Henry III gave Worfield to the Hastings family

By the medieval period there were three distinct administrative structures which made up Worfield, Worfield Manor, Worfield Parish and the Forest of Morfe. Worfield Manor was a secular area of administration under the Lord of the Manor and approximately the same in area as the ecclesiastical parish of St Peter's Church, Worfield is today. The Forest of Morfe covered the southern half of the manor/parish and was part of a national system of administration of royal forests.

Worfield Manor
Across England there are many small unspoilt villages which are off the beaten track; secret treasures known chiefly by those who live there. Worfield is such a village. Protected from development by its location, one wonders why it was chosen as the main village for the area at all,

Chapter 2 Early Medieval

for the land rises steeply behind the main street to the west and parallel to it, the River Worfe meanders. Only a narrow strip of land is available for building.

Yet it was Worfield which was the head of the manor as recorded in the Domesday Book and not its near neighbour, Hallon, or any of the other villages which, on the basis of location alone, seem to have much more in their favour. Hallon was a much more easily defended site being on a hill and it is a further mystery, which we have already mentioned, as to why the Parish Church was hidden away in a valley.

In 1086, at the time of Domesday, Worfield was in the Seisdon Hundred in Staffordshire and held by Hugh de Montgomery from the King. *Earl Aelfgar* [son of Earl Leofric and Lady Godiva] *had held it and there were 30 hides and land for 30 ploughs. In demesne* [for the lord's use] *were 4 teams and there were 5 slaves. There were 67 villagers with a priest, 10 smallholders who had 25 ploughs, 3 mills at 40s, a fishery at 15s, 16 acres of meadow and a wood 3 leagues long and 1 wide. 3 Englishmen had 5 ploughs with 18 villagers and 5 smallholders. 3 hides were waste. The value was £3* [before 1066] *and is now £18.* [By comparison Alveley was valued at £6 before 1066 and in 1086 100s and Claverley was worth £7.10s and now £10.] Earl Roger's son, Hugh, held 5 dwellings from the Earldom belonging to Worfield. Hardwicke suggests that these dwellings were Ewdness, Oldington, Catstrey, Ackleton and Hallon.

Within the area of Worfield Manor, Ackleton was part of Badger Manor. Ackleton held its own court but still had to present at the Worfield Great or Frankpledge Courts twice a year. There may have been other manors at this early period. Hardwicke says that it is documented that there were two manors even during the time of Hugh de Montgomery, *the Manor of Worfeld and the Manor of Wolpheresford so called because of its nearness to the castle which Wulfric Spot had erected as a guard over Hallon Ford*[1]. Hardwicke believed that Wolpheresford was Wyken but there is another contender with a very similar name. Ewyke was a village of some importance, judging from early records, which had completely disappeared by the eighteenth century. Ewyke was on the eastern side of the River Worfe, north-west of Rowley[App 2a]. There may be a link between Ewyke and Wyken we don't at present understand.

On the death of Hugh de Montgomery, the Manor of Worfield was inherited by his brother, the cruel and ruthless Robert de Belleme. Between 1101 and 1112 Belleme tried, without success, to depose King Henry I. Belleme was put in prison for treason and Worfield was taken into the King's hands. On Henry I's death, Worfield was inherited by Henry II who was probably delighted to receive it, because it was a wealthy manor. The wealth of Worfield came from sheep. Between 1238 and 1250 there was pasturage for 18 oxen, 3 boars, 12 cows, 12 sows and their litters and 500 sheep[A]. At the time of Henry II's accession in 1154, Worfield's fiscal value, ie the amount it had to produce in tax, was an eighth of that for the whole county of Salop (£32 0s 5d halfpenny). In 1204 the men of Wurfeld gave the King a fine of 10 merks to be free of tolls anywhere in the realm. The arrangement was supposed to include freedom from pannage but for some reason this was not included. The following year, King John put a charge on Worfield manor by giving his interpreter

18

Chapter 2   Chapter 2 Early Medieval

10 librates of land (valued at a pound a year) within Worfield manor. Wrenic fitz Meuric, the interpreter between England and Wales, held this land in lieu of his duties of carrying the King's writs throughout Wales[2].

In 1238 Henry III gave Worfield, together with Condover and Church Stretton in Shropshire, and others elsewhere, to Ada, sister of Henry de Hastings in lieu of her claims on the lands of the Earldom of Chester. The Hastings family very nearly lost the manor in 1267 when Ada's son Henry, who had inherited Worfield from his mother, joined with Simon de Montfort and others against the King in the Second Barons' War. In this case, after the King was convinced of Hastings' loyalty, the family were allowed to keep Worfield, which remained in their hands until 1324 when Worfield passed to John Hastings' widow, Julian, as her dower. Julian's second husband was Thomas le Blount and her third was William de Clinton, later Earl of Huntingdon. When Julian died in 1367 Worfield passed to her grandson, John de Hastings, Earl of Pembroke.

In a chest in the Church was a charter given by Edward I in 1287 [B] giving the same freedom from tolls for which Worfield had paid in 1204, freedom from the expenses of knights and freedom from serving on assize juries. The charter was enrolled several times, the last being in 1704. The charter was granted because Worfield was said to be of ancient demesne of the king.

Seal attached to the Worfield Charter. Photograph by F. R. Armytage

We have spoken of the history of the Manor without explaining how the Manor of Worfield operated. Some obvious questions arise such as, 'how were the boundaries of the manor defined and determined?' A paper (undated) was kept in the Parish Chest in St Peter's Church and reproduced in the Parish Magazine of October 1897:

These are the Meers and Bounds of the Liberty of Worffeild
In the High Way at the End of the Town of Brugenorth leading towards Worffeild, stands a small cross called Tyffyngs Cross and from that cross it extends to a meer between Batons Croft which is in the liberty of Worffield and Sollongs Croft which is in the Liberty of Brugg, along to the High

Chapter 2   Chapter 2 Early Medieval

Way which divideth the Liberty of Worffeild and the Liberty of Brugg, by the bank of the Severne even to Penstones Mylne and from Penstones Mylne the bank called Severne divides the Liberty of Worffeild and the Liberty of Brugg and Tasseley along to Gateston and at Gateston a certain meer divides the liberty of Worrfeild and the Liberty of Appeley,... the wood ... of Ewdness and from the wood of Appleley away to the gravell-pits and from the gravell pits a ditch divides the Liberty of Worffeild and the Lordship of Godystokton ...away to the High Road between Brugg and Stokton and from ... the highway a quicksett hedge goes even to the fields of Stapleford and then a certain hedge divideth the Liberty of Worffeild and the Lordship of Hugford and extends to the Bank of Worth and there the Worth divideth the Liberty of Worffeild and the Lordship of Baggesore so on to Mulnebroke and then Mulnebroke extends to the mill of Baggesore and then from that mill a small bank ...pol divideth the Liberty of Worffeild and the Lordship of Bager, away on to a certain corner called Mer ...and from that corner a certain hedge divides the Liberty of Worffeild and the Lordship of Patteshull, even to Sydwall Greene near to Stanlowe and from Sydwall Greene a certain small bank divides the liberty of Worffeild and the Lordship of Pattingham even to a certain small meadow called called Pastford a certain small bank called ... divideth the Liberty of Worffeild and the Lordship of Rugg even to Wyldmore and from Wyldemore to a certain small bank called Worbrok divideth the same even to Gradepoll and from Gradepoll the High Way which goes between Brugg and Hampton divideth the Liberty of Worffeild and the Liberty of Claverley, even to Shipellam Gate a certain hedge divideth the same even to a certain angle called Folford and from Folford a certain small bank called Payleford divideth the same even to Gattemore Style and from Gattemore Style a certain hedge divides the same even to a certain oak and from that oak a ditch extends to a certain furrow that leads to a small brook and from that brook a footpath goes away to a small meer which extends by its head to another called Almestr and ...that meer extends to a certain hedge, called Souleswall Yard and from Souleswall Yard a certain footpath goes along to Dedesmens Gate and from Dedesmens Gate a certain green meer goes to a certain furrow and extends to the head of the ridges even to a certain hedge which divides the Liberty of Worffield and the Liberty of Claverley, even to Wholpesbryche and from Wholpesbryche to the Green Meer ...

    Landmarks such as trees, stones and ditches were invaluable boundary markers. That such markers were needed can be seen by the number of people appearing in court accused of trying to move the stones. Under-ploughing boundary stones was a common technique for moving them but the court took a dim view of such misdemeanours, fining the culprit heavily for their actions.

    The Manor of Worfield in area has changed little since the boundaries were defined in medieval times. There was some loss of land on the west and south sides in the 1980s and perhaps, at an earlier time, there was some loss of land on the east. The number of townships has not changed much from the early days. Worfield has gained a few hamlets, such as the The Lowe, The Hobbins, Hartlebury, Bentley, Littlegain and Stanmore, and lost Wolstone (near St Peter's Well), Ewyke and Asterhull. In 1365[3] Worfield's townships were: Kingslowe, Stanlowe, Chesterton, Hilton, Bradeney,

Chapter 2　　　　　　　　　Chapter 2 Early Medieval

Rowley, Asterhull, Ewyke, Sonde, Roughton, Barndeley, Hokcombe & Swancote, Borughcote, Borughcote [Upper and Lower], Rindelforde, Bromleye, Catstre, Alvescote, Winnescote, Newton [which was then a new town], Stapleford, Akelton, Eudenas, Oldington, Wyken, Halon, Worfeld.

We know the names of townships in medieval times and also the names of some of the inhabitants. In 1327,[App 1] a tax was levied on wealthy and middle class individuals, whose names and the amount paid were recorded These were early days for surnames. They were derived from where they lived eg Roger of Chesterton, Robert of Alvescote, from the topographical features they lived nearby, such as Thomas at the Gate (Thomas atte Yate) and Agnes at the Brooke (Agnes atte Broke), from the jobs they did, Roger the Walker and Robert the Mercer, and were descriptive of the people themselves, such as Thomas Freeman or Thomas the Young. Some names seem odd to us today, perhaps coming from Anglo Saxon times, such as Gerbod or Merewalh.

We see from the taxes paid that Thomas of Ewyke paid the most tax, over 5s, and Roger of Eudenas 5s, Richard of Eudenas paid over 3s, William of Kyngeslowe 3s, John of Stanlowe 2s, Roger of Chesterton 2s, Thomas Colet 2s, Roger Walker 3s, Robert of Alvescote 2s. There may have been wealthier Worfield people who were exempt from the tax because they paid other feudal dues. The 1327 list is interesting and poses the obvious questions, what gave rise to Ewyke's wealth and what caused the village's demise?

Twenty years on from 1327 England was a much poorer country. In 1349-1350, the country was ravaged by the Black Death. It is estimated that, as a result of this epidemic, a third of the population died. We see the consequences in the manor court rolls of Worfield with farms left empty. One assumes the occupants had died and there was no-one to work the land. In the fifteenth year of the reign of Richard II (June 1391-1392), an Extent of the Manor[4] recorded that there was no manor house, the demesne land was not cultivated nor had the meadow known as Kings Meadow been mown. Perhaps Worfield forty years on from the Black Death was still underpopulated although there was a fulling mill and a corn mill.

Residence in Worfield, as in any other manor, carried with it strict obligations and privileges. The local laws to which residents had to adhere were laid down in a set of rules known as the customs of the manor which ensured that people were treated impartially. Worfield is fortunate in that records of some of these customs of the manor have survived. In this case, the lord of the manor, William Beauchamp (1237-1298), clarified certain obligations of tenants after some of them began to take matters into their own hands[c]. *The tenants ... must mow, rake and windrow all the meadows of the lord at their own proper costs and charges, receiving only from the lord as an allowance for the same a sheep of the value of sixteen pence.*

Every three weeks a small court, or court baron, was held, dealing with local matters and land transfers, and every six months a Great, or Frankpledge, Court was held to ensure that national and local laws were being enforced. Here we see breaches of laws such as playing football, drinking during a church service, not wearing woollen hats on feast days and not practising archery. The courts were held in the half timbered building at the end of the church path (see page 24).

Chapter 2 Early Medieval

The residents worked directly for the lord of the manor on his personal or demesne land in Hallon and indirectly for the lord in every other way. The manor was a financial asset which the lord owned. Access even to what grew naturally or lived in the wild was restricted and required payment of a fee. The fish and eels that swam in abundance in the rivers could only be caught with permission and payment, gathering of wood was restricted and acorns (pannage) in the wood were fodder to which access was limited. Even a swarm of bees belonged to the lord. It goes without saying that game belonged to the lord and while you may see a hare which you could kill for food, to do so would be a contravention of the law.

One couldn't wander from manor to manor and set up home without permission from the lord nor could one erect a house or subdivide one without permission. Those who gave shelter to a pregnant woman, a vagrant or a person from another manor, were fined for so doing.

For society to run smoothly there were rules of behaviour to which people had to adhere. You were expected to respect your neighbours by not using bad words or gestures to them, gossiping, or listening to their conversations. You did not swear in the churchyard and you did not chide your husband constantly or you would be dubbed a common scold. Minor skirmishes were common but had to be reported. The guilty party would then be brought before the court. Failure to report a crime was also a crime so snooping on one's neighbours was part of the manorial system.

Some rules and regulations were designed to preserve the natural resources of the manor and contributed to good husbandry. Early manorial records speak of permission being required for assarting, or the clearance of woodland so that the land could be ploughed. The lord of the manor might approve this for very small areas but if the King ordered it then trees would be felled in large numbers. In 1235, 1,700 oaks were sold from Worfield Wood and in 1621 the number of trees removed led to the almost complete loss of oak woodland in Worfield. Now the ancient oak woods are limited to valleys inaccessible to machinery, a reminder of what the landscape was once like.

Farming was carried out under an open three field system with tenants renting selions or strips in them. Crop rotation was practised and fields fertilised by turning livestock onto the stubble. This was a good system provided that the stock was not let loose until the crop had been gathered and the animals were removed before the new crop was sown. By the sixteenth century it was not an infrequent occurrence for stock to be grazing outside these times; put in too early, before the harvest had been carried away, and left to graze longer than they should have been. Perhaps this is an indication of shortage of grazing. Meadows were highly prized for providing fodder for livestock, particularly in the winter, and there were small parcels of enclosure, perhaps for holding oxen close to the farmstead. Each township also had common or waste attached. Picture a moorland landscape and that is what the commons would have looked like.

Rights of common were specific to each township. The fact that you might have the right of common for six sheep at Hoccom did not mean that you automatically had the right of common anywhere else in the manor. Common rights were often appurtenances to the occupancy of a house; lose the house and you lost the rights of common which went with it. Then you might have to resort

Chapter 2   Chapter 2 Early Medieval

to cutting the hedges of your neighbours and feeding the prunings to your stock. Of course that was a crime and you would be presented at the Frankpledge Court as a 'common lacerator of hedges.' How people survived when they had reached these extremes of deprivation it is impossible to imagine. Pigs running loose on the common had to be ringed to prevent them turning over the ground and stallions under 14 hands could not run free. Ponies wouldn't serve as war horses.

The purity of the water in streams and pools was safeguarded and heavy fines imposed on those who soaked hemp and flax in the common waters in order to break down the fibres. An alternative to soaking was to lay the hemp and flax in damp meadows to break down the fibres. This took longer and produced a better finish but was not as popular. Drainage ditches had to be cleaned out and hedges planted and maintained. Hurdles were used to contain stock in the common fields and fill in gaps in growing hedges and these had to be maintained in good order.

Any found live or dead stock, such as parts of ploughs or clothing, had to be reported and was announced in church, for example, one white sheep came as a stray on … and is in the custody of …If it was not claimed within a year and a day the goods were valued and either they or an equivalent monetary value was paid to the lord. Sometimes an animal would die but a fleece or skin still had a value. Livestock found straying on the highway would be taken to the pound and the owner could only take them from there on payment of a fine.

The Church[5]
The Domesday Book of 1086 notes that there was a church at Worfield and Eyton's view was that it was improbable that Earl Leofric, the father of Earl Aelfgar would have left one of his *principal manors spiritually unprovided for*. There would also have been monks within Worfield up to the time of the Reformation and there were monastic links with other Churches, particularly the Church of St. Mary in Malvern and the Church of Worcester.

1095-1098 Hugh de Montgomery gave the Church of Worfield with certain tithes, fisheries and other rights to the Monastery of Saint Marie de la Sauve-Majeure near Bordeaux.

1098-1102 The Abbott of Westminster, (to which the Great Malvern monastic cell was attached), gave Worfield to Malvern Church, along with Quatford. (There may have already been an association between Malvern and Worfield.)

1100-1135 Henry I gave land in Worfield and Quatt to the Church of St Mary in Malvern.

1292 Edward I in the twentieth year of his reign[6] gave the Church of Worfeld to the Prior and Convent of the Church of Worcester for the sustenance of three monks, and for maintaining two wax candles to be kept continually burning at the Feast of St Wulstan, and for eight days after, and to be lighted at the saying of high mass both at matins and vespers. This was done in accomplishment of a vow made to St Wulstan.[E]

1340 Roger de Worfield, a Benedictine monk at Worcester Priory, received two papal letters apparently because he withdrew from the Benedictine order he belonged to. The letters would have absolved him from excommunication & allowed his return to the Priory[7].

Chapter 2 Early Medieval

Sometimes, as we have seen above, land in one parish was given to support a church in another[8]. Wulfric Spot in 1004 endowed all his paternal inheritance to Burton Abbey. This included Shipley and Suthtune, thought to be Sutton Maddock. Also endowed was Halen which Hardwicke thought was Hallon in Worfield but is now believed to be Halesowen[9]. The picture of these donations of land is confusing and incomplete. We know that Buildwas Abbey owned a virgate (30 acres) of land in Hallon before the Reformation and that Hugh de Montgomery donated Burcote, complete with its eight fish pools or stakings, on the day of the foundation of the new church in Quatford in 1086. Earl Roger of Shrewsbury's first wife was murdered in Normandy in 1082, and when his second wife was on board ship crossing from France to England to meet her new husband, a terrible storm blew up. It seemed inevitable that all would drown but her chaplain had a vision that they would survive, as they did. To thank God for their salvation, a new church was built at Quatford, where she and her husband met, and dedicated to Saint Mary Magdalene.

At the end of the church path stands a half-timbered building which was once the Grammar School and Court House where the Manor Courts were held.

When Henry III gave Worfield Manor to Ada Hastings in 1238 he retained control as advowson over the Church of Worfield. The advowson's rights were the entitlement to tithes and the power to nominate the incumbent of Worfield Church to the Bishop of Lichfield, as head of the diocese, for ratification. The Royal connection with Worfield ended in 1318 when Edward II[10] exchanged the advowson of Worfield for Greenford owned by the Bishop of Lichfield. The contract was confirmed in 1321 by a Papal Bull. Bishop Langton lent 200 marks for the purchase of Worfield and another parish. In 1394 the debt was still outstanding and, in the same year, Lichfield reduced Worfield from a rectory[F] to a vicarage and set out the income entitlement of the vicar and the patron (advowson) ie the Dean and Chapter of Lichfield[G] giving proportionately more to Lichfield than Worfield, presumably helping to pay Lichfield's debt.

The Old Rectory, now known as Lower Hall, right & the Vicarage on the left. Circa 1938

So far we have said nothing about where the vicar, monks and chantry priests lived. Land opposite the church seems to have been church land from the early medieval period and probably before that. There was a principal house, barns and outbuildings and in the fourteenth century there were other church properties rented out for the support of the chantry at St Peter's. In 1422, three shops, which had been built by the Dean and Chapter of Lichfield, with the permission of the Lady of the Manor, were taken back into the Lady's hands, as they had fallen into decay[11]. Also opposite the Church may have been the almshouse mentioned in the churchwarden's accounts, and possibly an inn. In 1394 the Dean of Lichfield Cathedral stated that,[12] *The vicar shall have the principal place of residence and court yard with the buildings erected thereon, with the entire garden of the Rectory of the Church of Worfield as far as the court yard which extends from the entrance to the gate of the Rectory to the water of the river running to the mill of the Lord of Worfield as the said court is divided, for his convenient abode.* So what we have is a vicarage with land behind and buildings thereto and the Rectory next door with its own land and outbuildings. The picture above shows this arrangement clearly. The Vicarage was called the New Vicarage in 1617. We have seen that there was a Rectory on this site in 1394, so the 'mansion' which John Talbot built shortly after 1549 when he became advowson[K] must have either replaced it or been an extension to it. There was

Chapter 2 Early Medieval

also a Grange which in 1552 was transferred to Roger Smith[13]. (Roger Smith did homage for the Grange of Worfield.) This may have housed the monks of Worfield but the only Grange so-named now is in Hilton. Was there another which is now lost?

There were at least four churches in the parish before the Reformation; St Peter's Church in Worfield and chapels at Chesterton, Roughton and Newton. The location of Newton's chapel is indicated on the 1839 map by the field name Little Chapel Leasow but there is no trace of Roughton (St Ann's) Chapel, which was on The Green in Roughton. Chesterton (St John's) Chapel, has been a private house for many years (see page 174). Two other church references on the 1839 map are to Churchyard Field at Allscott and Church Hill in Bromley.

Stone coffin to the right of the main door to St Peter's Church

St Peter's Church, in the centre of Worfield, has been so victorianised that it is hard to get any sense of the architecture of the early church. The oldest part of the church visible today dates from 1180-1270 in an area at the north of the church extending as far as an exposed pillar in the Madeley rooms. If you walk round the back of the church from the main door and look up at one of the windows on the north side, you will see an example of Kentish tracery, a rarity in Shropshire, but why it is here is a mystery.

Other evidence for early building is a pillar at the south east of the nave which even Cranage[14] thought odd. His conclusion was that there had been transepts here. In other words that there may have been a section of the church which went from north to south just at the point where the chancel, the approach to the altar, now stands. Cranage went back to the church to see if he could make any more sense of the architecture, which he couldn't, but he then saw the doors which now hang in the church. Cranage[M] noted that, *since 1893 some doors have been placed against the west wall of the north aisle. I hear that they were found in an out-house at the vicarage. The iron work is very fine and has beasts, birds and serpents. The crescent hinge is used and the date is probably late twelfth or early thirteenth century.* The doors, known as picture doors, from the decorative

Chapter 2   Chapter 2 Early Medieval

ironwork they display, are a pair of only five doors *with extensive figural display* left in the country. (Geddes[15]). The others are at Stillingfleet, Staplehurst, Runhall and Old Woking although Geddes feels that *it is debatable whether the fragments of ironwork left at Old Woking amount to a picture door.* The Worfield doors are the only double picture doors.

Worfield Picture Doors.

There is no doubting the finery of the Worfield doors. The impressive C or crescent hinges dominate the top half of the doors, each hinge ending in a flourish of two snakes. Such hinges were in common use in twelfth century France and England and throughout the Holy Roman Empire. The square crosses would indicate a religious connection but the animal images in the circles, the lock keepers, perhaps, are a mystery. The ironwork has been rearranged and the handles and the locks have disappeared. On the left hand door as we look at it, there are keyholes, as there also are on the right. The initials WL have been carved in the wood in 1770. The group of picture doors in England is so small it is impossible to understand where the designs came from and how the tradition was passed from person to person to be used in Worfield.

Chapter 2   Chapter 2 Early Medieval

Left and right are details from the Worfield doors and centre from a door at Rogslosa in Sweden

There are only two examples decorative ironwork of a similar date near to Worfield[H]. Morville, has a door with elaborate ironwork dating from 1150-1200 and Highley may have a door with twelfth century hinges. This gives us no clear impression of how many picture doors there were in the twelfth century. Were Worfield's doors a rarity locally, or even nationally, or were they commonplace? Simple questions to which we have no immediate answer.

Geddes suggests that picture doors may have been introduced into England as part of the cultural heritage of the Vikings. Many of the picture doors remaining today are in Scandinavia. The doors we see now may look different from when they were originally hung. The newly-cut oak would have been much lighter in colour so there would have been a natural contrast between wood and metal and they may have been clad with leather to keep draughts out. They may even have been painted and the ironwork gilded.

Whether the doors originally came from the Church, is a good question. The suggestion has always been that the doors hung at the main entrance to the church, on the south side, prior to the 1862 improvements. To date I have found no reference to the doors in any of the church records. However, nor is there any record of the transepts which have disappeared. Prior to the restoration of the church there was a north door which led into the chantry. Perhaps these doors once hung at this entrance or they may have been interior doors. Geddes' view is that they probably were church doors as there is no other building of the right age still standing and there is no secular tradition of picture doors. There is also the use of the cockerel image (associated with St Peter) and the two crosses. Geddes identifies one of the beasts in the small circle of iron as a lion. The image on the left I would have thought was a deer and that on the right may be a griffin.

Before we leave the subject of medieval ironwork we need to make a mention of the church chests. Sadly, the earliest chest we know of is no longer in the church and its whereabouts are unknown. Dating from the thirteenth century this chest was described by Roe[I]. The following detail is from a late fourteenth to early fifteenth century chest[J] in the church showing that the tradition of decorative ironwork continued in the parish.

28

Chapter 2

Chapter 2 Early Medieval

Detail of decoration on the Worfield chest

The Forest of Morfe

The Royal Forest of Morfe[App 2] stretched from Kinver to Bridgnorth cutting across half the Manor of Worfield[E] and imposing forest law, a different set of rights and restrictions from that of the manor or the church. Instead of manorial courts there were swanimote courts[18]. Free men or swains attended the swanimote court as they did the hundred courts of Saxon times. We know that the forest court was held in a lodge on the road from Roughton near to where it joins the Stourbridge Road. When Randall wrote his book on Worfield in the late nineteenth century only the stout walls and cellar of the lodge remained[16]. The owner, Miss Stokes, told Randall that it had had large cheerless rooms and a spit big enough to roast an ox on. The lodge had been turned into cottages and at the wish of the tenants the fireplace was bricked up and some of the building taken down. The Forest was split into areas called bailliwicks, under the management of the bailiffs of Worfield, Claverley etc. The Swanimote Courts heard presentments by officers and justices heard claimants' cases. Apart from infringements of forest law, the familiar crimes we see recorded in the manor court rolls, such as assaults, petty theft and releasing stock from impoundment, were also dealt with.

Royal Forests were set aside for the exclusive use of the King and his entourage to enjoy the hunting of deer and hares. In 1235 a writ of Henry III ordered the sheriffs of Shropshire to take four knights and view the forests of the county. This was the report on Worfield:[17]

The wood of Worfield was much wasted by ancient waste, to wit, at the time of the great war [The Barons' War] *and also in the time of Ranulf late Earl of Chester* [Sheriff of Shropshire 1216-1223] *who, while he was Sheriff, sold 1700 oak trees there, besides other wastes made in his time for the purpose of enclosing the town of Bruges before it was fortified with a wall. And moreover the wood is much damaged lately through the very many deliveries made to the men of the manor of Worfield by order of the King and his Justiciars of the Forest. There are few beasts in the aforesaid woods because the beasts were destroyed in the time of war and in the time when liberty of the forest was conceded.*

The inhabitants of the nearby villages had rights of common[App. 2a] but their activities within the forest were restricted. Reading the records it feels as though a constant watch was kept by the Forest officers. It would be lovely to get an idea of what the Forest looked like and how people went about their business but the most difficult thing seems to be to get a picture of everyday life.

Chapter 2 Early Medieval

We can only try to piece it together from records not designed to reveal the uneventful and mundane. At best we get a glimpse of what life was like, at worst the picture is bewildering.

The administration of Forest Law involved a number of officers - a steward or chief forester, foresters, a verderer (a judicial officer who was sworn to maintain the law of the forest), a regarder (surveyor of the current state of the Forest and of activities within it who also kept a record of ancient agreements), an agister (an accountant who agreed terms for pannage or acorns and accounted for money paid for pannage and pasture), and a woodward (who looked after the deer's habitat and had the right, as did other forest officers, to apprehend law breakers). Later there were foresters in fee who held small estates in return for apprehending those who broke the law. Roughton was held in this way, first by William of Roughton (William Gerbod) who was given a virgate of land (about 30 acres) and a rood of meadow (a quarter of an acre).

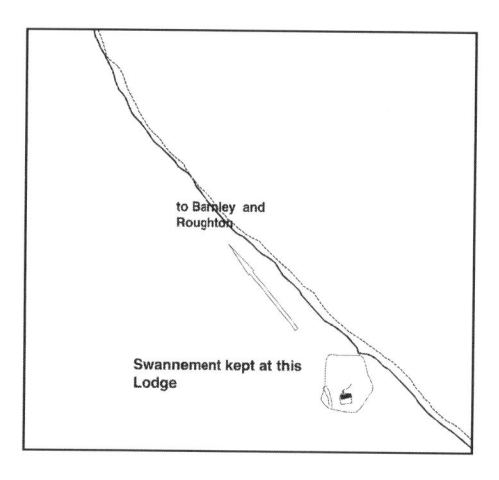

The Lodge as shown on the 1613 Samuel Parsons map of the Forest of Morfe[App. 2] *Scale: 2 inches to 1 mile*

The lodge, called 'Forest Lodge,' is now situated on the opposite side of the road ie the right hand side of the road from the Stourbridge Road to Roughton (alongside what used to be the Worfield Tip) as the course of the road has been altered.

While hunting within the forest was the right of the monarch, the local population took advantage of the wildlife to do the same. Deer were hunted with greyhounds, scent hounds and bows and arrows, hares with greyhounds, and rabbits were killed with ferrets. The names of Edward Grey, Thomas Hoorde and Robert Gatacre come up time and again in court. In 1495, Edward Grey, formerly of Bridgnorth and Thomas Hoord the younger, also of Bridgnorth, were hunting with a greyhound and killed a deer coming out of Bromley Hill. In the same year Robert Gatacre and Humphrey his brother, hunted in the Forest of Morfe with dogs. Humphrey Lee and Roger Hill of Morff in Staffordshire, yeomen, chased and drove deer in the King's Forest on the Feast of St Bartholomew and John Wotton of Quatt, a smith, was declared a common hunter in the Forest of Morff. Another serial offender was Humphrey Wolriche who kept a brache (scenting hound) which distressed 20 fawns. Wolriche was told many times by the forest officers, in the

Chapter 2 Early Medieval

King's name, to put the said brache away. Thomas Underhill of Bridgnorth and Richard Caldecote of Bridgnorth were found hunting with dogs in the Forest of Morff and they *kepith a ferett daily and so destroyeth the said coneys within the forest of Morff*. We might imagine that the punishments for these crimes would be severe but from the number of repeat offences the fines seem almost a licence to hunt rather than a deterrent not to do so.

The verderers had to see that the habitat for the deer was maintained. With permission, trees could be lopped to provide fodder for one's own livestock or the sheep and cattle could browse or eat the foliage and branches themselves. Evergreen foliage such as holly and ivy was used as a fodder crop for sheep and hawthorn and hazel would have a variety of uses including hedging, and firewood.

The number of trees felled in the Forest caused such deforestation that, after a perambulation in 1300[E], certain townships were taken out of the Forest of Morfe - Beobridge, Sutton, Gatacre, Whittimere, Broughton and a plain extending along the banks of the Severn near Pendleston to ancient earthworks at Quatford. Within the area of Worfield, Swancote, Hoccumbe, Barndeleye, Roughton and Wyke and three houses and a plain in Hilton remained within the Forest.

In spite of the difficulty of clearing the land of trees and tree stumps, parcels of an acre or half an acre were cleared, turned over, and finally sown; usually with oats. The whole process, known as assarting, took at least two years. In Fennhill in 1356:[19]

William atte Rylle occupied and held 1 acre
Edith of Wystanesiner occupied here 1 acre now held by William atte Rylle and Richard de Cuerton
Stephen the Tailloar occupied half an acre, now held by Thomas the Tailloar
Robert of Bromeley occupied and held half an acre

A group of dwellings within the Forest which have claimed special attention are the Hermitage caves. Tradition has it that in the tenth century they were lived in by a brother of King Athelstan, a nephew of Aethelflaed, Lady of the Mercians. Reliable evidence for this is lacking[20] but the caves were definitely inhabited as a hermitage in the fourteenth century and after[21].

Grant for life to Andrew de Corbrigge, hermit, of the custody of the King's hermitage of Adlaston by Bruggenorth (29 July 1333)
Grant for life, to William Chamberleyne, chaplain, of the hermitage of Athelardestone in the Forest of Morfe (15 March 1383)

Chapter 2　　　　　　　Chapter 2 Early Medieval

Lost and Found

Edward I Siver Penny 1301-1310
London Mint
HESH 5A0263
Long crosses were put on coins to make it easier to see if the coin had been clipped ie small pieces of silver snipped off.

Harness Pendant 1250-1450
HESH-EB5A47
Horse harness was decorated with colourful metal pendants. This pendant was made of copper alloy and was decorated with red and blue enamel. Some showed coats of arms but in this case a crudely drawn lion is the centrepiece

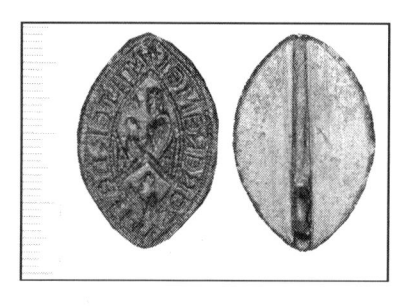

Copper Alloy Seal 1200-1300
WMAS 84EB67
In the medieval period there was an increase in documents which had to be personally assigned. Seals were the solution which solved the problem of most people not being able to write.

Papal Bulla 1352-1362
HESH-1517A7
A lead seal such as this would have been attached to a letter from the Pope, as head of the Church in England in pre-Reformation times. We know that Roger de Worfield received such letters while he was at Worcester in 1340. This may have been the seal on another letter to someone living in Worfield but it may not have been so. High status religious items were often bought as sacred relics and worn around the neck. In this case the hole in the middle is too large for this purpose so perhaps this seal ended up as a loom weight.

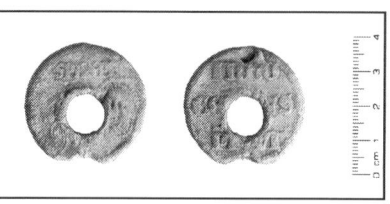

Images courtesy of Portable Antiquities Scheme
Finder of this group of artefacts, Frank Taylor

32

Chapter 2   Chapter 2 Early Medieval

References

1. Hardwicke, W. Collections for a History of Shropshire (William Salt Library)
2. Eyton, Antiquities of Shropshire Vol 3, p 106ff
3. Manor Court Roll 1374-1375. P314/W/1/1/61 (Shropshire Archives)
4. Extent of the Manor of Worfield 1391-1392 DL 43/14/3/fo74 (National Archives)
5. Eyton, Antiquities of Shropshire Vol 3, p 115ff
6. A History of the County of Worcester: Volume 2 (Victoria County History)
7. Logan, F. D., Runaway Religious in Medieval England 1240-1540 (Cambridge U. Press 2002)
8. A History of the County of Stafford: Volume 3, Houses of Benedictine Monks, P. 199-213
9. Sawyer, P.H. ed., Charters of Burton Abbey (OUP 1979)
10. Patent II Edward II
11. P314/W/1/1/261-262 Worfield Manor Court roll (Shropshire Archives)
12. Randall, J., Worfield & its Townships (pubd 1887) page 26
13. Record. Mich. Edward VI rot. 43
14. Cranage, Churches of Shropshire, vol 10 (Hobson and co, Shropshire)
15. Geddes, Jane, Medieval Decorative Ironwork in England (Research Reports, 59) (Society of Antiquaries of London, 1999)
16. Randall, J., Worfield & its Townships (pubd 1887) page 102
17. Eyton, Antiquities of Shropshire Vol 3, p 215ff
18. DL39/1/26 National Archives
19. E32/149 Regarders Accounts (National Archives)
20. Horovitz, D. 'The Hermitage Caves - a Myth explained?' in Transactions of the Shropshire Archaeological and Historical Society, Volume LXXXIV 2009
21. VCH Salop II, page 23

See also:
Dukes, Antiquities of Shropshire
5586/1/214 Glebe Terrier 1698-1699 (Shropshire Archives)

Notes

A. Extent or valuation of the Manor carried out between 1238 and 1250 when Henry de Hastings was Lord of the Manor of Worfield which details the value and economic activity in Worfield as follows:

Chapter 2 Early Medieval

3.75 virgates of arable land held in demesne realising £3.15s
8.75 virgates of meadow land at 3s per acre realising £1 6s 3d, Pasturage for 18 oxen at 2d per head, 3 boars at the same rate, 12 cows at 4d a head, 12 sows with their litters 4d per sow, 500 sheep at a halfpenny a head
Sudlegh Wood worth 40s
2 mills worth £7 6s 8d
4.75 virgates held in villeinage, some virgates containing 61 acres and some 62 acres
Burkott had 8 small fisheries called Stakings
Bradeney had 5 fisheries
Stapelford and Ewyke are separately valued. Esterhull is also valued
In Ewdness a certain free man holds a hide of land for a ferm of 4s or else by service of conveying the ferm of Worfield to London
Oldington hamlet held by service of taking writs of the manor in the County.
Roughton was held by service of keeping the wood of Morfe
In the hamlet of Halene (Hallon) there was a Smith (faber)
Pleas and perquisites of the Manor court - £20 per annum
Tallage of free men £3 14s 1d
The Church, which was in the King's gift, was worth 100 merks, £66 13s 4d
Total valuation £140.0s 3d[2]

B. Worfield Charter sealed with the Privy Seal of Edward I date 26 May 1288

Edward by the grace of God King of England and France and Lord of Ireland to all and singular his Justices, Sheriffs, Provosts, Ministers and all his lieges as well within the liberties as without to whom these present letters shall come, Greeting. Whereas according to the Custom in our realm of England, hitherto and approved that men of ancient demesne of the crown of England, are and ought to be quit of payment of toll as well as of expenses of Knights coming to Parliaments. And further that they should enjoy all customs in use from ancient times and not be placed on assize Juries or have any recognizances for land or tenements which are of ancient demesne of the Crown of England through the whole of our realm aforesaid. We charge you that the men and tenants of Wolveresford also called Worfield which is of ancient demesne of the crown of England as fully appears in a certain Certificate sent by us to our Chancery by our Treasurers and Chamberlains at our command and yet remaining in the files of our Chancery aforesaid- that they should be quit of payments of this kind and expenses of Knights as also of Assize Juries and any recognisances, you shall permit them as well to be quit of the customs aforesaid according to the custom before mentioned. And if you shall have made distraints of any kind upon the same me you shall release them without delay. In witness whereof we have caused these our letters patent to be issued.

C. Customary of the Manor of Worfield translated from the Norman French (William Beauchamp 1237-1298.) Shropshire Archives 2028/1/5/8

William Beauchamp Lord of Worfield. To all to whom these own letters Patent shall come, Greeting.

As we are informed and certainly understand that dissensions and disputes have happened and at this time subsist by and between our Officers and Agents on the one part and our Tenants of base tenure of our Barony aforesaid on the other part touching and concerning diverse usages and customs which our said Tenants there claim and follow. We now and at all times desiring and willing right government, peace and tranquillity between our Officers and agents and Tenants aforesaid have at the supplication and request of our said Tenants as well by the advice of ourselves and of our council as by their common advice and consent in order to remove doubt, ambiguities and obscurities to lay a foundation for peace in time to come and to fix by these presents certain customs and usages of our said Tenants and particulars of their tenure in a manner that shall exclude uncertainty. In the first place will that they and their heirs henceforth from time to time peaceably have hold and repossess their lands and tenements aforesaid with their and every of their appurtenances in manner and form as they and their Ancestors have had and occupied them in ancient time

Chapter 2 Early Medieval

without disturbance from us, our heirs or assigns. They performing, paying and rendering to us our heirs and assigns all and every the services and customs of right due and from ancient time accustomed to be paid to us and to those whose estate we have in the Barony aforesaid. Moreover that all and every our said tenants their heirs and assigns yield service and attendance at our courts of Worefeld from three weeks to three weeks and at summons attend there upon reasonable notice as from time whereof the memory of man is not to the contrary they have used, ought and have been wont to do. Moreover that all and every our said tenants and their heirs have in themselves liberty to dismember and alien their lands and tenements aforesaid to such persons as they shall think meet upon licence from us, our heirs and assigns in the said court of Worefeld provided that the purchaser of the same and the heirs to whom the aforesaid tenements of base tenure will descend after the death of their Ancestors enter into a compact with the High Steward in the court aforesaid to the use and benefit of the lord for the time being so that livery of the same may come from the family and possession of the lord in manner as from ancient time has been accustomed. Moreover that none of our said tenants their heirs or assigns shall at any time from henceforth be evicted or removed from their tenure on account of any default in attendance, appearance and personal service at our court aforesaid. We, our heirs and assigns reserving at all times to ourselves to discuss and determine our claim and seignorial right in the Barony aforesaid by and before ourselves and our Council in such place and at such time as we shall see meet. Moreover that none of our said Tenants and their heirs nor assigns grind corn elsewhere but at our Mills within our Barony aforesaid unless any default or stoppage shall happen so that our said Mills cannot grind by reason of not repairing the same. Provided always that the measures on our said Mills be lawful and approved from time to time by our Court according to what it shall be necessary to toll and take and the miller who shall be guilty of any breach of right or departure from upright dealing shall be punished. Moreover that the Tenants aforesaid their heirs or assigns from year to year make from among themselves at the accustomed times election of a Provost by whom they will answer to serve the law there in this said office. And that the Provost aforesaid associate to himself by his own proper act a Bailiff to serve the lord in the Office aforesaid. The said Provost to have yearly from the lord during the time of his said service six shillings and eight pence and the Bailiff three shillings and four pence without demanding or taking respectively any other fees or perquisites on account of their offices and service aforesaid. Moreover that the tenants aforesaid their heirs and assigns do yearly at seasonable and proper times under the superintendence of the officers aforesaid according to reasonable summons given to them mow, rake and windrow all the meadows of the lord within the Barony aforesaid at their own proper costs and charges, receiving only from the lord as an allowance for the same a sheep of the value of sixteen pence but the said Provost and Bailiff are respectively prohibited from taking any part of the hay made from the said meadows to their own use however the custom in this particular may have heretofore been to the contrary. Moreover that the said Tenants each in respect of his own person and lands are and is in duty and right subject to the payment and accruer of his and their heriots and escheats to the lord in manner as from ancient time to this day has been accustomed. Moreover that in case any one of the said Tenants being under the age of twenty years shall by himself or by his friend depart with or take lands coming to him by inheritance or by purchase within the Barony aforesaid it shall be lawful for him and his heirs at their full age to demand and recover possession of the same such Alienation made during the infancy of the Tenant or any custom to the contrary heretofore in any wise notwithstanding. Moreover that if any woman shall at any time henceforth after the death of her husband make alienation of any tenements held by the tenure aforesaid which came to her for her sole use during her life by the death of her husband provided such alienation goes or tends to the disinheritance of the heirs of her husband it shall and may be lawful to and for such heirs to claim, demand, enter into and recover possession of the same land by process of law in our Court aforesaid in opposition to such alienation however the practice in this particular may have heretofore been to the contrary. And lastly whatever has been declared by these our letters Patent special terms respecting certain customs and usages of our said Barony there are many and diverse good right and reasonable customs and usages still in force there which it

Chapter 2 Early Medieval

is not our intention in any way to weaken or disallow rather it being our aim by these presents to corroborate and uphold to the extent of our power whatever is conformable to equity and reason. Neither is it our intention that the right of any person be by these presents in any manner injured or affected. The rights of every person being in all respects saved.

Given under our seal the fourth day of June in the fifth year of the reign of King Henry the Fourth from the conquest.

D. Wulstan (1008-1095) was Prior of the Monastery at Worcester and was made Bishop of Worcester in 1062

E. In 1300 there was a written version of the **metes and bounds** called, 'The Great and Final Perambulations of 1300.' (National Archives DL 39/1/26.) These are the bounds of the Forest of Morfe as they relate to Worfield on the Forest's north western and northern edge.

From Pendlestone Mill going up the Severn to where the Worfe falls into the Severn and then along the Worfe to Worfe Bridge then along the bank to Rindleford Bridge and so along the bank to Chirle and upwards still to Chirlefords bridge and then along the highway to the village of Hilton and by road to Woghbrokesheth and so along the Stony Strete to Apewardes Castle ...

F. **Rectors and Vicars of Worfield** (from 'A History of the Rectors and Vicars of Worfield Salop 1205-1972' by R. M. H. Evans)

Rectors
1205-1213 Henry, Archdeacon of Stafford (alias Henry of London)
1215-1236 Walter de Cantelupe
1236-1254 William de Kilkenny
1254-1262 Henry de Wengham (alias Wingham)
1262-1295 John de Teford/Leford
1295-1310 John Benstead
1310-1316 Thomas de Boterwick
1317-1318 Humbert de Longville
1318-1320 Gilbert de Bruer
1320-1321 Walter de Thorp
1321-1325 Ralph de Salop
1325-1368 Sir William de Kyrkeby
1368   Thomas de Tenelby
1368-1369 William de Nenhagh
1369   William Lombe
1369-1393 Richard de Bemyncham

Vicars
1393-1395 Alexander Benet
1395-1396 Thomas Olynt (died)
1396-1404 Edward Flode (resigned)
1404-1420 William Aleyn
1421-1441 Thomas Manlove
1441-1474 Sir Thomas Staundon (died)
1474-1497 William Calton
1497-1536 Sir John Walker (died)
1536-1542 Richard Street (died)
1542-1545 Arthur Dudley (resigned)
1545-1562 Thomas Chedulton (removed. Refused to take Oath of Supremacy)
1562-1617 Humphrey Barney (resigned)

Chapter 2　　　　　　　　Chapter 2 Early Medieval

1617-1667 Francis Barney (resigned)
Chantry Priests (An incomplete list)
1345 Thomas de Worfield (resigned)
1345 Roger de Catstree
1352 John Hichecocks (Chaplain)
1481 Thomas Flosbroke
1497-1537 Sir John Lye (died) [Dominus William Janyns was also mentioned in 1503]
?1537-1549 Sir William Hampton

G. A summary of the "Copy of the **Original Endowment of the Vicarage of Worfield** and of a translation thereof procured from the Consistory Court of the Bishop of Lichfield and Coventry," which appears in full in Randall, Worfield and its Townships, pages 26 & 27.

Responsibilities of the Vicar: cure of the Church and the Parishioners thereof.

Place of residence: The vicar shall have the principal place of residence and court yard with the buildings erected thereon, with the entire garden of the rectory of the Church of Worfield as far as the court yard which extends from the entrance to the gate of the Rectory to the water of the river running to the mill of the Lord of Worfield as the said court is divided, for his convenient abode.

Income: the vicar shall have all the tithes of the small crofts near the house, cerage (for church candles and in gardens, apples, pears and other fruits of trees, flax, hemp, garlic, onions, and of the several mills, of hay as well as tithe in money as in the fields of Kingsmeadow and Eileshall, of fowls, of milking cows, calves, bees, geese, eggs, pigs, pigeons and other fowls and fisheries within the parish. And he shall have all oblations within the parish church of Worfield and the Church at Chesterton and within the manor however offered, and all personal tithes of workmen, artificers and merchants of the parish. And they shall have the herbage within the churchyard and the trees growing in the same.

The Dean and the Chapter of Lichfield shall have the whole residue of the fruits, profits, rights and obventions of the church aforesaid who thereout shall repair the chancel of the said church and shall bear and sustain all other burdens both ordinary and extraordinary incident to the same Church except, nevertheless, that the Vicar shall be bound to pay us and our successors St Peter's Pence every year at the accustomed times.

H. Examples of known medieval decorative ironwork in Shropshire: Condover (13th century chest), Wroxeter (14th century chest), Cound (13th century chest), Acton Round (17th century chest), Morville (door with elaborate ironwork 1150-1200 & chest twelfth century), Rushbury (chest 1175-1200), Munslow (door ?thirteenth century to late medieval), Stanton Long (door c1200-1250), Holdgate door ironwork lost fourteenth to fifteenth century), Highley (door, hinges ?twelfth century, ring plate fifteenth century), Silvington (ironwork lost perhaps late fourteenth century), Bitterley (chest 1350-1400), Ashford Carbonel (door front & top strap c1200) and Burford (door, late twelfth century).

I. Roe, F 1933. 'The fate of church chests,' Connoisseur, 92 July 26-28. Roe says the chest was bought by Mr G. Green of Claverley. Description: Thirteenth century style chest with a trefoil arch cut into the side of the legs, four vertical straps on the front and one at each end, all terminating in triple splits. Corner brackets with split curls. 'Found standing in a yard with a lot of old timber.'

J. Late fourteenth to early fifteenth century. Scrolls have been lost from the lid and replaced with plain straps

K. Recorded the 6 April 1650 transmitted to the surveyors Gratis the 10th of the same month. Oliverian Survey Volume 2 Lichfield Archives LD30/4/72. **A survey of the Rectory and Fee Farme of Worvill** in the County of Salop late parcels of the possessions of the Deane and Chapter belonging to the Cathedral Church of Lichfield.

Memorandum. The whole Rectory of Worvill aforesaid land and tithes were by the late Dean and Chapter of the Cathedral Church of Lichfield (as we are informed) granted in Fee Farme to …Talbott esq of Worvill

aforesaid deceased: under there served yearely rent of £51 payable at the Feast of St Michael and the Annunciation of the Blessed Virgin Mary by equal portions. But no deed was produced notwithstanding it was by us several times demanded. And by Mr Pearcy kinsman to Mrs Talbott who at last told us the deed was in time of the war with other writings delivered into a friend's hand to keep ….which is not … come to their hands. And still promiseth that it shall be produced to us before …and brought to be shewed at London
There is a Fair house belonging to the said Rectory which has been built by the Talbotts in which Mrs Talbott now lives. There is 3 several parcels of meadow ground belonging to it lying near the said house worth about £10 a year and a little croft or pasture containing about one acre
The whole tithes of sheafe and all grain which wool and lamb are worth for the year £260
There is a vicarage house adjoining to the aforesaid Mansion House with a yard and backside. The vicar hath the small tithes and the tithe corne of one little township member to Worvill all worth for the year £28
Richard Tayler and John Fisher, surveyors and George Smith and Samuel Foxcrofte, surveyors

L Lords of the Manor of Worfield Post Conquest
1086 Hugh de Montgomery
1098 Robert de Bellesme
1102 King Henry 1 & subsequent Kings
1224 Henry de Hastings
1313 John Lord Hastings Bergavenny
1325 Julian de Hastings (widow)
1325-1326 Thomas Blount (2nd husband of Julian)
1329 William Clinton afterwards Earl of Huntingdon (3rd husband of Julian)
1348 John Lord Hastings Bergavenny & Earl of Pembroke
to John, Lord Bergavenny (only child by Agnes daughter of Roger Mortimer)
1400 Reginald Lord Grey of Ruthyn
sold to William Beauchamp, Lord Bergavenny
1412 Richard Beauchamp, son of the above
Lady Joan Beauchamp
1435 Edward Neville and Elizabeth
1476/1477 ?John, Duke of Norfolk
1492 Sir George Nevill
1535 Sir Henry Nevill
1586 Edward Nevill Lord Bergavenny
1589 Manor split two thirds to Edward Nevill and William Sedley & Elizabeth, his wife, Lady Bergavenny one third to Henry Neville
… Henry, Lord Bergavenny
1624 Manor leased for 99 years by Sir George Whitmore, and Sir John Weld senior
1648 Sir George Whitmore and Sir John Weld senior hold the manor for their lives
… Sir William Whitmore
1699 Mary Whitmore for life
1868 Thomas Charlton Whitmore, Lord of Worfield Manor
M J. E. Auden in his book entitled, 'Shropshire,' (Methuen & Co 1912) noted that when he visited the church *some very fine ironwork of an old church door is preserved in the Reading Room*

Chapter 2	Chapter 2 Early Medieval

Between 1857 and 1861 Miss Theodosia Hinckes and Rebecca Moore, wife of the Archdeacon of Stafford, visited all the churches in the Lichfield Diocese and painted each one of them. These watercolours give us an idea of what Worfield Church was like before it was restored. As far as we know the picture below is the only interior view from that time.
Copyright: Lichfield Cathedral.

Chapter 3   Sixteenth Century

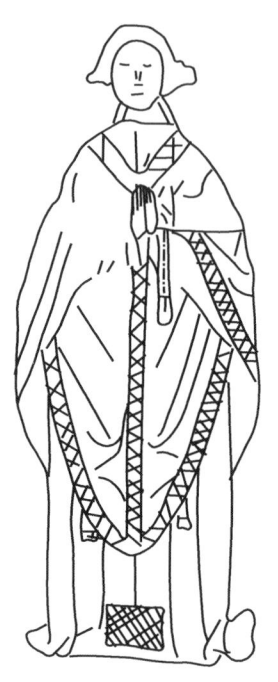

Sir John Lye tombstone set in the floor on the north east side of the church in front of St Mary's Chapel

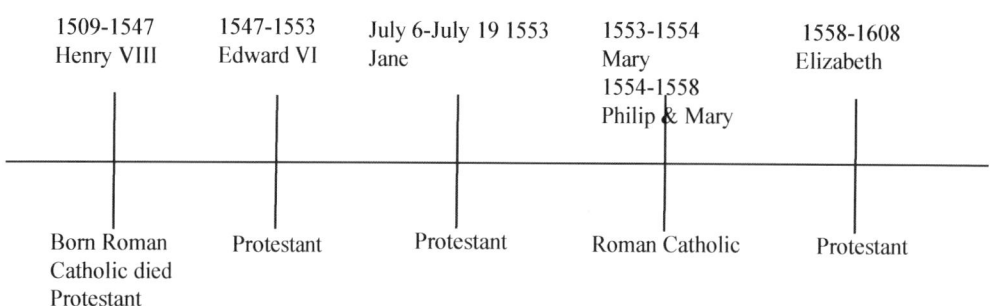

1509-1547	1547-1553	July 6-July 19 1553	1553-1554	1558-1608
Henry VIII	Edward VI	Jane	Mary	Elizabeth
			1554-1558	
			Philip & Mary	
Born Roman Catholic died Protestant	Protestant	Protestant	Roman Catholic	Protestant

The Reformation

The church played a significant part in the lives of those living in the sixteenth century. In an age in which many people suffered hardships beyond our imagination, attendance at church must have been a short respite from the daily struggles of life. Apart from spiritual guidance, the church was a hub for a variety of activities and functions and the perfect place to communicate with parishioners.

Chapter 3   Sixteenth Century

The Roman Catholic Church of St Peter's in early sixteenth century Worfield would have presented a very different picture from the church of today. Most of the windows were plain glass bringing more light into the church and in the St Mary's Chapel a huge gilded cross with a statue of the Virgin Mary beside it hung above the rood screen. The roof of the rood loft (which housed the organ), was gilded and the cross and statue were illuminated by a lantern. I believe there was also a rood loft over the chancel with a large gilded cross suspended. Elsewhere, painted images and statues decorated the church telling biblical stories to a congregation most of whom could neither read or write.

Enter the pre-reformation Church and these might have been some of the sights and sounds to have greeted you. In St Mary's Chapel, a chantry priest might be chanting for the souls of the deceased or for other benefactors of the chapel. You may hear an organ playing (William Corvehill, sub-prior of Much Wenlock is believed to have built the organ) or there may be minstrels playing. If you were in the church at the time of festivals there would be special celebrations. At Whitsuntide and Pentecost a play called, 'The King', was performed and ale was sold and served in church[1] at Whitsuntide.

Should you have visited the church in 1535 there would be no strangers worshipping here. In the previous year there was an order that[2], *it is agreed by the hole paresche that no person shall bryng no owt cummer nor go with them in the churche nor in the peresche to gether nother corne nor money a pon a peyne* [penalty] *of 10s as often as he so doys.* If it was a Sunday you would hear the Vicar conduct mass and unless you could afford to pay for a seat you would stand. The first seats were forms or benches (we know from the Churchwardens' Accounts there were forms against the wall of the chancel) but by 1597 there were also pews. John Baker of Bromley, John Hitchcockes of Chesterton and Roger Baker of Kingslow agreed, in that year, that *Mr Thomas Barkley of Yewdness and his wyffe should knelle in the pewe next our Lady Chancell for and during there natural lyves and no longer in the year of our Lord God 1597.*

Apart from the salaries of the vicar and the chantry priests, and provision for the poor, payments were made to an army of skilled workers, most of whom were local. The smiths mended the bells, glasiers the windows, roofers replaced the shingles on the church roof, carpenters cared for the wood work and masons the stone work, women washed the linen, and vestments were sewn by hand. Candles of all sorts had to be made, torches for carrying at mass, the paschal candle, processional candles and tapers, all made locally. Some wax was bought but bees were also kept, to provide wax and honey. In 1500, 2d was paid for two beehives and Margaret Billingsley was paid 4d for her work around the bees. In the same year, Margaret Billingsley was also the brewer who kept an inn. The interior of the church was decorated with paintings and statues were painted and clothed. The Churchwardens' Accounts detail other expenses: for riding to Lichfield, Brewood, 'Shrosbyre,' Lapley and Dudley, for travelling to London in 1531 about the lord's meadow, and for providing the mass book and the Bible, some copies of which had to be handwritten and bound. The picture we have is the church as the focal point of parish life.

Chapter 3　　　　　　　　Sixteenth Century

The income which appears in the Churchwarden's Accounts includes gifts and bequests of money, goods and property and what were effectively local taxes levied on the inhabitants. In 1515 the Churchwardens report that, *Hit is a greed at these accounts that every yard lond within the parish shall pay this yere to the reparacions of the church and for makyng the churchyord walles- 4d.* [A yardland is about 60 acres.]

In addition to gifts of money there were gifts in kind. Pots and pans appear as both income and expenditure. In 1518, Amy Bulocke, in her widowhood, and Sir William Bulocke, her son, have given, after their decease, the *Grettyste panne and the Grettyste pott that they have.* In 1532, Roger Cattsrei received a great pan for debts he was owed, which in turn had been given by Roger Bucknall. Horses, sheep and cows were other gifts often given to the church. In 1511, John Hytchcockes gave a horse, and in the same year, Richard Felton and Elizabeth his wife gave a cow, to St Peter, in the keeping of Richard Blakemon. In 1515, the same couple gave to St Nicholas a two year old heifer. Gifts were sometimes given for specific purposes. In 1518, there is a list of properties in the accounts for the upkeep of the Lady's Chapel.[A] Thomas Pytt of Shipley gave a cottage at the end of the bridge at the Sonde so that after his death the Lady Chapel would receive 4s. The Lamp Meadow was so named because it had been bequeathed to the church for providing altar lights. The name appears in this court roll entry in 1579[3]

Roger Rowley and Humphrey Potter, with a plough undercut the Queen's highway between Rowley Field and Bradeney Field which road leads to Lampas Gate up to Sonde Field.

At the time of the Reformation, on or near the site of the new parsonage, there were several dwellings, one of which may have been the almshouse referred to in the Churchwardens Accounts. Hardwicke,[4] writing in the nineteenth century, described the collection of properties thus:

On the north side of the house [Lower Hall] *is a brick and timber structure, the dwelling of the six former vicars since the reformation. On the same point are several miserable dwellings which had been given at times to form a revenue for the priests of chantry who officiated at St Mary's altar. In 1 Edward 6 (1547/8) the chantry priests were dispossessed. The crown took over these houses and in James I's reign the churchwardens bought the houses for the poor of the parish. At the north end of these houses is a small meadow.*

Henry VIII, apart from settling his marital difficulties by making himself head of the Church in England, had also set his sights on the wealth of the church. An assessment of church lands was ordered and an inventory of church goods made.

In 1549 the Worfield Churchwardens Accounts record, *Item in going before the Kings commissioners at several times having diverse of the parishioners in their company for the inventory of the church goods and the surveying of church lands - 10s 4d* (sadly this inventory has been torn out and lost.)

Chapter 3 Sixteenth Century

In 1553 the entry records: *Spent at Bridgnorth to appear before the King's commissioners for the lamp meadow - 15d. For laying before the King's commissioners for a melyus enquiry about our church goods - 4s 4d and for appearing between Mr Flowyd and Mr Jong the King's commissioners 4s 4d.*

In 1534-5 the Valor Ecclesiastes[5] recorded the rectorial and vicarial incomes from Worfield. The Dean and Chapter of Lichfield received the rectorial tithes, on average, £51 per year - £2 from land, £24 from corn tithes, £20 from wool and lamb, £4 from hay tithes and £1 from hemp, flax and other small tithes. John Walker, the vicar, had property and income valued at £16 16s 10d, that is, 10s for the house and garden which was provided, £6 13s 4d in the Easter book, 14s for the tithes of the two mills, 18s for oblations of Chesterton Chapel, 12s for the oblations from Roughton Chapel, £5 for the corn tithes of Chesterton, 14s from the oblations of the "three days," £1 13s 4d of geese, young swine and other small produce and 2s 2d for candles. The only charge on this annual income was 6s payable every third year to the Bishop of Lichfield.

The Reformation and the years that followed were turbulent times. Henry VIII was followed by Edward VI, a confirmed Protestant, he by Mary, a Roman Catholic and she in turn by Elizabeth, a Protestant. The to-ing and fro-ing of activities in response to denominational requirements was costly, confusing and potentially dangerous. In 1552, when Edward VI was on the throne, the altars in Worfield Church were twice defaced at a cost of 10d and replaced by two trestles for the Lord's table at 8d. The Chantry was shut down by the Chantries Act of 1547 and the last Chantry Priest was William Hampton. The Lady Chapel was dismantled and made into a school house, pictures were defaced and the images pulled down. The walls once embellished with paintings were whitewashed, but no sooner had Edward VI died at the age of fifteen and Mary come to the throne in July 1553 than an altar stone was put back into the Lady Chapel and it seemed to be worship as before. There is an entry in the accounts of 1555-1556 *for stone to our lady altar and for hewynge of the same stone and carriage of the same from Bacher* [probably Badger] *mill 4s 8d*. Worfield was perhaps a little hasty in making this purchase because in 1562, after Elizabeth's accession, the altar stones had to be removed again and were carried away at a cost of 18d.

The Vicar of Worfield also found himself at odds with the new religion. After the Acts of Supremacy and Uniformity were passed in 1559, every vicar had to swear allegiance to the Queen; to acknowledge the monarch as the head of the Church in England rather than the Pope and the Prayer Book as the only legal form of worship. Thomas Chudleton, Vicar of Worfield, refused to take this Oath of Supremacy and in consequence was removed from office.

In 1549, Lichfield Cathedral sold the advowson of the Church to Sir John Talbot of Pepperhill near Albrighton. This seems an odd arrangement whereby when a vacancy for vicar arose, the holder of the advowson nominated a new incumbent to the Diocese. Worfield Church continued to be in the Diocese of Lichfield as far as church matters were concerned but the rectorial tithes would go to the new owner and in return the advowson would provide housing for the vicar and also a stipend. Shortly after taking over as Rector, Sir John Talbot built the house now known as Lower

Chapter 3   Sixteenth Century

Hall which stands opposite the church. Described in the Oliverian Survey of Worfield's Church lands in 1650 as *a fair house belonging to the Rectory which has been built by the Talbotts... and a vicarage adjoining.* Some years ago, a silver vervel, a ring around a hawk's leg, was found in the Worfield area, inscribed John Talbot.

Attached to the ring is this crest showing a talbot passant. A talbot, now-extinct, was a hunting dog. Finder Frank Taylor. Image courtesy of the Portable Antiquities Scheme. Item no. HESH-3A6AE5

On entering Worfield Church your eye will probably be drawn towards two alabaster memorials in the church and you may wonder what contribution the people so honoured made to the parish. George Bromley was the first son of George Bromley of Hodnet by Jane, daughter of Sir Thomas Lacon of Willey. Born in 1526, Sir George was only seven when his father, George, died. Without the benefit of paternal care, George Bromley's career was shaped by his cousin, Sir Thomas Bromley, and his mother's family, the Lacons of Willey. Perhaps it was here he met his future wife, Jane, the daughter and heiress of John Wannerton of Worfield. John Wannerton was the second husband of Alice Barker, her first husband having been William Day. Alice Barker was the sole heir of the Barker family of Hallon, the male line having died out. The marriage to John Wannerton produced one child, Jane (sometimes written Jone), who married George Bromley.

The Barker family came to Hallon from Calverhall near Whitchurch. Another family which came from the same place at the same time were the Smythes and they also seemed to have settled in Hallon for a time before moving down the road to Hilton. The Manor of Calverhall was owned by Bartholomew de Badlesmere who unwisely decided to rebel against King Edward II. Bartholomew de Badlesmere was hung, drawn and quartered, but he had put those associated with him and living in the manor in grave danger of a similar fate. It is thought this was the reason why William took the name Barker rather than William de Calverhall by which he had also been known. Barker might have been an occupational name, either a shepherd from the French, 'bercher,' or a stripper of bark for tanning. It was 'prudent' for William to put some distance between himself and Calverhall but why he came to Hallon we don't know. By 1327 he had been granted land in Hallon and that is where the family remained. It seems that the Barkers married well, marrying into the family of Whorwood, Lollestick and Colynson of Rowley so that by 1480 they are described by Hardwicke as *enjoying great estates in Hallon*[B].

George Bromley settled at the Barker's house in Hallon, but must have spent a great deal of time away from Worfield. The Bromley family had worked in and around court and parliament in their capacity as lawyers and MPs and George Bromley followed in their footsteps. Trained at the Inner Temple, George Bromley soon rose to positions of considerable authority. In 1554, during Queen

Chapter 3   Sixteenth Century

Mary's reign, he was a Steward of Crown Lands. From then on was appointed to a range of civil and ecclesiastical appointments, significantly, Chief Justice of Chester 1580, member of the Council in the Marches, Ecclesiastical Commissioner 1572, Custos Rotulorum (Keeper of the Rolls) 1574, Attorney General of the Duchy of Lancaster 1566-1580 and MP 1558-1572.

The only personal mark of George Bromley's life in Worfield is the address on a letter he wrote[8] on January 9 1577/8, *From my howse at Hallon*. This was the Bromley house, situated on the left hand side of the road from Hallon to Rindleford before Mere Pool.

The picture is taken from a plan of roads as altered by William Davenport[7]

Sir George & Dame Jane Bromley memorial in Worfield Church

On his memorial in Worfield Church, George Bromley is described as *a just man and a great professor of the Religion now established*, a fitting inscription since he played an active part in the establishment of the Protestant Church. In 1573 he was appointed a member of a commission set up to impose the Act of Uniformity of 1558. The Act required everyone to attend church at least

45

Chapter 3   Sixteenth Century

once a week on penalty of a fine of 12d. In 1577, George Bromley was then chosen with another man to compile a list of suspected recusants at the Inner Temple. Recusants were those who refused to attend Anglican services, mainly Roman Catholics. Bromley found fifty nine in all and listed them according to their level of complicity.

Baker's Cottage, Bromley. Houses of timber structure became fashionable in the late fifteenth and sixteenth centuries and were an ostentatious expression of wealth and creativity.

The Forest of Morfe

By the late sixteenth century the Forest of Morfe was becoming almost impossible to manage as a hunting forest. The Commoners' rights to graze their animals, take firewood, timber for building, hedging material and loppings, had taken a heavy toll of the tree cover in the forest. And yet there were still oaks growing. A parkland landscape it may have been but there must have been coppices of wood or how else would Lord Dudley have been able to take 4,000 oaks in 1592?

    Forest wood was used in the building of houses across all the manors associated with the Forest of Morfe and contributed to the loss of the woodland, of oaks in particular. Randall's[9] description of Baker's Cottage explains how essential good quality oak timbers were to the building of the most important houses in the parish.

Timber was unsparingly used in its [the cottage's] *construction. Great balks were laid down to build on; a framework was then raised upon them and bound together with iron clasps. The original windows are small and the rooms low and the doorways so diminutive that one must stoop to enter. "The door is so heavy," the woman of the house remarked," that when taken off the hinges for repair it took two men to remove it and it was like a plate of iron." There was no plaster ceiling*

Chapter 3   Sixteenth Century

to the chief room. The oak flooring fitted in between the joists so that the bare boards were exposed to view.

Firewood, too, was a vital and saleable commodity. Humphrey Wolrich[10] *felled great birches and also cropped 12 oaks in Worfeld and will not forbear.* John Hoord took 16 loads of wood at Christmas for his fuel.

The grazing of livestock impeded hunting in the forest. The sheer number of sheep, cattle and pigs meant a chase was impossible; the deer simply stood in disarray in their midst. Of the villages on the 1582 map[App 2a] with common rights in the Forest, each owner of a yardland (60 acres) had the right to graze 100 sheep, 12 cows and 2 horses. In Henry VII's time, in Bromley, Burcote, Burcote (Upper & Lower), Rindleford, Wyken and Swancote, there were around 1,500 sheep grazing in one year. It is recorded that, *they grazed all through the year, winter and summer.* One of the lovely things about looking at these old documents is the detail they contain. In this account of sheep, in Bromley, *John Hitchcock hath and his mother together -100 sheep,* and in Wyken, Richard Barker, the fletcher, had 80 sheep. In Summer the stock would be able to graze but in Winter the loppings of greenery from trees were an essential part of the animals' diet[10].

The Queen's tenants within the manor of Worfield and in the Forest of Morfe were listed in 1583 (Appendix 1.) The number of tenants were as follows: Bromley (4), Burcott (4), Swancott (2), Occom (3), Barnesley (1)), Roughton (12), Hylton (8), Sond (2), Rowley and Bradney (3), Chesterton (6). Rowley, Bradney and Chesterton were outside the Forest but had rights within it. Multiply that number by the number of commoners from Claverley, Bridgnorth and Quatford and those who took loppings without any rights at all and one can see how quickly the growth would disappear. Humphrey Wolrych took advantage of the opportunity to sell loppings when he cropped or lopped 36 oaks, carried the crop to Bridgnorth, and sold it to diverse people at diverse times for £10. He paid a penalty of this amount for so doing. In 1571-1572 William Jannes was presented[10]

for falling one hollow oak against Christmas and diverse others in both the Parishes of Worveld and Claverley and has made great waste in cropping of oaks to the value of 100 loads of wood the like of which was never seen before this year and they [the regarders] *say they will traverse the matter in law with the Queen's Majesty before they will lose their custom wood.*

Others who were brought to court were:

Thomas Aston of Bridgnorth felled holly, hawthorn and hazell
Roger Underhill of Bridgnorth for browsing and felling diverse grenes
William Heyns, labourer, for browsing and felling diverse grenes
John Therne for browsing
William Crompe, labourer, for felling holly and hawthorn ....
John Colyns for browsing
(crossed through) Raynold, the tinker, for felling grenes
(crossed through) George the labourer for felling holly, hawthorn and saplings

Chapter 3   Sixteenth Century

William Elcock, butcher, for browsing
(Crossed through) John Caldecote for browsing
William Elcock, butcher, & Thomas Nicholl, baker, felled 6 oaks in the Forest of Morff
Isabel Fleming, widow, for browsing
John Heyns cut growing branches
Thomas Cliffe for browsing and felling of grenes
William Gylis, labourer, for browsing
William Tucke, labourer, for cropping of oaks

Unauthorised felling of trees was an increasing problem which the supervisors of the Forest were unable to prevent. Even the keepers, themselves, were part of the illegal activity. In 1571 Francis Horde, gent, had three oak trees which, he said, he was permitted to take by the keepers. In the same year, the keeper is presented *for felling diverse elms in the forest but by what authority they know not.* Other forest officials carried off wood, made great waste and spoil, and cut down the underwood, *and now enter upon the oaks but by what authority we are ignorant.* The poor old supervisors of the Forest referred the matter to a higher authority in a rather despairing letter[10]

Present that the keepers of the Forest of Morfe do not regard the Queen Majesty's Commission but that they neglect and disobey the authority unto us committed and appointed concerning the preservation of the forest

Worfield men were some of the transgressors. In a postscript to the above, the regarders, John Hayward and Thomas Betterton wrote:

William Brooke under forester of the Forest hath a tenant one John Groome dwelling in Roughton in the Parish of Worveld within the County of Salop unto which tenant the said Brooke findeth wood all the year to his house out of the Queen's forest and the same tenant of his, John Groome sayeth he will fall trees by the root at his pleasure we know not by what authority.

Meanwhile, if the Forest officials were making merry with the resources of the forest, others probably felt they could do likewise. Dorothy Wolrich, a widow, *carried much wood out of the same Forest and made great spoil there but by what authority was not known.* Others claimed a right to wood which couldn't be proved. The Priory of St James had 12 oaks a year and the Hospital of St James, 8 oak trees *but by what authority we are ignorant.*

The Queen's advisors must have decided that it was time to dispose of the Forest and in 1588 the whole of the Forest of Morfe, its wood and herbage was leased for a period of twenty-one years to Hugh Sotherne,[11] at an annual rent of forty shillings. The villagers in and around the Forest were incensed. The inhabitants of fifty-two townships delivered a complaint to Edward Bromley specifying their grievances and the lease was revoked. The consequences of loss of grazing and other rights were unthinkable and for a short time at least, the status quo was maintained.

Chapter 3   Sixteenth Century

Lost and Found

Spindle Whorl (pronounced whirl)
Natural fibres had to be spun to be knitted or woven. Apart from wool, hemp and flax were grown to produce a coarse cloth from hemp and linen from flax. The whorl is a weight which attaches to the spindle affecting the rate of spin and twisting the fibres. Women were able to spin as they walked, in contrast to a spinning wheel.

Lead Tokens
Made locally, lead tokens had a variety of uses, for example, as small value coins, gaming tokens and tickets. They are difficult to date and hence usually given a broad date range of 1500- 1800
Finder: Frank Taylor

Chapter 3   Sixteenth Century

References
1. Worfield Churchwarden's Accounts 1502-1503 (Shropshire Archives)
2. Worfield Churchwarden's Accounts (Shropshire Archives) & Transactions of the Shropshire Archaeological Society 3rd Series Vol VII, 1907
3. Worfield Manor Court Rolls 5586/1/237 (Shropshire Archives)
4. Hardwicke, William. Collections for a History of Worfield (William Salt Library)
5. Valor Ecclesiastes (Shropshire Archives)
6. Oliverian Survey LD30/4/72 (Lichfield Archives) & Chapter 2 note K
7. Worfield Court Roll 1727 William Davenport alteration of roads (Shropshire Archives)
8. Manuscripts of Shrewsbury and Coventry Corporations Fourth Report, Appendix: Part x. Originally published by Her Majesty's Stationery Office, London, 1899.p 43-45
9. Randall, J. Worfield and Its Townships
10. Regarders' Accounts E32/149 (National Archives)
11. P314/Q/1/4/1 Revocation of the lease of the Forest of Morfe (Shropshire Archives)
Also: Michaelmas 6 Edward VI Rot 43

Notes
A. In 1518 the **Churchwarden's Accounts** record the following properties belonging to the Chantry:
The Sonde
Half a virgate of land of William Haslewood now in the hands of Dominus William Hasylwood - 4d halfpenny
Ditto for one cottage here - 1d
From William Sond for half a virgate of land - 4d
From Thomas Pytt of Shipley for several parcels of land and a cottage with curtilage - 4d halfpenny
From the house of the Rector of Quatt - a halfpenny
The Lowe
(2 illegible lines and one erased)
From Roger Catstrey for one garden at the Lowe on the left part leading to the Rector's meadow - torn
From the same for one meadow adjacent at Brade [Bradeney/Broad Bridge]
Separate entry for one cottage in the Lowe given by Nicholas Sadyllar and Humphrey Barret [in 1511 it is explained that Nicholas Sadler had given the cottage in his will]
Worfeld
From Agnes wife of Thomas Barker … for a parcel of land in Halon - torn
Ditto for one cottage - 3d
Ditto for half a virgate of land
From Roger [torn] for half a virgate of land - 4s 8d
From John Barker of Aston for a croft lying in Worfeld now in the hands of George Barker - 22d
From Richard Calo for a cottage - 10d
…for the Redhyll 1d
…for a garden - 3d
[rest torn]
Walston

Chapter 3 Sixteenth Century

From Thomas Glover for a cottage and a meadow - 10d
For a cottage lying at the well of St Peter in the hands of Dominus John Lye
Of the holding by the gift of Agnes Grene in Worfeld in the tenure of John Smyth - 10d
Of the holding formerly in the tenure of Robert Taylor now in the hands of Thomas Baret - 4d

Halon
From John Brown, miller, for one toft formerly in the hands of John Price of Newton - a halfpenny now in the hands of James Brown as testified by Humphrey Barret and others

Bradeney
From William Bradeney for parcels of land unseparated - 2d
Ditto for other parcels of land unseparated with the meadows of Richard Bradeney - 1d
From John Gold for other parcels of land unseparated - 1d

Brugenorth
From Roger Walker for the house of the Blessed Virgin Mary in the tenure of Henry Castell - 4d

Ewyke
From John Hychekockes Junior of Chesterton, son and heir of William Hychekokes for the land of Ewyke and the meadows here himself paying annually to the Chantry of the Blessed Virgin Mary of Worfeld from the gift and grant of Thomas Harley, Stephen Rowlowe and William Hychecockes aforesaid and all the heirs of the said John Hychecockes - 2s
Entry erased
From Thomas Undrell for a virgate of land - 13d
From William Foxall - 6

B. The Barkers held Winter's Place, Yeldon's Yard, Buryland, Chemehill near the Hollow Way in Hallon, Lollsticks, Massie's land and Chamberlaine's Yard. The family acquired a lot of property, but there were issues with other tenants over their holdings. In 1514 Richard Barker had to answer a claim to some land made by Thomas Alden. In the same year John Perry complained against George Barker in a plea of land and challenged over one messuage, a toft and fifteen acres of land called Lollstickland. Perry said that the property was a gift from Roger Catstree to William Perry of Bylston.

The Tailors' Platform at Lower Hall so named because it is believed tailors worked here when they came to make clothes for the family.
Source: Oliver Leese photograph album. Date of image estd. 1950s

Chapter 4   Seventeenth Century

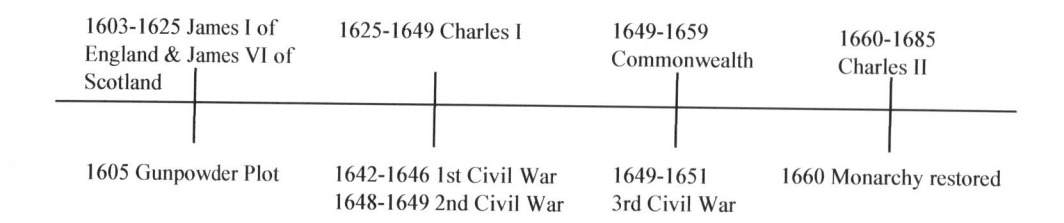

1603-1625 James I of England & James VI of Scotland	1625-1649 Charles I	1649-1659 Commonwealth	1660-1685 Charles II
1605 Gunpowder Plot	1642-1646 1st Civil War 1648-1649 2nd Civil War	1649-1651 3rd Civil War	1660 Monarchy restored

As the century dawned, Queen Elizabeth was still on the throne. On her death in 1603, her cousin, James VI of Scotland, was crowned James I of England. James was the first monarch to unite Scotland and England but he is probably best remembered for the fact that the Gunpowder Plot took place while he was on the throne. James proclaimed the day of the near-disaster, the fifth of November, a holiday. Each year thereafter, bonfires were lit and gunpowder exploded so that the day would not be forgotten. Charles I, James's son, who came to the throne in 1625 had none of his father's ability to hold the country together, and after a head-on clash between Crown and Parliament, the Civil War started in 1642. Four years later, the First Civil War ended with the capitulation of the Royalists at Oxford. The word of Parliament was supreme. The Royalists rallied troops and fought back in the Second Civil War but were defeated at Preston in 1648. Reluctantly, Cromwell sanctioned the execution of Charles I in 1649, but his son, who would later became Charles II, was not about to give up his claim to the throne without a fight. Charles's plan was to rally troops in Scotland, march south, enter London, and reclaim the throne. Events did not turn out as planned. Charles got as far as Worcester where he was defeated in battle and had to flee for his life. The story of how Charles made his escape and hid, firstly at Boscobel, and then at Moseley Hall, is well-known. Local families, loyal to the Royalist cause, such as the Penderel, Whitgreave and Lane families, facilitated the future monarch's escape to France and enabled his return in 1660 to be crowned King of England.

Shropshire was one of those counties which the King had to hold in order to win the Civil War[1]. If Shropshire fell, Wales was vulnerable. This poses the question as to which side Worfield was on at the start of the War. Royalist, almost certainly, but it is impossible to know how many parliamentary sympathisers there were in the parish. The Rowley family were the most prominent, but this was a war in which brother fought against brother so some family members may have been royalists. William Rowley, a maltster, from Worfield, was a well-known Puritan who had moved to Shrewsbury in the 1590s where his business as a wool merchant (draper) and brewer grew. We know that Roger Rowley was also a Parliamentarian and Francis Rowley, a tenant of Ewdness at one time, was probably of the same persuasion. It is interesting to speculate on Worfield's history had the monarchy not been reinstated in 1660 and the Whitmore fortunes restored.

Chapter 4   Seventeenth Century

If ever there was a family which took advantage of the benefits which Worfield had to offer, it was the Rowley family[2]. They were clever, enterprising and had great business acumen. In the sixteenth century, John Rowley had married Mary Barrett, a widow, of Astley Abbotts. As well as a substantial amount of money, Mary brought to the marriage the estate of Severn Hall, Astley Abbotts. When John Rowley died in 1566, his elder son, Roger, inherited Rowley and the younger son inherited Severn Hall. Roger married Ann, the daughter of William King of Birmingham and it was three of their sons who built the Rowley business up to be so successful. William, the eldest, built Rowley House in Shrewsbury, formerly the Shrewsbury Museum, and either John or Richard built the farmhouse and malthouse at Rowley. John was a maltster in Ackleton. The Rowley malthouse supplied breweries which the family owned in Bridgnorth and Shrewsbury, shipping the malt up the Severn by trow.

The Whitmore family, on the other hand, were typical of many of the lesser gentry who supported the King. During the Civil War, Apley House was used as a meeting place for prominent Royalists and it was during such a meeting, in February 1645, that Parliamentarians surrounded the house. Sixty common soldiers, and others, were captured, including Sir William Whitmore and his son Sir Thomas Whitmore. Some of the victors urged that Apley should be burnt to the ground, but it made more sense to make money from the situation. The Whitmore estate, including all the goods, chattels and personal estate of Sir William Whitmore of Apley[3] was thus sold to Roger Rowley, for the sum of £582 3s 2d. Of those who were captured at Apley, some were imprisoned but most of the commissioners remained in Bridgnorth Castle until they finally surrendered to the Parliamentarians in 1646. At the Restoration, Apley was returned to the Whitmore family.

Towns and other strategic points in Shropshire had to be held if the King was going to win the war but by the end of 1644 the Parliamentarians were in control of a swathe of land across the north of the county including Oswestry and Wem. Bridgnorth held out longer than many towns but in 1644 was vulnerable to attack after Prince Rupert's army had left. Worfield, being exactly east of Bridgnorth, must have played an important role in ensuring that the Roundheads did not come through the parish. Roads, river crossings and open land would all have been guarded. In Stableford, the house which stands on the hill, The Old House, was renamed Hayes Bank by John Collis who believed that a Colonel Hay was responsible for guarding the river crossings at Stableford and Rindleford during the Civil War. Whether there was such a man is not known but bridges and fords would certainly have been guarded.

The Parliamentarians did take Bridgnorth, but not from the east. A plaque on the Northgate of the town reads as follows:

On the 31st March 1646 Bridgnorth was captured by the Parliamentary forces; but the next day, Wednesday 1 April 1646 nearly the whole of the High Town was destroyed by fire started by the Royalist defenders of the Castle. More than 300 families were thus rendered homeless and destitute.

Chapter 4   Seventeenth Century

George Bellet wrote[4]:

The misery of the inhabitants of Bridgnorth is described as having been most severe. Rich and poor alike were left homeless and sought shelter where they could, in the fields around the town, in thickets, and under rocks: all their property destroyed and their life itself in jeopardy. Many a wretched invalid would be forgotten and left to die a more awful death than they had hoped for...

If only we had the Worfield Constables Accounts for this period we might be able to see the direct effect of the fall of Bridgnorth on the parish but the accounts are missing for the years 1641-1646. It is quite likely that some Worfield men were part of the Bridgnorth garrison. They may have been some of the large number killed or injured in the siege or caught up in skirmishes.

Crossed swords on the side of the Old House (Hayes Bank) in Stableford, which may date from the time of the Civil War

Even before the Civil War there was a system across the country for maintaining a fighting force to protect the country against invasion. The parish constable had to keep a list of those eligible for service, all able bodied men between the ages of 16 and 60. Periodically those listed had to assemble, or muster, for training or inspection. In 1650-1651 the eligible men were summoned to appear at the Old House with their horses and arms. The training was in addition to practising archery as required by law. The Constables Accounts record that there were shooting buttes at Sonde and Wyken Green. While the evidence for this activity in Worfield has long since disappeared, the walls of St Andrew's Church, Shifnal, are pitted with the marks of arrows. After church was a convenient time and the churchyard a very handy place for practice.

How seriously training was taken and how many attended is not known. These are the expenses which were incurred in peacetime and which would rise significantly in the Civil War[5].

Chapter 4 Seventeenth Century

1625-1626
Spent when the trained men met their Captain one day at Claverley and for shot and powder 4s 6d
laid out at Bridgnorth when the trained men were 2 days with their Captain for their charges and more arrows 21s 2d
laid out when we had a warrant to bring the trained men and their maintainers before their captains and the muster master 13s
for fetching the muster master at the lodge 2d
laid out when we and the trained soldiers went to Wenlock 9s
for powder, match and bullets the same time £12
to William Clark for carrying the armour to Wenlock 18d
for making our presentment and a roll to the High Constable of all the able mens names in the parish before the quarter sessions 6d
laid out when the trained men met in Morfe 4s
for match, powder and bullets the same time 12d

Each soldier had to be properly armed and there had to be a sufficient stock of weapons for the parish. The more well-to-do might have their own sword or dagger, the less wealthy might have a billhook. Other weapons were provided by the parish and their adequacy was assessed periodically. In 1591-1592 the 'furniture' was taken to Bridgnorth to be reviewed and was presumably found to be wanting. There follow a number of purchases to upgrade the armoury such as:

for 2 pikes 3s 6d
for 3 arrows and the heads 4d
for pointing a sword 1d
for a black bill and the halne 20d
for 3 rivetts and 2 buckles 2d
for train and choke to store and trim the harness 9d
for an headpiece for bow and arrows 2s 6d
for an headpiece for a musket 4s
for a mould 12d
for scouring the harness and mending the leathers 2s
for 3 flaske leathers 12d
for 2 girdles 8d

An inventory of all the parish armour delivered into the charge of the parish constables was made in 1601-1602 as follows:

2 corsletts (armour over the torso) *wanting on part of a pair of poldrons* (armour over the shoulders), *and 2 pikes* (ash poles with a spear at the end) *whereof one is in the keeping of Francis Westbury*

Chapter 4   Seventeenth Century

2 calivers (an improved version of the arquebus), *and a musket one belt 3 flasks* (for keeping gunpowder) *and touchboxes* (sometimes called matchboxes, match being a flax rope used for priming gunpowder), *one rest for the musket and 5 head pieces with 2 bullet bags, 3 mouldes* (for making musket balls) *and 2 wormes* (a corkscrew device for removing unexploded shot)
a bow and a sheffe of arrows, a skull cap, a black bill (similar to an agricultural billhook) *and one dagger*
one sword and dagger in the keeping of Stephen Rowley with the girdle and hangings and another sword and dagger with the girdle and hangings in the keeping of Roger Barret

Soldiers had to be properly clothed as well as armed. In 1596, the constables went to Shrewsbury to buy cloth for coats, at a cost of 3s. In the following year, 7s was paid for for the soldiers' apparel and in 1599 we have an account of all the items a soldier was supplied with when joining the army. John Jugmetrot first received 6d press money (ie for being pressed or conscripted) and then the following:

for his dinner and supper 12d
for a girdle and hangers 12d
paid to the high constable towards half the furnishing of John Jugmetrot 35s
for a shirt cloth and the making for the soldier John Jugmetrot 3s
for a pair of gloves for the same 4d
for a pair of shoes for the same 2s
allowed the soldier for half his own dagger 15d
spent when we bought his apparel 4d
our charge at the muster and at the delivering of the soldier John Jugmetrot to the conductor 2s 8d

Apart from John Jugmetrot, other soldiers were named in the early Constables' Accounts. In 1599 there was Thomas Hakins/Hankins, *then the soldier,* and in 1602, Edward Jones went to serve in Ireland. William Millens, John Beech, Thomas Bradburne, William Smyth, John Brooke and William Bowen each received 4d press money in the same year and William Millens was *hired to allow the sword* (6d). Thomas Berkeley had a troop of light horse at Ewdness in the early part of the century and between 1626 and 1632-1633 Berkeley was paid by the parish constables to show his troop. The entry the following year was crossed out so perhaps the troop was disbanded or transferred elsewhere. Later there is a reference to a troop of dragoons in Worfield. There was also a group of trained men whose job was a defensive one, to guard the parish itself. It was these trained bands who were called upon to defend the eastern boundary of Shropshire in 1644.

Soldiers had to be given food and lodgings when asked for. Sometimes 'quarter' was provided in the local church. Worfield Church was not used in this way but in Wolverhampton soldiers were housed in St Peter's Church for five days. As a result, many old records were destroyed. Thomas Bradney, a soldier, (surely from the Worfield family of the same name,) had an issue with his

Chapter 4   Seventeenth Century

landlord, Mr Lee, and destroyed the title deeds of the property concerned. In Worfield in 1642-1643, the manor court rolls were destroyed by the soldiers. This was recorded by the under steward, William Perry[6], as follows:

The Court Book of this manor between Michaelmas in the seventeenth and eighteenth years of the reign of King Charles being plundered and taken away from the under steward Mr William Perry by soldiers, these copies ensuing which were of the same year in the tenants own hands are by the tenants desired to be entered and enrolled being brought and delivered in full court.

Whether there was a particular reason for the destruction of this court roll is not known. Perhaps it was because the Whitmores had declared for the King in 1642, because the soldiers wanted to demonstrate their power, or because there were personal scores to be settled. It is one of the few descriptions we have of how the war disturbed the peace of the parish.

There are many references in the Constables' Accounts to quartering, as shown below. In 1645, Worfield was quartering Royalist horsemen from Lichfield and oats and peas were sent from Stockton to feed the horses. In 1647, William Billingsley was reimbursed 3s 4d for his costs in quartering five soldiers for one night. From 1647 until 1651 quartering was an onerous cost on the parish. One cannot imagine that the men would have been your ideal house guests. Some carried disease, others were injured; not with clean, dressed wounds, but festering, suppurating battle wounds. Others who had to be quartered were simply out of control and hell-bent on taking whatever they could. Captain Young's men were a a rebellious group which had refused to disband when ordered. Having stayed in Bridgnorth for a time, the town bribed them to leave. Worfield was their next home, arriving on 21 November 1647 where they were just as troublesome. Eventually it would seem that Worfield, too, managed to move Captain Young's men on.

1647-1649
to Robert Barrett for going to Badger about Captain Younges soldiers
our charges for bringing Captain Young money and one to go with us - 1s 4d
paid to Thomas Rowley for going to Shrewsbury about Captain Young's soldiers 2s 6d
for quartering 2 soldiers one night and another night and their horses 5s 6d
paid to Thomas Tyror for quartering one soldier and horse one night 1s 6d
for quartering 5 soldiers at Vernons as before one night 5s
for quartering 5 soldiers one night my self 3s 4d
for quartering soldiers one other night 2s 8d
Given to John Best for quartering one soldier 2 nights and one day 2s 4d
to a troop of soldiers which would have quarter one night in the parish 8d
given to John Best when soldiers were quartered here 1s 6d
paid to William Newton and John Sadler for quartering soldiers who came for money before it was due 3s 4d
spent quartering soldiers as before 1s 6d

Chapter 4   Seventeenth Century

paid to Captain Cresett £1 8s
1648-9
paid to Thomas Rowley for going to Shrewsbury about the soldiers 12s 6d
1649
paid to William Newe for quartering soldiers who came for contributions before it was due 2s 4d
paid to Captain Cressett £4 10d
Paid to Captain Crooe £10 10s
1649-1650
for charges for quartering soldiers at Widow Stiches 1s
for relief of one Thomas Brooke a soldier who had a pass to travel to his friends 6d
for giving summons to the parishioners for to take the engagement 6s 4d
for quartering 2 soldiers who had been to see their friends 1s
paid to Captain Broadhurst and a horse for taking of soldiers who were a plundering and carrying home to Shrewsbury ordered by the justices 4s 6d
paid to a soldier for quarter one night who was to guide his company 10d
paid to Edward Frichart a soldier for his quarter one night 1s
aid to John Pernum for quartering one foot soldier one night having a passage to his company in Leicester1s
spent at the quartering of soldiers Feb 1st- 6d
1650-1
for bringing an hue and cry to Badger who came after a mare was stolen from Worcester 2d
for relieving 2 maimed soldiers which came from Worcester fight having a pass 1s
given to a maimed soldier being disbanded and having a pass to travel towards his own country 6d
Paid to William Palmer for quartering soldiers who came for contribution before it was due 2s 8d
to 2 of the General's men who had quarters and a peck of oats 1s
hue and cry to Bridgnorth 2d
for 4 soldiers who were on their march to Ireland 1s 6d
for a brass half crowne put upon us by Captain Crompe 2s 6d
paid to Captain Crompe for quartering soldiers more then gathered 8s 4d
paid to soldiers which were upon their march and would have quarter 2s 6d
1651-1652
for dining 4 maimed soldiers who came from Worcester and were travelling towards Chester having a pass 1s 4d
for quartering a soldier 2 days who had ?news for Captain Croo charges for himself and horse 2s 6d
Paid to Captain Detton who had a pass and was going towards London 1s 8d

Chapter 4   Seventeenth Century

By 1649, the war had become so expensive and disruptive that people were weary, and it became increasingly difficult for the constables to collect the taxes which were due. The parish constables had a thankless job in carrying out orders. There were meetings to be attended, soldiers to be accompanied, summonses to be received and carried out and money to be collected. Parishioners, too, were sent hither and thither as the war dictated.

1650
spent at Shifnal when we were called in to give the names of the soldiers and contributors 4 September 1s
for summoning the maintainers and soldiers with my charges going to Shifnal to make return of the warrant 1s
paid to two soldiers of their coming to take up arms at Shifnal September 24 3s
for giving summons to the trained soldiers to repair to their colours at Shifnal and making return of warrant 6d
for giving summons to the parishioners to appear at Lilshull hill with my charges to going in to make return of the warrant 1s 6d
for giving summons to the parishioners to appear at Old Heath with my charges for going thither 2s 6d
spent at Worfield at a meeting re maintained soldiers' pay 6d
for going in with provision to Bridgnorth for soldiers which were quartered there with any expenses there Sept 6d
spent when went to Wenlock and Shrewsbury the first time to take in men to be imprest £1 12 10d
spent the second time when we went to Shrewsbury to bring in men to be imprest 14s 9d
1650-1651
for moving the trained soldiers and their maintainers to go in to train at Newport and making a return of the warrant 8d
given to a soldier who came by entreaty not having a pass - 2d
for giving summons to the maintainers of the Dragoons to send in their horse and men upon 17 December and returning the warrant 6d
spent at Shifnal by the maintainers January 8 1s 8d
for giving summons to the maintainers and trained soldiers to come in and my own charges going in to make returne
for summoning the trained soldiers and giving notice to the maintainers to send in their soldiers with their arms complete to Newport and 10 days pay and making a return of 6d
for the return of the warrant requiring the maintainers and ...to meet at John Bach's July 3rd to ... business 4d
spent at Wellington bringing in the trained soldiers to deliver up presentments 2s

Chapter 4 — Seventeenth Century

for overseeing summons to let maintainers of the dragoons to send in their horse with horse maintainers to Shifnal 6d

spent at Worfield, Wenlock and Salop when we took in the men to be imprest £1 16s 8d

spent at Shifnal when we were charged by a warrant to summon in all inhabitants to bring in all their horses and mares to Lilshall hill and for giving summons and making return [August] 1s 6d

spent at Shrewsbury and by the way going thither and coming home when we went to make return having summoned all persons within the age 16 and 60 to appear at the Old House with their horses and arms 2s 6d

spent at Worfield at a meeting concerning the trained soldiers and captain 1s 6d

spent going to pay part of a fortnight's pay for the trayners unto the High con[stable] 4d

spent at Worfield July 12 by prest men and their keepers 2s 6d

for the return and execution of the warrant requiring watch and search to be set forth for the apprehending of all Scotts and others 6d

paid to the High Constable for the relief for the Scottish prisoners 8d

William Pendrill and the famous oak tree at Boscobel in which the future King, Charles II hid after his escape from the Battle of Worcester.

The 3rd of September 1651 marked the end of the Civil War when King Charles's Scottish army was soundly defeated at the Battle of Worcester. 2,000 soldiers died and 3,000 were taken prisoner but the remnant of the army was left to make their own way home. Search warrants were issued for any hiding in Worfield.

| Chapter 4 | Seventeenth Century |

1651-1652
paid to a leaven maimed soldiers who had a pass to go to Ludlow for their relief 1s 8d
and for carrying one of them to Bridgnorth with a horse 6d
for relieving 2 soldiers who were travelling towards Bristol having a pass 6d
for relieving 2 maimed soldiers which came from Worcester fight having a pass 1s
given to a maimed soldier being disbanded and having a pass to travel towards his own country 6d
given to a souldier who came out of Shipley and had a pass to travel to Ludlow 6d

It is a wonder that during the ten years of Civil War normal life could continue in any sense at all, yet it seemed to have done so. In 1641-1642, the same year in which the soldiers had seized the manor court rolls, the Churchwardens Accounts record that the cock on top of the Church was gilded. The needs of the farm had to be met, too, or there would be no food to eat. In 1634 two books were bought for the improvement of husbandry and while the Civil War may have put such improvements on hold, work on the farm was essential to survival. In Wyken, in 1647, the Reeve set out the manor's obligations in harvesting the lord of the manor's hay[7]:

To cause the lord's meadows to be mown and the hay made having notice given him for that purpose every half yard land sending one mower and two hay makers till it be made ready for carrying. And then they are not to be troubled any more with it but to tell the lord it is made and deliver it up. Three days warning for mowing and making the meadows is usual. When the mowers have mowed the meadows they are to have drinking. The lord to spend 12d and the reeve 6d. And likewise when the haymakers have made the hay they are likewise to a drinking and cakes that is every hay maker a farthing cake and drink. The lord then spends 12d and the reeve 18d in the whole the lord 2s and the reeve 2s which is the due. What more they please.

The Constable, in his accounts of 1651-1652, records his irritation that the demands of his job have got in the way of getting in the harvest.

Had to remove a woman out of our parish which the said John Pugh had begotten with child which was afterwards delivered at Hallon spending a day in the busiest time of the Burley [barley] *Harvest with my expenses 1s 6d* [September]

Oliver Cromwell died on 3rd September 1658 and King Charles 11 was restored to power by popular demand of the people on May 29th 1660.

Bromley-Davenport Inheritance
George Bromley died in 1588, followed four years later by his eldest son, Francis. The Bromley estate then passed to Francis's eldest son, Thomas, who died in 1609 without issue. Against all the

Chapter 4   Seventeenth Century

odds the Hallon lands descended to the second child of Francis Bromley - Jane. Perhaps it was fitting that it should be so because the Barker land which Jane Wannerton took with her into her marriage with George Bromley also came through the female line. This is a summary of the relevant genealogy:

George Barker's only child was Alice who married (1) Richard Day of Hallon and (2) John Wannerton. By (1) there was a son, William Day, who died without issue and by (2) there was a daughter, Jane Wannerton.

Jane Wannerton married George Bromley (died 1588) and there were ten children. The eldest boy was Francis.

Francis Bromley (died 1591) married Joyce Leighton of Wattlesborough who married (2) Walter Wrottesley. By Francis there were three children, Thomas (died Feb. 1609-1610), Jane and Charles. Jane Bromley married William Davenport (1603-1604).

It was in this way that Jane Davenport legitimately inherited the Bromley lands but it was an inheritance contested by the Bromley family and by Peter Gyfford, who had taken the tenancy of the lands in question. William Davenport was the outsider from the parish who met his future bride in a manner reminiscent of a Bronte novel. This is the story as told by Randall in 'Worfield and its Townships.' Shortly before Francis Bromley died, the family were living at Hallon House and one night a stranger was riding towards his home in Chorley, Cheshire, and lost his way. Hallon House being on a hill, the rider saw the lights of the house, knocked on the door and was invited in. The stranger was particularly taken with the daughter of the household and vowed that she should be his wife. The girl was Jane Bromley and the stranger was, of course, William Davenport. After Francis Bromley's death, Joyce Bromley married Walter Wrottesley and it was from Wrottesley Hall that William Davenport took Jane away and married her against her mother's wishes.

William Davenport, baptised in 1585 at Wilmslow, Cheshire, was the son and heir apparent of Henry Davenport of Chorley in Cheshire and it was there that the young couple initially set up their home. Shortly after their marriage in 1603-1604, William Davenport and Jane brought an action in the Court of Chancery[A] against Walter and Joyce Wrottesley concerning the estate of Francis Bromley, deceased. William's claim was that Francis Bromley had goods etc. to the value of £2,000 and had intended to give Jane £1,000 on her marriage. On his death bed, according to William's claim, Francis had stated this intent and asked that Joyce Bromley care for their children and carry out his wishes. There were three children, Thomas, the eldest who would inherit from his father, Jane, and Charles, the youngest. When Joyce Wrottesley married Walter Wrottesley an agreement was made that Walter Wrottesley would taken over the fatherlike care of the children.

The outrageous claim of William and Jane Davenport must have made the Wrottesleys gasp. Their answers were succinct. No, Francis Bromley had nothing like an estate of £2,000, he had no more than £350 and he died intestate. His annual income was no more than £100 per year since his mother, Lady Jane Bromley, was still alive at the time of his death. Yes, Joyce Bromley, was given £580 by Lady Jane Bromley as part of a promised £800 and Joyce had given William Barker £400

Chapter 4   Seventeenth Century

to invest but William Barker died and the money appeared to be lost. Joyce's intention had been to confer the greater part of the £580 to Charles and Jane. This would be the only money the children would receive and therefore Joyce tried to restrain her daughter from making an unsuitable marriage. If she followed her mother's advice, Jane would receive £300, if she did not do so, she would be entitled to the same sum as her younger brother Charles, £100. Walter and Joyce made this statement to the Chancery Court:

... about September, last past twelvemonth, the said complainant Jane, being then young, was by some practices and persuasions of the other complainant, William Davenport (a man in worth and estate far unworthy of such a match), privily enticed and stolen away from the house at Wrottesley and married to the said complainant, William without the probity, notice or consent of the defendants.[A]

William Davenport answered that he was in every way a worthy match for Jane and that he did not entice or steal her away. Chancery claims were notoriously convoluted and lengthy and often never came to a conclusion. In this case I have found no more. Perhaps William Davenport let the Chancery claim lapse when a bigger prize came into view.

The next challenge William and Jane made was to the right of Peter Gyffard to the Wannerton holdings. In 1608 Richard Day came to the Worfield Manor Court and surrendered land in Hallon, *as the son and heir of Alice Wannerton.* This was the correct procedure by which the tenant would surrender the property into the hands of the lord and then the property would be taken out of the lord's hands by the new tenant. The new tenant of the Wannerton lands in 1608 was Peter Gyfford. In 1610 Richard Day died, as did Thomas Davenport (Jane's elder brother) and in 1611 William and Jane Davenport made a claim in Jane's name on the Bromley estate, contesting Peter Gyfford's tenancy of the Hallon lands[8].

The case rested on how the estate had been left many years before which was as follows. When Alice Barker died, the estate was to go to William Day and his heirs, then to Richard Day and his heirs. Here was the problem, Richard Day died in 1610 without heirs. In this event the estate was to go to Alice's other child and her heirs. That child was Jane Wannerton, who married Sir George Bromley. Lady Jane Bromley, wife of George Bromley, *the virtuous Lady Jane* had died in 1607 and with the death of her father and elder brother, Jane Davenport was the next in line to inherit.

The Davenports asked for a jury to enquire into the legality of the land transfer to Peter Gyffard. Jurors were named but twice failed to attend court[B]. One can imagine that being a juror in such a difficult case was an unenviable position to be in. Eventually twelve men were sworn and did attend. The steward summarised an interim position as follows:

We find that John Wannerton and Alice his wife were seised of the aforesaid holdings in fee according to the custom in the right of Alice and did surrender with respect to Henry VIII 37 and that Richard Dey son and heir apparent of Alice was accordingly seised and did surrender in these words. And that afterwards 19 February Elizabeth 4, John Wannerton etc as shown in the copy. But

Chapter 4 — Seventeenth Century

if on all the matter etc the law fall out for the demandants then we find for the demandants and if otherwise then we find for the tenant.

In 1614 the steward made his decision and it was in favour of Jane Davenport who was admitted to the Barker lands in Hallon[C]. At stake had been the Barker family home at Hallon which of course had also been the Bromley family home.

The Bromleys contested the legality of the Davenport claims until the end. Edward Bromley in his will[9] in 1625 doubted the legality of the claims suggesting that he was the rightful heir to the estate having paid Thomas Bromley's debts but by that time it was too late.

Whereas William Davenport of Hallon and Jane his wife, daughter and heir of Francis Bromley, pretend a right to certain manors, lands and inheritance of Sir George Bromley deceased, my father, which were conveyed to me by a declaration of uses... whereas the said Thomas Bromley in consideration that I paid his debts, gave me in fee all his Manors, lands etc and that I have paid £700 ...

We know from the Constables' Accounts[5] that Baron Bromley was in Hallon in 1617 and Lady Bromley in 1634. After that date there is no further mentions of the Bromley family in the Constables Accounts. Hallon is such a small place that it must have been very uncomfortable with the Davenport and Bromley families living there at the same time and yet it seems that was probably the case. In 1616-1617 there was a warrant to bring William Davenport before Mr Kinnersley in Newport but in connection with which case we don't know.

Forest of Morfe

Around the same time as the Bromley Davenport drama was taking place there was another major event in the manor, the sale of the Forest of Morfe. This would have affected the grazing rights of many of the villagers who had common rights within the Forest. Even under the monarch's ownership, enclosures had been taking land out of the 7,000 acres of forest thus restricting the area of common grazing. We saw in the last chapter the reaction of the villagers to a twenty-one year lease to Hugh Sotherne, of the whole of the Forest of Morfe. In 1652 feelings ran high when Thomas Wolrych was given permission to enclose 25 acres called The Bind[10]. Several tenants broke into the area and destroyed fences and hedges.

The sale of the Forest of Morfe would go ahead eventually to other buyers but a valuable by-product of the intention to sell the Forest was a map of the townships and their inhabitants drawn by Samuel Parsons [App 2].

Care of the Poor

The Merrie England of the Tudor period was not quite so merry if you happened to meet some of the gangs of vagrants who wandered around the country. In the sixteenth century the population grew and common fields in many areas were enclosed for sheep grazing. In Worfield this enclosure

Chapter 4   Seventeenth Century

did not happen until later but the effects of enclosure elsewhere were undoubtedly felt within the parish. Squeezed out of any means of making a living, an underclass of poor and dispossessed grew in numbers and disaffection. Without a roof over their heads and with no means of making a living, they took to the road. Travel outside one's parish was only permitted with a pass which entitled the traveller to food and lodgings within the parish they were passing through, and help in getting to the next parish. Many roamed without passes and were treated in a similar way - fed, watered and moved on. Others with fewer prospects took to a life of crime. Even begging was denied to them as begging was illegal.

Rather than allowances being made for the circumstances which had made people poor, poverty was seen as being caused by the individual. To deal with their condition they needed to stop wandering, get back to their home parish, and start work. The lazy or incompetent were only a small part of the problem, however. If Worfield's Constables' Accounts in the Seventeenth Century[F] were typical of what was happening across the country, large numbers of people were on the move. There were soldiers going to or from war, those who had lost their their homes through fire, had losses at sea, or who had had their goods stolen. There were the infirm, the diseased, orphaned children, cripples and Eygptians (gypsies). Many of those on the tramp would never work again.

Most of the travellers walked. If they were lucky, a group might have one horse between them. One mother walked, carrying her two children in panniers. People walked great distances, in all weathers, from Northumberland, Cumberland, the Low Countries and Ireland with goodness knows what cladding on their feet or clothes on their backs. The lodgings and food they were given were a lifeline and sometimes they received a small amount of money to travel with. One poor boy *that was like to perish in the snow,* was saved by John Felton who kept him at his home in Worfield for a week. Pregnant women might fall into labour during their journey and were kept at the expense of the parish. In 1616, the parish paid 4s for bringing to Bridgnorth a poor man and his wife and 2 children of which she was delivered at Hilton and finding them relief for a fortnight. Others were less fortunate and died unknown becoming merely an entry in the Constables' Accounts, *For burying a poor woman ...*

Queen Elizabeth's Poor Law dealt with the poor, rogues and vagabonds by punishing, feeding, and moving them on to the next parish. The whipping post or a night or two in the stocks, was the usual punishment. Whipping posts stood in Worfield[F] and Hilton and there may well have been others in the parish. Evans, in his book, 'The Rectors and Vicars of Worfield,' says the Worfield stocks were on a patch of grass by the north west gate to the church. The stocks in Hilton were probably on the Green which begs the question where the Green was. In 1597 a poor boy was whipped, in 1601 three rogues were whipped and in 1633 a woman and a wench were kept two days and a night and then whipped. A deterrent to both victims and onlookers alike one would imagine.

Chapter 4   Seventeenth Century

The other part of the treatment of travellers was to move them on to the next parish. The infirm, women and small children were often taken by cart, in a barrow, or on horseback. In 1619 the constable took three poor folk to Bridgnorth *one of whom was lame and I carried on horseback.* Those who could walk were accompanied to the next parish. There are some heartbreaking stories. In 1632, a dumb man who had had his tongue cut out was taken to Claverley. I wonder how long the poor man survived the trauma and why his tongue cut? A woman whose husband was killed and her child burnt in a house fire was another poor wandering soul. How on earth did people who had suffered in this way rebuild their lives?

Apart from the poor and needy who came from outside the parish, the parishioners themselves could fall on hard times and the Parish had to support them. The Churchwarden's Accounts in 1604-1605 show a payment to Joan Vallance, *for keeping the bastard*, and in the same year *poor* Thomas Taylor, by consent of the parish, was given 18d. In 1612, Stockhall, a mason, was commissioned to hew out rock in a cave at St Peter's Well to provide a house for a poor person who had none, and in 1608, John Vallance, a lunatic, was brought home.

Before the Reformation, care of the poor had been the responsibility of the church and the Chantry at St Peter's had a pauper's house. After the Reformation, caring for the poor became a parish responsibility. The law required Overseers of the Poor to be appointed and a means of raising and distributing money put in place. A book had to be kept for recording the recipients of money which was raised by a rate levied on land. The church continued to collect money for the poor, and a box was put in the church for this purpose. In 1648, a box, since lost, was made with the inscription, 'Bee sure as you remember the poor.'

Bequests were another source of income. In 1609, Thomas Woolley[D], a servant of Sir George Bromley and Lady Jane Bromley, left £100 to buy land which would generate an annual profit. The following property was purchased, a cottage and land in Brierley [we would now call it Brierley Hill] called The Toft, three cottages and an acre of land in Worfield (1613) and a cottage and a garden in Bridgnorth. The first beneficiaries of the bequest were:

Jerome Warter 2s 6d, John Frodgesley 2s 6d, Francis Hatton 2s 6d, Thomas Lowe 2s 6d, Robert Maynard 2s 6d, Johanna Weaver 2s 6d, Eleanor Warter 12d, Susan Walker 12d, Alice Freewoman 2s, John Groome 2s, Richard Hatton, 12d and his brother Roger Hatton 12d, Hugh Yeat 12d, to his sister Mary Yeat 12d, George Staunton 2s

In 1624, George Bromley, son of Sir George Bromley, left £100[E] to be used to buy land to generate an annual profit to be distributed to the poor. Although George Bromley had made his home in Albrighton, he felt a love towards *the Parish of Worvile, my native soil.* The profit was to benefit twenty-four poor inhabitants *in the same parish, none of them being juveniles but aged, impotent people or decayed householders of honest conversation.*

Chapter 4   Seventeenth Century

Crime and Punishment

Fighting crime in the seventeenth century was a social duty. If a crime was committed it was the duty of the victim to report it and, if the perpetrator was still at large, a hue and cry was raised. Neighbours were obliged to help catch the criminal as well as the constables of the parish. In 1603[5] the hue and cry was raised when Mr Brooke's silver plate was stolen and in 1618 the hunt was on for those who had robbed John Barrett of Alscote. If the suspect escaped out of the parish the hue and cry had to be taken to the next parish and the constables there had to search for him/her. Some of the hues and cries were carried long distances, from Coventry when silks and velvets were stolen, from Wellington after horses were stolen and from Stafford after a man in a black doublet, and riding a black horse, murdered a man. In 1619 a hue and cry was raised from Kinlet when Sir Francis Lacon was robbed. Livestock were common targets of hungry thieves and poultry were an easy prey. Other items were stolen for their monetary value. Tails and manes were 'trimmed' from horses as the animals grazed. In 1625 a woman was caught in Worfield with eleven pounds of horse hair[F]. Once caught the suspect had to be watched until they could be taken to Bridgnorth. For lesser crimes the punishment might be a day or two in the stocks, a good whipping or a stay in the house of correction. More serious crimes were tried at Shrewsbury. The job of a constable included many duties we would today see as outside the scope of the police such as transporting transients, military matters, weights and measures and licences for brewing.

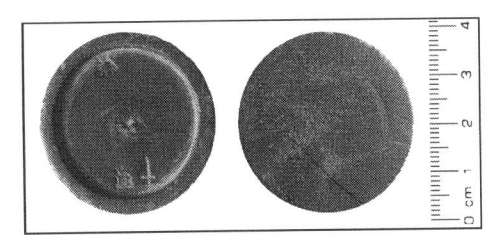

Weight HESH-829485
The front face is marked with a series of stamps - a crowned EL (Queen Elizabeth), the dagger or sword of the London Guildhall, and the ewer (coffee pot) of the Worshipful Company of Founders. 1588-1603

On the left is a Commonwealth coin found in Worfield/Rudge. The St George's cross and the Irish harp have replaced the royal arms. The found coin has been clipped and should look like that on the right. An anchor above the shields is visible but the writing round the edge has gone. 1658-1660

Chapter 4 Seventeenth Century

Cloth Seal HESH-8328B8
The two discs were clasped either side of a piece of cloth to guarantee its size and quality.
1400 -1700 AD.

Charles I coin HESH-829485
A high value coin to lose. Very fine condition.
1625-1626
Finder of these items: Frank Taylor
Images courtesy of Portable Antiquities Scheme

News from the Parish
Births
December 7 1602 Alyce, daughter of Elizabeth from the Lodge, a base daughter as she saith, of Roger Walton of Hilton, husbandman and servant
July 14 1605 Yeekin, Jane, daughter of Richard of Acleton, cooke & Jane
May 9 1605 Bradney, Ann, daughter of William of Winscot, fisher and Jone
Burials
Jan 18 1600-1601 William of Hoccum, householder, husbandman, died in the Church upon a January between Thomas Gyldon of Bradney and Humphrey Lythall of Enville.
1601 Alice Jymetrot of the Armitage, widow, pore.
Jan 30 1658/59 Abraham Jones son of William of Barnsley, a glover and Ann. Died 29th Jan

References
1. Worton, Jonathan, To Settle the Crown (Helion & Co 2016)
2. Caradoc & Severn Valley Field Club Transactions, 1915-1916, p170 & Ionides, J. and Howell, P. G., The Old Houses of Shropshire in the Nineteenth Century. The Watercolour Album of Frances Stackhouse Acton (The Dog Rose Press, Ludlow, 2005)
3. The Garrisons of Shropshire during the Civil War 1642-1648 (Leake and Evans, 1867)
4. Bellet, Rev George, The Antiquities of Bridgnorth, page 170
5. Worfield Constables Accounts, series P314/M (1617 for making a certificate to the Right Honourable Baron Bromley concerning Walton's examination 4d. 1634 a hue and cry from the Lady Bromley.)
6. Worfield Manor Court Rolls P314/W/1/1/944 (Shropshire Archives)

Chapter 4   Seventeenth Century

7. Reeve's Book of Rents from Worfield & Wyken 3007/4 (Shropshire Archives)
8. Worfield Manor Court Rolls 5586/1/268 - 5586/1/272 (Shropshire Archives)
9. Transactions of the Shropshire Archaeological Society 2nd series vol. 5 1893
10. Revocation of Lease of Forest of Morfe P314/Q/1/4/1. The Bind Enclosure Riot, 1652, 2922/1/5/14 (both in Shropshire Archives)
11. Moran, Madge, Vernacular Buildings of Shropshire (Logaston Press, 2003)

Notes

A. Davenport versus Wrottesley C2/Jas1/D13/27 (National Archives)
Sir Walter Leveson and …Humphrey Gifford, John Fowkes esq, Samuel Pyper, gent with William Davenport and Jane his wife petitioners before us in Chancery versus Walter Wrottesley and Joyce at Westminster 11 February 1st year of the reign of James I

William Davenport, son and heir apparent of Henry Davenport of Chorley and Jane his wife.
Whereas Francis Bromley of Haunde in the County of Salop esq late father of the said Jane was in his lifetime lawfully possessed of and in diverse goods, chattels, household stuff, plate, jewels and sums of money to the value of two thousand pounds as of his own proper goods and chattels and whereas the said Francis Bromley being so possessed did by good assurance thereof in the law give, demise and assign to the said Jane in money and other goods and chattels for her proferment in marriage amounting to the whole to the sum of one thousand pounds and did constitute and appoint Joyce Bromley then his wife and mother to the said Jane to have the safe keeping and proceeding of the said assurance so made as aforesaid and further willed and required the said Joyce upon his death bed that she the said Joyce would have motherlike care of the said Jane and to perform his said intent and mind to the uttermost value according to the content of the said assurance so made as aforesaid and afterwards died by and after whose death the said Joyce did marry and espouse Walter Wrottesley of Wrottesley in the County of Staffs esq betwixt whom there were indentures of covenant made and settled for the more speedy effecting of the said marriage in which said indentures it was especially concluded and agreed that the said Walter Wrottesley should perform all and every such act and acts which her other late husband did make in his lifetime for the payment of the marriage money of the said Jane and as was by him required as he lay on his death bed and should likewise give the said Jane £300 more for increase of her portion but now so it may please your lord that they the said Walter Wrottesley and Joyce his wife having gotten into their hands custody and possession [of] the said assurance made unto the said Jane or unto her use as aforesaid and pretending that there was never any such gift or grant made of the goods, chattels and premises for that she the said Jane being but of a young and tender years at the time of the death of her late father neither she nor your orator William Davenport know the contents and particulars thereof neither the kind, quality, quantity or value of the same they the said Walter Wrottesley and Joyce his wife have and do refuse and deny to deliver unto your said orators the said goods, chattels and premises so given and demised to the said Jane or to make any due satisfaction for the same in tender consideration of the premises and for as much a the said Walter Wrottesley and Joyce his wife have diverse and several times confessed and acknowledged that the marriage of the said Jane was worth in money, goods and chattels to the value of £1,200 at the least and for that your said orators knowing not the …date or contents of the said assurance nor of the said goods, chattels and premises and that the said Walter Wrottesley and Joyce his wife do deny to satisfy and pay unto your said orators may it therefore please your good lord to grant unto your said orators the kings majesties writ of ?spirit to be directed to the said Walter Wrottesley and Joyce his wife commanding them thereby etc
The joint and several replies of Walter Wrottesley and Joyce his wife.

Chapter 4   Seventeenth Century

The said defendants having the benefit and all advantages of exceptions to all and every the incertainty insufficiency contrariety and imperfections of the said Bill of complaint now and at all times hereafter to them and either of them saved and reserved for answer thereunto say and first the said defendant Joyce for herself says that Francis Bromley her former husband did not have the goods, chattels, household stuff, plate, jewels and sums of money to the value of two thousand pounds as of his own property nor anything like that amount nor was it probable that he should have that sort of money because he died shortly after his father, Sir George Bromley and in the life of Dame Jane Bromley his mother and in the life of his father he never had more than £50 over the charges of the diet of him and his family and never attained to the substance of his living and estate yet carried himself in porte and shewe to the uttermost limits of his habilitie and therefore was unlike to raise any such portion of goods as in the said bill is pretended neither had the said Francis any other means to raise the same save only out of his lands which (his mother living) were but of small yearly value to him in possession and not above £100 by year to this defendant's knowledge neither did the said Francis Bromley by any assurance in the law give, devise or assure to the complainant Jane in money or any other goods or chattels for her proferment in marriage or otherwise the sum or value of £1,000 or any other sum or value as in the said bill is untruly surmised For this defendant sayeth that the said Francis Bromley this defendant's said former husband, having issue by this defendant Thomas Bromley his eldest son Charles Bromley his younger son and the said Jane his only daughter, died intestate being possessed at the time of his death of goods, credits and chattels under the value of £350, 5s 8d…..As by the inventory thereof taken after his decease whereunto she this defendant referred herself may appear. The administration whereof was committed by the Competent Ordinary to this defendant Joyce and the overplus thereof his funeral and debts discharged was of very small value and little benefit to defendant: howbeit this defendant sayeth that after the death of the said Francis Bromley this defendant Joyce having received of the said same Jane Bromley, widow relict and administratrix of the said Sir George Bromley the sum of five hundred and four score pounds part of a sum of £800 by the intent and true meaning of one indenture of covenant made between the said Sir George Bromley and Sir Edward Leighton this defendant's late father upon the marriage of the said Francis and this defendant. By which indenture the said sum of £800 was appointed or meant to be paid to the ?survivor of the said Francis and this defendant as by the same indenture to the which in this behalf for more certainty this defendant she referred herself more at large may appear. She this defendant Joyce had then a purpose upon the receipt of the said sum of five hundred and four score pounds in her widowhood out of motherly love and affection and the tender care and respect she then had of the said Charles Bromley her younger son and the said complainant Jane then her only daughter to bestow and confer on them a good part of the sum of five hundred and four score pounds by her received as aforesaid and that rather for that the said Francis Bromley their father was then dead and had not in any sort to her this defendant's knowledge provided or left unto them any portions at all to maintain or advance them with. And therefore and because the said Jane this complainant was to reap her only advancement by the free gift of … this defendant; she this defendant as she remembers as well to restrain her the said Jane this complainant from making unfit choice in her marriage as otherwise to reserve a power in her self this defendant to dispose of all of the greatest part of the said portion meant to be bestowed on the same Jane this complainant to any other of her children or kindred as to her the defendant should seem expedient in express terms as she now remembers declared her intention and meaning to be in that behalf that she the said Jane would be advised and ruled by her this defendant in her marriage that then she should have had of the said money by her this defendant so received the sum of £300 with all the increase thereof otherwise she should have no more than the value of that she this defendant then intended to bestowe to and upon the said Charles brother of the said Jane which was but £100 and to that end and under that caution and fore prise she this defendant did as she remembereth disbursed and delivered out of her hands to one William Barker now deceased in whom she reposed trust in that behalf the sum of £400 of lawful money of England being the proper money of her this defendant to be set forth for them to the best

Chapter 4 — Seventeenth Century

increase and benefit, and shortly after these defendants intermarried between whom there were not any indentures of covenants sealed or made for payment of any sum or sums of money to or for the said Jane as in the Bill is currently surmised and the said Jane one of the complainants before the said marriage and sythence by many years hath been maintained and kept with meat, drink, apparell and all other competent necessaries for her estate at the charge and responsibility of these defendants. And these defendants further say and trust that this honourable court will be of opinion that there is no cause why these defendants or either of them should be compelled to yield to the complainants or either of them any advancement at all in money or otherwise use the proceedings of the said complainants be duly respected for these defendants say that about September last past was twelve months (as their defendants remember) the said complainant Jane being then young was by some practices or provisions of the complainant William Davenport as the defendants truly think (a man in worth and estate far unworthy of such a match) privily enticed and stolen away from their defendants house at Wrottesley and married to him the complainant William without the probity, notice or consent of the defendants or either of them or of any other the good friends of her the said Jane to these defendants' knowledge and to the great discomfort of them … she the said Jane then overlooking the care of her self and much forgetting her own parentage and worth, and the dutiful and good respect she ought to have had of the defendants and others her said good friends and kindred of which undue proceedings the defendants trust this honourable court will have good consideration without that that the said Francis Bromley was possessed of goods of any such value as is mentioned in the said bill or did by any assurance or otherwise give, deliver or appoint any such sum to the complainant Jane as in the said bill is surmised was possessed of such charge or make any such request to the defendant Joyce in that behalf as is supposed in the said Bill neither have these defendants or either of them now ever had in them or either of their hands custody or possession any deed, devise, writing or assurance containing any such gifts, devise or grant from the said Francis Bromley to the said Jane or to her use as is supposed ……or denied is true. All which matters these defendants are ready to aver and prove as this honourable Court in the said Bill contained material to be answered unto and not herein by these defendants sufficiently answered confessed and avoided reasonable costs and charges in this behalf wrongfully sustained

The Replication of William Davenport and Jane his wife to the answers of Walter Wrottesley Esq. and Joyce his wife defendants

All advantages of exception to the uncertainties and insufficiencies of the said defendants answers unto these respondents always reserved then for replication thereto they say and either of them saith in all and every thing as in their said bill of complaint they have already said and further they do and will aver justify maintain and prove their said Bill of complaint and all and every the matters and things herein comprised to be just and true in such sort manner and form as in and by the same their bill they being set forth and declared without that that the said Francis Bromley former husband to the defendant Joyce was not in his lifetime possessed of goods, chattels household stuff, plate, jewels and sums of money to the value of £2,000 of his own proper goods nor anything were of that value or that it is not probable he should so be for the causes in the said answers suggested and without that that the said Francis Bromley did not by any assurance in the law give demise or assure to the Repliant Jane in money or any other goods or chattels for her proferment in marriage or otherwise the sum or value of £1,000 or any other sum or value as in the said defendants answers is untruly alleged and without that that the said defendant Joyces former husband having such issue by her the said Joyce as in the said answers is declared died intestate and was possessed at the time of his death of goods, credits and chattels under the value of £350 6s and 8d or that it so appeareth by the inventory taken after her said first husbands decease and that the said Joyce having the administration of the said goods and chattels committed to her by the competent ordinary the over plus of them (his debts discharged and summarily performed) were of very little value and benefit to the same defendant Joyce as in the said answers it also untruly surmised and without that that the defendant Joyce after the death of her first husband Francis Bromley received of Dame Jane Bromley widow in her said answer named the sum of

Chapter 4 — Seventeenth Century

five hundred and four score pounds due to the said Joyce in such sort and for such cause as in the said answers is alleged and that the said Joyce upon the receipt of the said five hundred and four score pounds in her widowhood did out of her motherly love and affection and for the respect she then had of this repliant Jane and Charles Bromley younger brother of this repliant intend and purpose to bestowe on them a good part of the said sum of five hundred and four score pounds by her so received as aforesaid and that she did so purpose because the said Francis her late husband had not in any sort (to her the said defendants knowledge) provided for or left unto them any portions at all for their advances as in their said answers as also pretended and without that that the defendant Joyce did according to this her said purpose disburse and deliver out of her charge upon trust to one William Barker deceased the sum of £500 of lawful money of England (being the proper money of her the said defendant Joyce) be set forth to the best increase and benefit of this repliant Jane and the said Charles her son but did as well to restrain this repliant Jane from unfit marriage as also to reserve power in her self to dispose all or the greatest part of such portion as intended to the repliant Jane to any other of her children or kindred at her pleasure declare in express words that the said Jane should have the sum of £300 of the money delivered over as aforesaid with the increase that came thereof under this caution viz that is she would be advised by her this defendant in her marriage but otherwise she should have no more but £100 as in the said answers is also untruly surmised and without that that the complainant Jane being young was by the other petitioner William Davenport (being a man far unworthy to marry the said Jane) about September last past was twelve months by practises and persuasions privily enticed and stolen away from the house of these defendants at Wrottesley and married without their consent or the consent of any other their friends to the great discomfort of her said friends and that therefore this honourable court should be of opinion that the plaintiff ought not to have any advancement yielded there at all in money nor otherwise as in their said answers is likewise untruly suggested for this repliant William Davenport saith that he was every way worthy to match with the said Jane and that the said marriage was no disparagement at all to her neither did he the said William Davenport entice or steal her away in such sort as is pretended but with the good liking of her the said Jane (being then of good discretion) was married unto her and since their said marriage this repliant William Davenport had maintained his wife in fit sort according to her degree and reputation and without that that any other matter or thing in their said answers contained material or effectual in the law to be replied unto is true in such sort as in the same they being set forth and declared and is not herein already sufficiently replied unto and avoided trans..sed or denied all which matters and things these defendants are ready to justify, maintain and prove as this honourable court shall think fit and humbly prove as in and by their bill of complaint they have already proved   Signed: William Brooke

To the Right Honourable Thomas Lord Ellesmere Lord Chancellor of England
Humbly complaining showeth unto your lordship your daily orator William Davenport of Chorley son and heir apparent of Henry Davenport of Chorley in the County of Chester, gent and Jane his wife that whereas Francis Bromley of Hawnde in the County of Salop esq late father of the said Jane was in his life time lawfully possessed of and in diverse goods, chattels, house … plate jewels and sums of money to the value of £2,000 in money and other goods and chattels for her proferment on marriage amounting to the whole to the sum of £1,000 and did constitute and appoint Joyce Bromley then his wife and mother to the said Jane to have the safe keeping and preserving of the said assurance so made as aforesaid and further willed and required the said Joyce upon his deathbed that she the said Joyce would have a motherlike care of the said Jane and to perform his said intent and mind to the uttermost value according to the content of the said assurance so made as aforesaid and afterwards died by and after whose death she the said Joyce did marry and espouse Walter Wrottesley of Wrottesley in the County of Stafford esq between whom there were indentures of covenant made and sealed for the more speedy effecting of the said marriage in which said inventories it was especially concluded and agreed that the said Walter Wrottesley should perform all and

Chapter 4 Seventeenth Century

every such act and acts which her said late husband did make in his lifetime for the payment of the marriage money of the said Jane and as she was by him required as he lay on his death bed and should likewise give the said Jane £300 more for increase of her portion. But now so it is may it please your Lordship that they the said Walter Wrottesley and Joyce his wife having gotten into their hands custody and possession the said assurance made unto the said Jane or unto her use as aforesaid and pretending that there was never any such gift or grant made unto her the said Jane and if any were that your said orators have no remedy by the …. course of the common law for recovering of the said goods, chattels and premisses[/promises] for that she the said Jane being but of young and tender years at the time of the death of her said late father, neither she nor your orator William Davenport know the the certainty and particulars thereof neither the kind, quality quantity or value of the same they the said Walter Wrottesley and Joyce his wife have and do refuse and deny to deliver unto your said orators the said goods, chattels and premisses so given and demised to the said Jane or to make any due satisfaction for the same. In tender consideration of the promises and for as much as the said Walter Wrottesley and Joyce his wife have diverse and sundry times confessed and acknowledged that the marriage of the said Jane was worth in money, goods and chattels to the value of £1,200 at least and for that your said orators knowing not the certain date or contents of the said assurance nor of the said goods, chattels and premisses and that the said Walter Wrottesley and Joyce his wife do deny to satisfy and pay unto your said orators may it therefore please your good Lord to grant unto your said orators the King Majesty's writ of subpena to be directed to the said Walter Wrottesley and Joyce his wife commanding them and either of them thereby at a certain day and under a certain pain therein to be ? prefixed and appointed personally to appear before your honour in his majesty's high Court of Chancery to answer the p..omsses And further to stand and abide such order and direction herein as to your good Lordship shall be thought most meete to stand with right and equity and your said orator shall daily pray unto god for your good Lordship being to live in health
Signed: William Brooke
Writ April 20 1604 to Walter Wrottesley esq and Joyce his wife. Signed: Walter Leveson, John Fowkes, Samuel Piper

B. John Walker the beadle presented the following panel of jurors, namely, Roger Rowley, John Yate, William Brooke, John Beech, Richard Bradney junior, John Warter, John Foxall of Stapleford, John Marrall, John Newton, John Barbor, John Granger, John Hitchcocks sen., Thomas Beech, John Vane, Nathaniel Barrett, Stephen Bradney, John Foxall of Hylton, Thomas Sadler and John Gould, pledges by John Doe and Richard Roe. [John Doe and Richard Roe were fictitious names used to cover a technicality]
Actually sworn were: William Brooke, John Beech, Richard Bradney junior, John Warter, John Foxall of Stapleford, John Marrall, John Newton, John Barbor, John Granger, John Hitchcocks sen., Thomas Beech, John Newe (Worfield Court Roll 5586/1/268 Shropshire Archives)

C. 5 April 12 James (1614) William Dey, gent, died seised of one messuage and half a yardland in Holland one toft and half a yardland in Hallond late Wermotts, one toft and one nook called Lollysticke land, half a toft and half a yardland called Barker's land and one dole of meadow in half meadow in Hallon. And that Jane Davenport, now wife of William Davenport, gent, sister and heir of Thomas Bromley esq, deceased son of Francis, son of George Bromley, knight, and Jane his wife ought to be admitted and at the same court they were admitted. (Worfield Court Roll 5586/1/272 Shropshire Archives)

D. Bequest of Sir Thomas Woolley
Sir George Bromley, Knight, late of Hallon in the parish of Worfield, Chief Justice of Chester and the Council in the Marches of Wales amongst others had attending on him Thomas Woolley, gent, who was also his kinsman, his mother being a Bromley, sister to Sir Thomas Bromley as heretofore Lord Chief Justice of England which Thomas Woolley having attained to a good estate of wealth in the service of the said Sir George Bromley with whom he continued during the life of the said Sir George and some years after his decease with Dame Jane Bromley his wife, growing somewhat into years and giving over service, ever

Chapter 4   Seventeenth Century

carrying a pious and charitable mind towards the poore and a love to the parish of Worfield where he had long dwelt in the service of the said Sir George did by his last will and testament give and bequeath one hundred pounds for the purchasing of lands of inheritance to remain for ever according to the use of the poor of the said parish which lands were purchased accordingly, 20s issuing out of the rents & profits thereof for 4 sermons to be preached there yearly for ever as is more at large expressed in his will.

The said Thomas Woolley reposing special trust in the family of the Bromleys did constitute and ordain Thomas Bromley of Hallon esq, son and heir of Francis Bromley esq son and heir to Sir George Bromley and Margaret, youngest daughter of Sir George Bromley & wife of Francis Wolriche of Dudmaston esq, overseers of that part of his will for the perfect disposing of his charitable legacy to the use and behoofe of the poor and Thomas Woolley shortly afterwards departing this life the said Margaret Wolryche by the advice of her brother Sir Edward Bromley, knight, one of the Barons of the Exchequer second son and next heir male to the said Sir George did establish the following to be observed perpetually.

First that the number of the poor to whom the charitable almes is to be given shall be just under 24 and that there shall not be above 5s nor under 12d yearly given to any of the poor and that there shall be kept by the vicar for the time being, who is to have for his paines 2s yearly a book fair written wherein the names of all such poor as are to have any part of this alms shall be registered

Item. That the churchwardens for the time being shall yearely at the day apoynted receive the rents comoditys and profits whatsoever rising or any way accruing of the lands be only to the use of 24 poor registered except the 20s yearly for 4 sermons and 2s for he who keeps the book ...

The poor born in Hallon and Worfield shall have preference, elder rather than younger. When one dies another replaces at the choice of the vicar and churchwardens and by advice and consent of the Bromleys ?if they know them say if appropriate. No drunks, no one who lives out of the parish for more than a year

Thomas Woolley died 6 August 1609

The first poor to receive were: Jerome Warter 2s 6d, John Frodgesley 2s 6d, Francis Hatton 2s 6d, Thomas Lowe 2s 6d, Robert Maynard 2s 6d, Johanna Weaver 2s 6d, Eleanor Warter 12d, Susan Walker 12d, if they live in Hallon or Worfield, Alice Freewoman 2s, John Groome 2s, Richard Hatton, 12d and his brother Roger Hatton 12d, Hugh Yeat 12d to his sister Mary Yeat 12d, George Staunton 2s

With Woolley's money a cottage and land in Brierley called The Toft was bought and, in the 10th year of the reign of James I, 3 cottages and an acre of land in Worfield and a cottage and a garden in Bridgnorth bought.

E. Will of George Bromley 25 March 1624. 2/JasI/D/13/27 Cheshire Record Office.

George Bromley the unprofitable servant of God now inhabiting at the manor of Shifnal being sick in body but strong in mind etc do after my expenses and debts have been paid give

- to the poor of Albrighton Parish £3 to be distributed
- to the poor of Worvile Home 40/- to be distributed
- to the poor of Sheriefe Hales 20/- to be distributed
- to the poor of Shifnal 20/- to be distributed

the vicars to take 2 of their honest parishioners for the distribution

- to my brother Edward Bromley one gold ring value 30/-
- to my 3 sisters viz Susanna Puleston, Mary Cotton and Margaret Wolrich to every one of them one gold ring value 30/- in remembrance of their love to me and mine to them. These words being engraved on the ring, *'Death is the Gate of Life.'*
- I give to Margaret Barrett £3
- And first to remember the place from whence has come my maintenance of late, Albrighton, my will is that two years after my death my executors will disburse £200 on land for inheritance of the clear value of £5 yearly which land 6 or 8 substantial persons of the said parish should be in charge of for the use of the parish for ever in the following manner a) 40/- to be distributed to 20 poor people living in the parish being all of the poor decayed householders or aged persons or poor fatherless children and to be paid on

Chapter 4 Seventeenth Century

Good Friday. b) 40/- yearly towards the paving of the streets of the town of Albrighton c) 20/- to the Church annually to ring the bell every night …beginning at the Feast of All Saints and ending at Candlemas. The Churchwardens to distribute the £5
- Bearing a love to the Parish of Worvile my native soil I do in like manner will that within 2 years my executors will disburse £100 upon land of inheritance of the clear value of £5 yearly to be bestowed as follows a) 15/- to be distributed by equal portions, the one on St George's Day and the other on the Feast of St Michael the Archangel to 24 poor inhabitants in the same parish, none of them being juveniles but aged, impotent people or decayed householders of honest conversation, the most to have not more than 5/- and the least not less than 2/- yearly and the poor of the township of Hallon especially and Worvile next to have the best alms. And the other 5/- to be given to the vicar for the time being to keep a book fairly written with the names of the poor and to distribute it at all times aforesaid making mention that it is the legacy of George Bromley esq who was the fifth son of Sir George Bromley, knight and that the churchwardens for the time being receive the [profit] of this land yearly and pay it over according to this my will.
- Provided that if any of the money bequeathed to Albrighton or Worvile or whatsoever else be wasted … or bestowed to any other use than that in my will then the lands and profits shall remain with St John's College Cambridge where I had part of my bringing up
- I give to the Free School in Shrewsbury 12 books, 8 of which are in written hand - 4 books of the Chronicles of England vis Jefferey of Monmouth, Henry of Huntingdon, William of Muberviensis and Palpe a monk of Chester called Policromicon in the English tongue, John Gowre and Geoffrey Chaucer's Canterbury Tales.' Of printed books 2 books of Gildars Sapioncie and Bead's Book of the Chronicles of England and John Leland's The History of King Arthur
- I give and bequeath to my servant Richard Barney £100 in money and also all my apparell
- To my good brother George Cotton I give my signet ring
- To my good sister Mistress Margaret Wollrich, my sister, a cup

George Cotton & Margaret Wollrich executors

F. Extracts from Worfield Constables Accounts (P314/M)

1597
for fetching the Egyptians from Bridgnorth to Worfield 10d
for cords to bind them 6d
1598
for whipping of rogues and beggars and food bestowed upon them this year 6s 6d
1599
to Hugh Yeate for whipping a rogueish woman and bringing her to Bridgnorth and for her diet for a whole day and a night in the stocks 6d
1601
to Hugh Yeate for whipping 3 rogues 3d
to Freeman for whipping another rogue and bringing her to Higford 4d
in sending out precept after one that broke out of the stocks 4d
1605
for staples and shackles of iron on the whipping post at Worfield 4d
for the like at Hilton 4d
1619
for bringing 2 poor wandering persons of Bridgnorth that were taken at Wolverhampton and there whipped for stealing of poultry and so directed to [take]… from constable to constable 4d
precept for Rebecca Hakins and Lewis Lloyd for keeping a begging woman 8d
for making a poor man a passport to go into his own country 2d

Chapter 4　　　　　　　Seventeenth Century

1624-5
laid out for 5 diseased persons having a pass to travel from London to Cardington 2s and for hiring a man and an horse to bring them to Bridgnorth
paid for a woman who was travelling from Whitchurch to Worcester who fell in labour in the field and for keeping her and her sister 4 days 3s
1626
for taking a poor woman on suspicion for cutting horses' tails that had 11lb of hair found about her
1631-1632
Paid to Shrewsbury to maintain them that were infected with the plague £4
1632-1633
paid to a poor man who had losses by fire who would have had a gathering in church - 12d
given to 3 soldiers who came out of Ireland who had a pass and lodging them at night - 6d
given to the poor people that we punished 6d
for wandering about the parish 3 weeks for the avoiding of beggars
given to 4 vagrant persons 12d
given to a seafaring man that had losses by sea
given to a dumb man that had his tongue cut out of his mouth and taking him to Claverley 2d
given to a merchant that had losses by sea - 6d
1633-34
for keeping a woman and a wench 2 days and one night and for whipping her 2s 6d
1634
For lodging a poor cripple and his wife who lost their house by fire and bringing them to Bridgnorth
For lodging a poor cripple and bringing him to Quatford
given to a man of Stanton Lacy who lost by surety ship by one John Newton, gent - 11d
given to a lame soldier and finding him meat and drink
for mending the butts
Given to Katherine Gerrards the wife of Richard Gerrard who had lost £600 on the sease being taken by the Turkes - 12d
to John Felton for relieving a poor child that was like to perish in the snow and keeping him a week 12d
given to Eleanor Grant who travelled with 2 small children carried in panniers - 12d
To John Marrall for being our deputy and punishing vagrant people
1650-1651
paid for suping lodging and breakfasting 17 of a company of Cumberland people who were dressed in the habit of Egyptians with a pass and for bringing them to Norton 24 October 4s
for bringing a hue and cry to Norton that came from came from Hartlebrough after 2 men with their wives who broke out of the stocks 2d
1651-1656
for two rogges [rogues] which were taken by Roger Barrye and were had before Mr Wolrich there charges and those that went thither 2s 2d there were in the stocks two nights
1665-1666
for apprehending a felon, men to tend him at night who robbed Roger Rowley's hen house 2s
for taking him on the morrow to Bridgnorth 1s
for going myself about the same business 4d
paid to a man for the whipping him 1s
1671-2
for lodging John Bowman, being blind, all night and bringing him to Bridgnorth having a pass 8d

Chapter 4　　　　　　　　Seventeenth Century

Bradney Farm. This section of the house is box framed with brick infill probably replacing wattle and daub. It is thought to date from the mid to late seventeenth century when the house was altered. The house was built as a hall house and some of the timber from this part of the house has been dendro-dated to 1487. Boomerang-shaped oak 'blades' were used to support the roof and a louvre system released smoke from an open hearth through the roof. Known as cruck construction, this was a style of building common until the supply of raw materials ran out. The blades were cut from pedunculate oaks which produce naturally curved timbers perfectly suited to cruck construction and ship building. Worfield had extensive oak forests in which the pedunculate oak was common. Box framed buildings, on the other hand, could make use of the straight timber provided by the sessile oak[11].

Chapter 5   Eighteenth Century

Most of the property in the Main Street of Worfield dates from the eighteenth century.

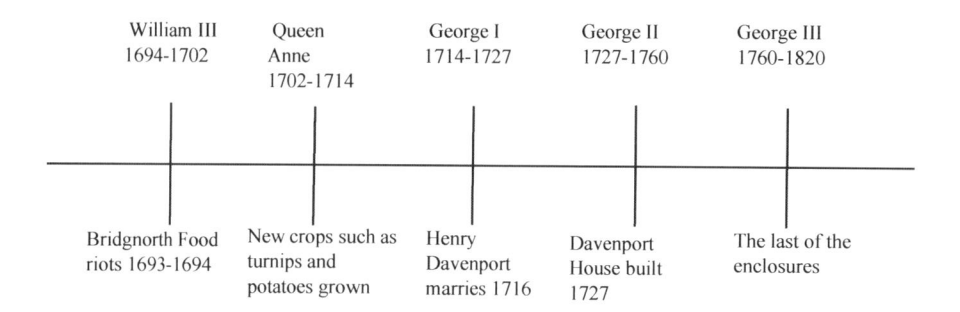

William III 1694-1702	Queen Anne 1702-1714	George I 1714-1727	George II 1727-1760	George III 1760-1820
Bridgnorth Food riots 1693-1694	New crops such as turnips and potatoes grown	Henry Davenport marries 1716	Davenport House built 1727	The last of the enclosures

    In the mid seventeenth century, Cromwell and his followers brought about an unimagineable change in the social hierachy of the nation. If they were in Worfield at this time, the Davenport family were noticeably silent, perhaps having observed what had happened to their neighbour at Apley. In the event, the Parliamentarians' ambitious attempt to change the old order was over in just twenty years. With the return of Charles II to the throne in 1661, most of the old landed gentry were restored to their former power and possessions. Wealthy merchants emulated the lifestyle of these old families by buying manors and building stately homes. Together, both new and old gentry

Chapter 5 — Eighteenth Century

spearheaded a movement to enclose common land and so brought about changes in the physical landscape of the countryside which endure to this day.

The effects of enclosure were profound. No longer would farmers have to walk to the open field to till their strips of arable land and no more would they graze their livestock on the open commons. Both were replaced by farms surrounded by enclosed land, similar to the pattern we have today. The three field system of winter grain, a spring crop, and fallow land or peas and beans worked because villagers collaborated. Enclosed fields did not demand the same kind of co-operation. The population became divided into the haves and have nots, profitable for those lucky enough to have their own farms, but not so for those who had relied on an odd strip in the common fields to grow their corn and the commons or waste on which to graze their livestock. The more egalitarian, pre-enclosure society, gave way to a hierarchical structure of master and servant, farmer and labourer. To mark the new order each farm had a farm house, farm buildings, barns, wain houses and fold yards, the size and elegance of which reflected the success of the new system.

The Agricultural Revolution

Prior to the eighteenth century, even those who were not farmers had livestock and grew corn. Richard Colley, a thatcher, had a cow and a pig when he died in 1665 and and William Barker,[A] a day labourer, died in possession of five sheep and some rye. A day labourer would supplement his income from casual farm work by spinning or weaving. There were farmers whose wives spun and weavers who farmed, for this was a local economy which was self sufficient. There was William Gravenor of Hilton, a shoemaker (died 1692), John Parsons, miller at Rindleford in 1687, John Rofe, the mason (died 1706), John Barney, the dyer (died 1693) and John Blakeman from Ackleton, the tailor (died 1684). There were bonnet and basket makers, wheelwrights, blacksmiths and, most numerous of all, farmers.

Crops were broadcast on strips (selions) in the common fields, mixtures of different grains such as muncorn, a wheat and barley mix, dredge, a mixture of spring barley and wheat, and maslin, a mixture of wheat and rye. Rye was grown and used for making bread. Some of the barley was malted for brewing and hemp and flax were grown on small pieces of land and spun into cloth. Vegetables such as onions, garlic, carrots, peas and beans and herbs were grown in gardens adjacent to houses and peas and beans were also grown in the open fields.

Before we get the impression that a self-sufficient way of life was somehow idyllic, disease and bad weather were always knocking at the door and when they entered, hunger and hardship followed. Disease of livestock was a problem for which there was no adequate treatment. Movement restrictions were frequently imposed when an outbreak of distemper in cattle broke out and murrain in sheep was an infectious disease whose spread was made worse, no doubt, by open grazing on the commons. Bad weather affected crop yields and therefore the price and affordability of grain.

Chapter 5   Eighteenth Century

Two years of poor harvests in the early 1690s led to food shortages made worse by dealers, known as badgers, raising the food prices beyond the reach of ordinary people. In the spring of 1693, attacks were made as grain was being transported from Bridgnorth Market to Wolverhampton. The first incident happened on the 22 April 1693. Several agents for Wolverhampton bakers, mainly servants of Compton Mill, were at Bridgnorth to buy grain but the shortage of corn meant that the buyers left without being able to meet their requirements. Henry Pemberton of Perton could only buy enough grain for two of his six clients. Having bought the grain Henry's problems were far from over, it still had to be transported safely home.

Corn was traded in some of the Bridgnorth inns, and William Evans, landlord of one of the main trading inns on the High Street, instructed Francis Lacon to transport some grain belonging to William Farmer of Wolverhampton down the Cartway to the Vine Inn. John Lloyd and a man called Head stopped the cart in Cartway and a crowd unloaded the corn and carried it away. A Wolverhampton chandler was then stopped in Cartway and his wheat was stolen by a group of people.

Two weeks later, also in Cartway, Thomas Clemson, a Wolverhampton baker, was attacked as he went down the road with his packhorses laden with grain. There was a mob in the street threatening to seize badgers (dealers) and corn and Rebecca Crudgington with whom Clemson had just dined, feared for her guest's safety[1].

Enter three people who had ideas about how food production could be increased, Thomas Townshend (Turnip Townshend as he was known), Jethro Tull and Robert Bakewell. Townshend recommended a four course crop rotation, which included turnips and clover, to replace the fallow field in the three course rotation. Turnips suppressed weeds and when sheep fed on them in the field, soil fertility was improved. Tull was concerned with soil structure and fertility and how to increase crop yields. His invention was a seed drill to replace the old system of broadcasting seed so that the crop was more evenly spread. Robert Bakewell focused on the breeding of livestock, pioneering in-breeding to fix the characteristics he wanted in his stock. He also improved grassland management.

Changes, no matter how positive they are in the long term, can bring tensions in the short term. One of the areas of dispute was tithes, a local tax levied by the Church, usually a tenth of a particular product. When Worfield was sold by the Deans of Lichfield to the Talbot family, a natural battleground was created between the vicar's right to small tithes and the patron's (advowson's) right to the great tithes of corn, wool and lamb, except in the township of Chesterton. Worfield was a poor living for a vicar, as we have already seen, and tithes were an important part of his income.

In 1683, Henry Davenport became the advowson or patron of the church, having bought Lower Hall and property at Wyken from Thomas Talbot. He thus became an impropriator or lay person holding church properties. The properties in Worfield and Wyken went together and were referred to as the Rectory of Wyken and the Rectory of Worfield. (In medieval times the Deans and Chapter

Chapter 5   Eighteenth Century

of Lichfield had some special relationship with Wyken and had the responsibility for maintaining the bridge at Wyken. They also owned a fulling mill there.) With the patronage or advowson went the rectorial tithes some of which Henry Davenport leased out by area. Towards the middle of the eighteenth century Robert Barrett held the tithe rights for Allscott, John Bradney for Hilton and the Boycotts for Swancott and Burcot. It was a system open to abuse with tithe owners trying to collect more tithes than they were entitled to and inflicting fear in so doing.

    Tithe disputes were heard in the Consistory (Bishop's) Court in Lichfield and the witness statements present a picture of life which is both unexpected and enchanting. In 1786[2] the vicar, Reverend Bromwich, claimed tithe of pigeons, fish and eels. He said he had never received the tithe of pigeons although *there were ancient dovecotes in Chesterton village and other parts of the parish and boxes about the houses from which the young have been sold* nor had he received tithe of fish *although there are ancient wears on the River Worfe rented of different owners where fish are caught for sale and also ponds or pools in the parish (although one or two people have paid him tithe of fish for about 2 years past when he discovered the tithe of fish and pigeons was due.) From the tithe of fish due, expenses incurred must be deducted, the weir, the twigs to catch the fish, labour in catching and trouble and expense in selling.*

    In another dispute there was the question as to who was entitled to the tithe of the new crops favoured by Townshend which had been increasing in popularity since the turn of the century. Turnips and potatoes had not been grown in the parish before 1700 but the value of these new crops soon became apparent and by 1719 most of the farmers were growing large quantities of carrots, turnips and potatoes. Edward Pratt of Burcote grew a quarter or half an acre of turnips and carrots in 1719 and by 1731 he was growing ten acres of turnips. Both vicar and impropriator tried to collect tithes of these new crops but the parishioners resisted. In Hilton, Joseph Bradney, husbandman and blacksmith, leased some impropriate tithes and tried to gather turnip seed tithe from Mr Smith *whereupon Mr Smith turned the sheep on them.* The matter was settled.

    Henry Davenport, shortly after he became patron, tried to collect tithes of clover seed but the parishioners refused to pay. Davenport threatened a lawsuit and several farmers grouped together to buy him a silver gilt cup in lieu of payment. Those who paid towards the cup were given exemption from the tithe while those who didn't were forced to pay. Over the next twenty years more clover was grown. With the benefit of hindsight, Davenport would have been better off had he held out for the tithes[3].

    Carrots were a good cash crop and well suited to the light, sandy soil of Worfield. John Nock of Bushbury rented a farm in Worfield and in one year took twenty waggon loads of carrots to market. The tithe on carrots was worth collecting but Robert Barrett, who held the right to tithes in Allscott, only approached small farmers so he probably knew he had no right to them. Barrett must have thought Widow Beddowes, who had a good crop of carrots, would be an easy target, but he was wrong. He went to the field where Mrs Beddowes was piling up carrots and a heated exchange took place. Carrots went to and fro from one heap to another as Barratt grabbed a bunch to add to his

Chapter 5   Eighteenth Century

tithe pile and Mrs Beddowes flung them back onto her heap. Barratt took some carrots but Widow Beddowes took him to court, contesting his right to the tithe, and won the case.

In 1745 the vicar tried to claim a tithe on rape which was grown to extract oil from the seed. The precedent was that the vicar was already entitled to tithe on flax seed also grown for oil. Rowland Smethyman[3] had been growing rape at Rindleford for the previous twenty years and was the first man to grow the crop in Worfield. The oil was extracted at Rindleford Mill which was owned by Smethyman.

Enclosures

Apart from the crops grown in the open fields, livestock, mainly sheep, were a major part of Worfield's agricultural economy. For centuries, sheep had grazed the common fields after the harvest had been gathered, and the commons or waste, but by the seventeenth century the open landscape was under attack from enclosures and encroachment. The Royal Forest of Morfe had been sold and much-enclosed in the seventeenth century with the Whitmores, as Lords of the Manor, taking a favourable line towards other enclosures. In 1677 Richard Bradney of Hilton asked for permission from the Lord of the Manor, Sir William Whitmore, to enclose two yardlands in Hilton (about 120 acres). The Lord of the Manor retained the right to fish and fowl and Richard Bradney paid 40/- for a licence to enclose by fences or hedges. The only proviso was that Bradney had to put wickets and gates in so that Whitmore's pursuit of game was not hindered[4]. A year later there was another request to enclose a further area of the common field of Hilton, then there was a request to enclose part of Cranmore Field. In the eighteenth century the Lord of the Manor permitted many 'improvements' on the waste such as new buildings, enclosures, encroachments and the rerouting of watercourses, charging a rent in return. John Williams built a cottage and, encroached onto the Morfe[B] and William Green built a brewhouse on the Green in Hilton. In Roughton and Barnsley, Thomas Bell built a flax oven and hovel and enclosed a garden, Edward Pratt built a flax oven and workshop and enclosed and encroached on Barnsley Green and Widow Littleford built a barn and made an enclosure on Morfe.

Prior to enclosures, lanes leading to commons and open fields had to be kept open. With the open fields gone, or about to be gone, there was no need for the lanes which once allowed access to all. Quite the reverse, it was in the owner's interest to restrict such access once land had been enclosed. By 1744[B], Ewke Lanes, Fenn Lane, the lane from Mutland Green to Broadbridge and from Kingslow to the common were all enclosed. The inhabitants of Ackleton in 1759 ordered *a penalty of 2/6d on any of the inhabitants within this manor who do not keep the usual foot ways over the lands within this manor after notice.* New roads were required by enclosures and new gravel pits permitted for their foundations.

The final enclosures, known as the Parliamentary Enclosures, came at the end of the eighteenth century and the beginning of the nineteenth and were the death knell for the old rights of common. It is hard to imagine the impact of enclosure on the lives of those who had nowhere to graze their

Chapter 5   Eighteenth Century

livestock but also no rights to firewood and hence no means of keeping warm in winter or cooking food. Coal may have been an affordable substitute for firewood for the wealthy but too expensive for the ordinary man. The map below shows the large area of Worfield which was common or waste around the time of the Parliamentary Enclosures. Between 1801 and 1811 the population of the parish fell by 100 people. Could this be due to migration to nearby parishes and towns caused by enclosures? There is no conclusive proof but it is certainly possible.

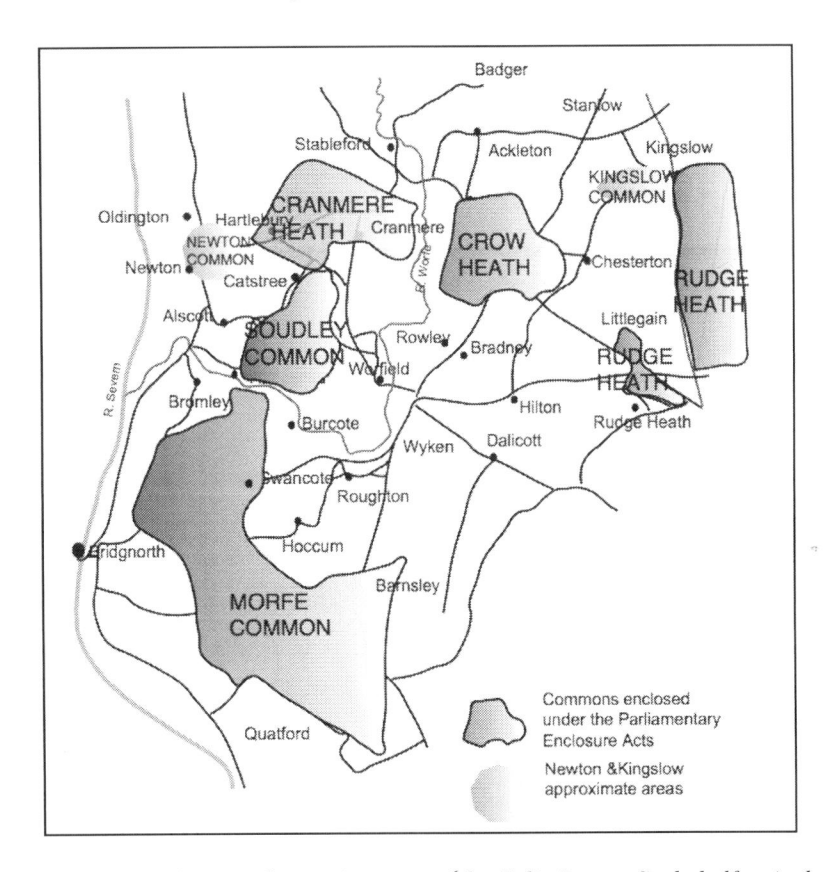

Enclosures: map drawn from Enclosure Agreements[6] by Colin Brown. Scale half an inch to 1 mile

There were, almost certainly, agricultural benefits in the enclosure of the common fields. Growing crops in fields over which one has sole control is undoubtedly a much more efficient system than having a strip bordered by a weedy bank. Grazing on the commons was also restricting expansion of flocks and herds. The quota system was strict and could only be exceeded by coming to an arrangement with someone who had unused quota whereby the animals were branded with that

83

Chapter 5 — Eighteenth Century

person's mark. Alternatively, you might risk grazing on commons where you had no rights but the consequences of that were not to be taken lightly. Thomas Green, who lived at the Heath Side in Claverley Liberty, was careful not to venture on Rudge Heath[5] *for fear of mischief.* Flogging of the shepherd or stockman was the common punishment. At the same time, the Whitmore flock was never less than 800 sheep, an inequity which wouldn't go unnoticed. The question was how long could the commons sustain the current level of grazing let alone allow for expansion of flocks and herds? The pressure was on to enclose the commons.

Instrumental in mapping out the allotments for the Parliamentary Enclosures was Valentine Vickers of Cranmere who surveyed a large part of England and Wales for enclosure and would have known these local lands so well. In the letter below he gives his approval for the enclosure of Barnsley Common.

Dear Sir,
I have this morning received your Letter on the subject of the Inclosure of Barnsley Common Land which I think ought by all means to be done; therefore shall not object.
I attended a meeting of Proprietors on the same Business at Shrewsbury in December 1814 ...
I am Sir, your obedient servant,
Valentine Vickers

The reason given for enclosure was always the same - *whereas the common or waste referred to is incapable of improvement in its present state and all those entitled are desirous of enclosing ...* The significant phrase here is, 'those who are entitled.' Not all who lived in a village were entitled to a share of the enclosed common. Houses less than twenty years old, for example, carried no entitlement and became the property of the Lord of the Manor. Entitled to a share of Cranmere Heath when it was enclosed were Thomas Whitmore, William Yelverton Davenport, Edward Davenport, Edmund Sherrington Davenport, Joseph Scott of Great Barr, Baronet, John Jasper of Stableford and Elizabeth his wife, and John Jasper the younger, Richard Taylor of Tasley, farmer, Mary Taylor, widow, also of Tasley, James Marshall of Roughton, William Butcher of Ackleton, Richard White of Alscott, gent, Samuel & Elizabeth Ridley of Hopstone and Thomas Haslewood of Bridgnorth, gent. The 86 acres of Kingslow Common was enclosed in 1787 and split between Thomas Devey, Thomas Bache, Robert Piggott and Thomas Whitmore. 700 acres of Morfe Common, in Worfield, Quatford & St Mary's Bridgnorth and 150 acres of Crows Heath were enclosed in 1806 and in 1807, 350 acres of Cranmere Heath and 250 acres of Sowdley Common were enclosed. Over 1,500 acres of common land disappeared within a few years[6].

Chapter 5   Eighteenth Century

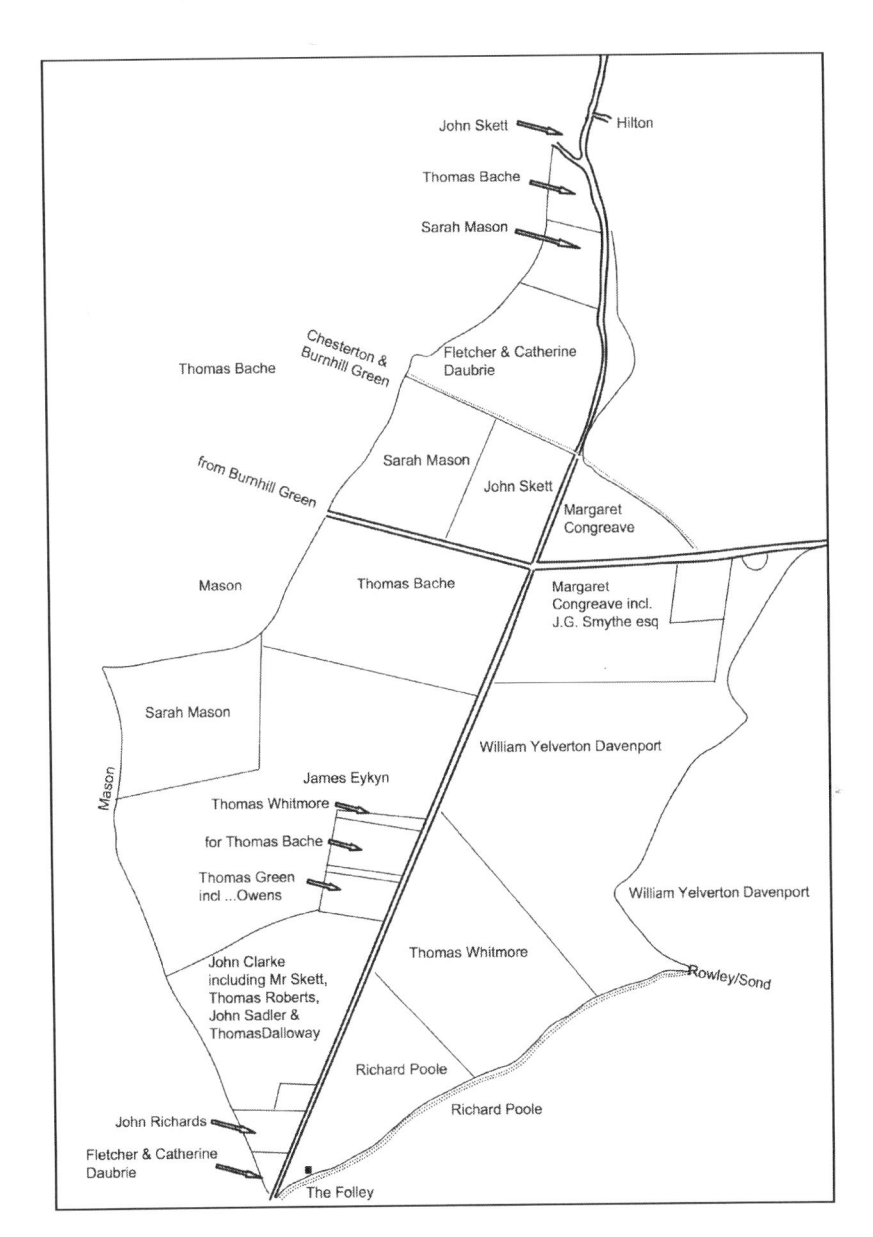

Crows Heath Enclosure 1806
Scale: 4 inches to a mile (5586/13/5 Shropshire Archives)

Chapter 5   Eighteenth Century

With enclosure the principles of the agricultural revolution were embedded in tenancy agreements. The Forest of Morfe Allotments stipulated that[4]

- *The land to be split into 15 enclosures with post & rail fencing & wickets. Whitmore to allow for gates & gate posts only*
- *Whitmore to allow £500 for the erection of a barn, stables, sheds & labourer's house & fencing a fold yard to be made out of the rents as they become due and vouchers to be produced by tenant for the expenditure*
- *Land to be cultivated by 1810 & limed for the first or second time with at least 2 good waggon loads of burnt clod lime per acre & after 4 years to apply at least 60 waggon loads of lime to the whole*
- *Within 4 years to lay down at least 24 acres of permanent grass & within 2 succeeding years 17 more*
- *At the end of the term of 14 years to leave all the produce on the farm. Straw & fodder can be cut and eaten till the May day after quitting*
- *Tenant not to take more than 2 crops of grain in any one course of tillage, fallowed for turnips & manured with at least 12 ?cubic yards of rotted dung or 2 good waggon loads of well burnt clod lime per acre. 30 acres of turnips to be grown each year*
- *With the second crop of grain to lay down the lands with clover & grass seeds being paid for all such seeds at the Spring seedness before quitting the same being hayed up at Christmas preceding*
- *New tenant to be allowed on to land before taking over to allow acts of husbandry.*
- *Tenant to preserve & nurse up the fences and such young trees as the Landlord may think fit to plant*
- *Tenant not to sow any hemp, flax or rape on any part of the lands except flax on the first breaking up of the lands*
- *Tenant not to sow more than 40 acres of winter corn at the Michaelmas seedness before the expiration of the term & liberty to house and thresh out his share on the premises that is two thirds of the fallow and one half of the Brush (tithe first deducted) between end May day following leaving the straw & chaff to the use of the next tenant*
- *Land sown with turnips at the Michaelmas seedness to be preserved for the Lent grain*
- *Tenant in all respects to manage the Lands in a good and husband like manner and such other covenants and reservations as are usual between Mr Whitmore & his tenants to be inserted in the lease*

The Rise of the Apley and Davenport Estates

At the same time as the yeoman farmers were creating their own farms, those with even more wealth were creating estates. Merchant money bought land available from enclosures and large houses appeared in many townships such as Allscott, Swancote, Roughton, Hilton, Ackleton,

Chapter 5   Eighteenth Century

Stanmore and Stableford. None could rival the grandeur of Davenport House nor the size of the estate of Apley with its even larger house standing just outside the parish.

Davenport House. Engraved by J. Tye from a picture by H. Harris. Published 1830

In the late seventeenth century the Whitmore family began to acquire a substantial estate of lands near to Apley and within the manor of Worfield. The Whitmores were farmers from Whittimere in Claverley Parish, hence the surname. The family gained considerable wealth and standing locally and built Ludstone Hall in 1607. One member of the family, William Whitmore, travelled to London in the sixteenth century and worked as a haberdasher's apprentice. William became a merchant and in 1582 invested some of his wealth in acquiring land around Apley. In 1607, William's eldest son (1573-1648), also called William, joined a consortium investing in Crown lands, many of which were sold to the sitting tenants. The investment was highly profitable and in three years the group had made 50% on the capital invested and were in a perfect position to buy properties for themselves. More investments followed and William also lent money to his neighbours, including Thomas Hoorde, from whom he acquired the Manor of Apley. William held high office in the County, including Sheriff of Shropshire, and with the acquisition of the Manor of Apley came representation of Bridgnorth in Parliament. The Civil War could have been a disaster for the Whitmores as the family had close connections with the Royal family. William Whitmore

Chapter 5 Eighteenth Century

declared for the King in 1642 and Apley was seized but their property was restored to them after the Civil War.

In 1624 the Whitmores had taken a 99 year lease on the Manor of Worfield from Henry, Lord Bergavenny.[C] Being Lord of the Manor conveyed status but also an opportunity to build up an even larger estate. As Lord of the Manor they owned the majority of the land in the Manor of Worfield but not as distant landowners such as the Bergavenny Lords. Towards the end of the seventeenth century the Whitmores begin to take into personal ownership land to the west of Worfield Parish,[D] for example, in Newton, Ewdness, Hartlebury, Allscott, Bromley and Catstrey. William Bridgen was the agent for purchasing land on behalf of the Whitmores. In 1686 William Warter of Swancott surrendered a close or pasture in Newton called Amnestre, a quarter of a nook formerly Crudgingtons to the work and use of William Bridgen but to remain in the hands of William Whitmore, the Lord of the Manor.

Henry Davenport likewise began to acquire land around his existing holdings in Hallon, including Lower Hall, Worfield Mill and Wyken, together with the advowson of the parish which he bought from George Talbot. There was a Talbot connection here, as Henry's wife was Elizabeth, the daughter of Sharrington Talbot of Lacock. Henry Davenport died in 1698 and was succeeded by his elder son Sharrington, who was a military man. Sharrington died in Dublin in 1719 and his younger brother, Henry (born 1678), succeeded to the Davenport Estate. Henry had worked for the East India Company from the age of eighteen at Fort St. George in Madras, now known as Chennai. In 1707/8 Henry married Mary Lucy Chardin, the daughter of Daniel Chardin, a merchant, also of Fort St George in Madras. Mary Davenport died in 1712 after the birth of her third child and in 1713 Henry Davenport brought his children and mother-in-law back to England. Henry returned to India in October 1713 and the family finally came to live permanently in England in 1714. The East India Company must have been an exciting place to work in every sense of the word, sometimes rather too exciting for comfort. At one point, Henry Davenport was chosen to replace Robert Raworth as Deputy Governor of Fort St George, but as Henry approached to take his post Raworth fired at him and his party. Henry described it thus: *Mr Raworth was so kind as to salute us with an eighteen pounder*[7]. Pirates were a constant problem, ships laden with goods were an easy target and profitable prize. Captain Jones of the Greyhound wrote:

... the pirates came on board the Greyhound in a forcible manner and took from John Bennet and myself the sum of 12,500 pagodas. [A pagoda was worth eight shillings]

Henry's time with the East India Company made him a wealthy man. On his return to England, he continued to work as a merchant in London, and around 1716 he married Barbara Ivory, the daughter of Sir John Ivory of Ireland and Anne Talbot[7].

Henry's merchant activities in London were many and varied. In modern parlance, he had a broad portfolio. He traded all over the world, in diamonds, fabrics, wines and spirits, and possibly

Chapter 5   Eighteenth Century

opium, having trade links with China. He also bought stocks and shares through brokers in the area of Exchange Alley in London, dealings which were carried out in various coffee houses used by brokers as their offices. Henry had shares in many companies, including the East India Company, but he couldn't fail to notice a company offering astonishing returns on investment. The South Sea Company had been set up in 1711 to trade with Argentina and the Americas just at the time as the government was grappling with enormous debts as a result of recent wars. The government saw an opportunity to offload its debt and the South Sea Company saw a way to make huge amounts of money. The result was a giant Ponzi scheme in which many lost their fortunes. Henry was one of the smaller investors since he never trusted the viability of the Company. While his losses caused him to reduce his household expenditure in the short term, seven years after the collapse of the South Sea Company, Davenport House was built. Many were ruined as they staked all on the returns promised but Henry was clearly too shrewd to gamble everything in this way.

When Henry inherited the Worfield estate in 1719, a survey was made of the Davenport land in Hallon[E] so we know exactly which properties were then owned. Henry then continued to acquire land in the parish to increase and consolidate his estate. Rowley Farm passed to the Davenports in this way. Having been in the hands of the Rowley family since the house was built, the farm passed to Anne Rowley who married Richard Shalcrosse of Derby in 1656. Rowley Farm was left to Anne's son, John Shalcrosse, who sold it and it was bought by Henry Davenport in 1722.

The main house in Hallon was the Bromley house, referred to in the survey of lands as the *Ancient Messuage at Hallon.* Sadly for us, Henry knocked down the house and the only hint that it was there is a stone wall alongside the road. Walking from Hallon towards Mere Pool, the Bromley house stood on a hill on the left hand side, just before a drive, also to the left, which leads to Davenport House. Henry replaced the family home at Hallon with a magnificent new house h set in parkland. The design and construction of the new house was placed in the safe hands of Francis Smith of Warwick, formerly of the Wergs. The house was completed in 1727 and the grounds were later landscaped by William Shenstone of Halesowen. What prompted Henry to build Davenport House is, at the time of writing, not known. Perhaps the Bromley house at Hallon was too old-fashioned for Henry's taste, perhaps he wanted a home which could display his wealth, or perhaps he simply wanted a fitting home for his family. What is certain is how different Davenport House was from any other house in the parish. It wasn't just the sheer size, nor the fact that it stood in its own grounds which made this house exceptional but the fact that its function was simply to be a family home.

Houses in the eighteenth century were inextricable linked to one's occupation, as they had been for centuries. They were not designed as places for relaxation, but somewhere to eat, sleep and work[A]. Davenport was an exception to this rule. As an expression of the owner's wealth, status and aesthetic preferences, the new house was a very different type of dwelling inspired by fashion rather than the reality of daily life in Worfield. At a time when many lived in one or two rooms it is

Chapter 5   Eighteenth Century

hard to imagine what Worfield people made of this new mansion or what they made of a parkland created out of what were formerly common fields.

Davenport House. Source: Sir Oliver Leese Photograph Album. Date estd 1950s

Sandstone and timber were the building materials for many of the houses in the parish and, of course, brick. The tithe map of 1839 shows the following field names associated with brickmaking.
- Brick Furlong and Near Bricknel east of Roughton
- Brickkiln Leasow & Clay Pit Leasow between Cranmere and Hallonsford
- Brickkiln Leasow at Hartlebury
- Brickkiln Piece north of Stanmore Grove
- Brick Furlong near Hoccum
- Big Brickkiln and Little Brickkiln east of Hilton
- Brickkiln Leasow with pits adjacent to Stockton east of Ewdness

When the first brickyards started in Worfield we don't know, but there was one family whose name was associated with brickyards in several places within the parish. William Wood started his

Chapter 5   Eighteenth Century

brickyard in Hilton around 1711. George Smith giving evidence at the Rudge Heath dispute[5] in 1731 mentioned that about twenty years before, *William Wood first set up his brick kiln in the way to Hilton.* Later the Wood family had brickyards in Cranmere and Hartlebury.

Lost and Found

Crotal Bell

Bells have been put on livestock since the thirteenth century. The initials on this bell are of the maker, Richard Wells, the O being decorative. The bell foundry was in Aldbourne, near Marlborough, Wiltshire from 1755-1825 when it went bankrupt.
Finder: Frank Taylor

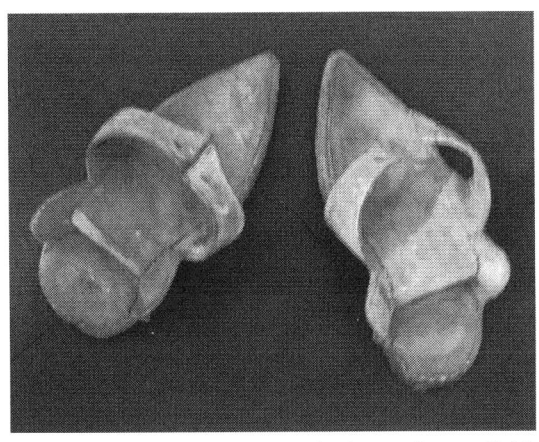

These pattens were found in the chimney breast of a house in Worfield Parish. They date from the 1790s and were worn to protect one's shoes from the mud and muck on the roads. You put on your shoes, slipped them into the pattens and hopefully kept your shoes clean and dry.
The idea of concealed objects was to bring luck to a newly built or altered house or barn. A variety of objects were concealed including money, cloth and even dead cats.

Chapter 5   Eighteenth Century

News from the Parish
Births, Deaths and Marriages
April 11 1778 (baptism) Griffith, son of Thomas Broadhurst and Elizabeth. The father and mother of this child are travelling chimney sweeps. She was delivered of the child in a barn of Mr Colley in ye Hopes on Wednesday without the help of a midwife, her husband having outrun her; and yet the Saturday following at noon came 2 miles to me to baptise the child and afterwards walked four more miles in search of her husband and return'd at night safe to her barn to two more children which she had left there.
(H. Bromwich vicar.)
Aug 13 1756 (burial) Thomas Warter son of Samuel of ye Parish of Astly Abbotts and Elizabeth died at Stanlow of ye smallpox ye 12th. Buried here.
June 4 1755 Thomas Walton of Stableford, blacksmith, died suddenly in the fields, ye 2nd
June 9 Thomas, son of Benjamin Vaughan of ye Hermitage, labourer and Mary died 7th and being drowned was buried
29 July John Bache, a servant to ye widow Worral of Oldington, was drowned the 28th
Wyken Court Roll 1786[8]
John Rowley, maltster, of Ackleton and Elizabeth his wife (she examined separately) surrenderered into the hands of the lord a cottage and garden (formerly Nicholas's) in Worfield to the use of William Slater of Winscote, his heirs and assigns. Fine 10s 6d

References
1. Malcolm Wanklyn, Bridgnorth Food Riots 1693-1694. Transactions of the Shropshire Archaeological Society in 1993 (Volume LXVIII) (Shropshire Archives)
2. Worfield Tithe Dispute 1786 D30/5/56 (Lichfield Archives)
3. Worfield Tithe Dispute 1758 B/C/5/1746/106-238 (Lichfield Archives)
4. Precedents of the Manor of Worfield 5586/1/214 (Shropshire Archives)
5. Rudge Heath Dispute 1731 BOY/5/6/R299823 (Shropshire Archives)
6. Enclosures: Cranmere Heath QE/1/2/19 & P314/7/1/2 (Shropshire Archives), Sowdley Common QE/1/2/17 1806 250 (Shropshire Archives), Newton, Winscott etc QE/1/2/16 (Shropshire Archives), Crows Heath and Part of Rudge Heath. Award & map P314/T/1/1(Shropshire Archives), Kingslow Common D3074/H/1/1-2 (Stafford Archives)
7. Henry Davenport's archives including those relating to the East India Company and Davenport are in Lacock Abbey Archives held at Wiltshire Archives
8. Minute Book for the Manor of Wyken beginning 15th March 1785 ending 1850. 1190/1/448 & /449(Shropshire Archives.)

Chapter 5   Eighteenth Century

Notes

A. **Inventories**

A TRUE AND PERFECT Inventorie of all and Singulr the goods Cattells and Chattells late of Richard Colly of Chesterton in the parishe of Worffeild, Thatcher taken and praysed July the thirtieth day 1665 by us whose names are hereunto subscribed:
Imprimis. The Testators apparrell and money in his keeping £5
Item. one fether bed, tow flocke beds three Coverlets fore blankets one rudge £2
Item. five flaxen sheets three peare of hempen sheets eaight peare hurden sheets twelfe napkins & other linnes £2
Item. tow fither bolsters & tow pillowes 10s
Item. five bras Ketells one posnet tow Irone potes eaight dishes of puter one flagon one bras Candell Sticke tow salts £1 5s

A TRUE AND PERFECT Inventory of ye goods and chattells of William Barker late deceased of ye parishe of Worfeild day labourer taken and apprised by us whose names are under written March 8th 1674 as followeth:
Item. one flocke bed & steds & cloth & 2 spinning wheels & other small things 10s
Item. one feather bed & steds & cloths & steds 10s 4d
Item. 2 barrels & 2 pails 5s
Item. bras and pewter 6s 4d
Item. one little table & 1 fourm Cheirs and Stooles 5s
Item. one grate 1 pair of pothooks & other things belonging to them 3s 4d
Item. 5 sheepe 10s
Item. one strike and half seeding of rye £1
Item. his wearing apparel & money in his purs 10s
Item. 6 pairs of sheets & other lining 15s 4d
Item. for all things forgot & out of sight 3s 4d
The mark of John Hitchcox, Thomas Clout
ex. 23 March 1674 Maria Barker, widow

An Inventory of all and singular the goods Chattels Catle and debts of John Bache late of Chesterton deceased taken the 24th March 1684 by Richard Billingsley, Joshua Piper, Thomas Bache & John Bradburne as ffoloweth:
Imprimis. The deceased's wearing apparel books and moneys due upon bond £62 4s
Item. plate viz. one silver pole and 6 silver spoons £4
Item. 200 sheep old and young £48
Item. 6 oxen and one horse £34 10s
Item. 12 cows and a bull £42
Item. 2 twinters and 4 yearlings £8
Item. swine & poultry £4 6s 8d
Item. corne & grain in the house barne and fields £145 15s
Item. barley for seed and several other things in the new house £18 12s
Item. household furniture in the hall £6 15s
Item. household furniture in the new parler £7 19s 8d
Item. bedding and other furniture in the chamber over the new parler £7 11s
Item. household furniture in the closet £4 15s
Item. bedding and other furniture in the old parler £11 3s

93

Chapter 5　　　　　　　　Eighteenth Century

Item. bedding and other furniture in the little parler £6
Item. bedding and other furniture in the chamber over the little parler £14 9s
Item. bedding and other furniture in the chamber at the stairehead £8 14s
Item. household furniture in the storechamber £10 9s
Item. malt and several other things in the malt chamber £34 9s 6d
Item. brass and pewter and several other things in the bras house £8 13s
Item. bedds and bedding furniture for servants with some other furniture in their chambers £2 15s
Item. barrels and other things in the sellar £1 15s
Item. lynnen of all sorts £30 4s
Item. household provision of all sorts £15 19s
Item. household furniture in the kitchin £3 10s
Item. goods in the welhouse £1
Item. household furniture in the malt house £4
Item. implements of husbandry of all sorts and bees £12 9s
Item. land taken of John Newe for tyme yet unexpired £23
Item. all other things of small moment not formerly prized forgotten & out of sight 10s
Sum £588 18s 4d
Richard Billingsley, Joshua Piper, Thomas Bache & John Bradburne appraisers

An Inventory of all and singular the goods Chattels and Catle and all other the psonall Estate of John Barney late of Worffield deceased taken and aprized by us whose names are hereunto subscribed the seaventh day of November Anno Dom 1693 as ffoloweth:
Imprimis. **The goods in dwelling house**
A table board two joyne forms one side table two joyne stooles & two carpets £1 10s
Item. A jack, two spits, a gale, fire shovel, a sevrg & one paire of cobbards 13s 4d
Item. A cleever, and a hacking knife, an iron dreeping pan, a frying pan, a flesh fork & a iron basting spoon 5s
It. Brass & pewter & tinnen ware £5 15s
It. A fouleing peece a smoothing iron and heaters & a chafing dish 18s
Item. **In the parlor**
One Joyn bed & bed steeds a feather bed & the furniture thereunto belonging £5
Item. Two chests & a livery table three chaires five cushions & two carpets £2 2s 6d
Item. The deceaseds wearing apparel bookes & moneys in his purse a silver can & eight silver spoons & a silver dish £8
A glass crate & whitemeat in it, a fire plate, a maid to hang clothes on & a flasket 8s
Item. **In the Buttery**
Seaven barrels, Earthen ware and trinnen ware & other wooden vessels £1 15s 6d
Item. Three furnaces & a mault mill five pair of sheeres and a tainter and implements of & belonging to the trade of a dyer & a hot presse £5
Item. A piece of white woollen cloth £1
Item. **In the chamber over the dwelling house**
Two joyn beds and two feather beds and furniture thereunto belonging £5 10s
Item. One chest a side table a desk boxes and trunkes £1 5s
Item. In the chamber over the Parlor
One half headed bedstead & a feather bed a bolster and Blanketts £2 2s 6d
Item. One cubbard one chaire some whiteware 8s
Item. One trunk with linnens £5

Chapter 5   Eighteenth Century

Item. **In the chamber over the Shop**
One feather bed a flock bed two bed steeds the furniture thereunto belonging & two boxes with some other trumper there £3 10s
Item. Lynnens of all sorts £4
Item. Corn in the barn & house of all sorts viz. rie and barley £6
Item. A cart & cartrope, horse geers & lather 16s
Item. Coals & an iron pott £1 15s
Item. Hemp £1
Item. A cow & six sheepe £5
Item. Muck 10s
Things forgotten and unaprized 5s

Note: I am indebted to Barrie Trinder for these inventories
B 1744 Extract of the fines and amercements of the Court Leet and Court Baron of Sir Thomas Whitmore Lord of the Manor of Worfield for incroachments on the Lord's waste (Precedents of the Manor 5586/1/214 Shropshire Archives)
Roughton & Barnsley
Thomas Bell for part a flax oven and part of a garden and an hovel on the waste
Edward Pratt for a flax oven & workshop thereto belonging
Ditto for part of a fold yard
Ditto for an inclosure and incroachment in Barnsley Green
Widow Littleford for a barn and inclosures on Morfe
Hoccum & Swancott
Widow Wright for a Cott and Inclosure on Morfe
Samuel Walker for a barn on ditto
William Walker for part of a fold yard & barn & Cottages
Thomas Hoccum for an inclosure
Burcott & Burcott
Incroachment for a cottage and inclosure on Morfe
William Ridley for an inclosure on Morfe
Richard Hardwicke for the like
William Bell for an incroachment
William Davies for a cottage and pigstie
Bromley
Richard Littleford for a cottage and inclosure on Morfe
John Massey for the like
Isaac Madeley for the like
John Baker for 2 incroachments
Joseph Taylor for a cottage & Inclosure
James Oldfield for an inclosure
Ewdness & Oldington
John C… for a cottage & inclosure on Crowmore Heath
Thomas ?Harries for part of an edifice and inclosure on ditto
William Rowley for an incroachment
Thomas Worrall for inclosing Fenns Lane
Samuel Thomason for the like
Newton
William Cox for an inclosure on Crowmore Heath
Allscott, Winscott & Rindleford
William Groom for an inclosure on Sowdley

Chapter 5   Eighteenth Century

Thomas Billingsley for the like
Nathaniel Roads for a stable
Moses Jones for a cottage & inclosure
Richard Edwards for a garden
Mary Billingsley for a cottage and garden on Sowdley
Rowley, Bradney & Sond
Joseph Jellico for enclosing Ewke Lanes
Robert Groom for enclosing the lane leading from Mutlands Green to Broadbridge
Thomas Shaw for a pigsty on the Waste
Thomas Billingsley for an encroachment in Bradney Lane
Hilton
John Cluet for enclosing Hilton Green & for a Brew House
Richard Billingsley for inclosing part of ditto [Hilton Green]
John Grainger for a cottage & 2 inclosures in Willmore Hill
Ditto for another
William Whitbroke for 3 huts
Edward Barker/Baxter for an hovel
John Smith for another
ditto for an incroachment on Willmore Hill
Kingslowe & Stanlowe
John Bache for inclosing part of the lane leading from Kingslow to the Common
Thomas Devey for inclosing part of the lane leading from Kingslow to Stanlow
Ditto for an incroachment on the common
ditto for an incroachment on the Wallen
Chesterton
Joseph Parker for an incroachment at Hodgemans Meadow
Mr Bradburne for an incroachment on Chesterton Green
Joseph Parker for a waggon house on Chesterton Street
Joseph Barney for an incroachment at Hodgemans Meadow
William Ely for an incroachment and cottage on the waste
John Bache for an incroachment on the Wallen
James Bradburne for the like
Joseph Parker for an incroachment on the waste
Jonas Pratt for letting his piece lie open to the Wallen
Hallen and Catstrey
Henry Davenport Esq. for an incroachment adjoining to Worfield Yard
Ditto for water course on Crowmore Heath and incroachment adjoining
Thomas Bache for a pigstie & wainhouse on ditto
Thomas Slater for a wain house on Sowdley
John Butcher for an incroachment on Crowmore Heath
Stableford
John Richards for a cottage and 5 little inclosures on Cranmore Heath
James Richards for the like
Joseph Barney for a watering place on Crowmore Heath
Ditto for suffering his sheep to lie in the lanes
Thomas Mills for the like
John Heynes for the like
Andrew Poyner for the like

Chapter 5   Eighteenth Century

C Mortgage of the Manor 20 James [10 November 1624] 5586/2/1/300 (Shropshire Archives)
Henry Lord Bergavenny and Katherine his wife and Sir Thomas Nevill. *Lease of the whole manor of Worfield for 99 years for £500 and an annual rent of £5 to Sir George Whitmore and Sir John Weld all messuages, cottages, mills, lands, tenements, meadows, leasowes, pastures, feedings, commons, woods, underwoods, wastes, free warrens, wayes, passages, tolls, waters, watercourses, pounds, ponds, pools, stanges, dams, flood gates, fishings, mines, quarries, courts leet and frankpledge.*

D Worfield Court Rolls series 5586/1 (Shropshire Archives)
Court Baron Feb1683
William Whitmore came to court and gave this understanding
Robert Eldrington parishioner of St Andrew Holborn, Middlesex Looking Glass Maker and Mary his wife customary tenant of Worfield manor, daughter & heir of Thomas Barrett of Allscott now deceased. Robert Eldrington junior and Mary his wife and surrender three parts to be divided as one nook customary with appurtenances in Winscott to the use of William Bridgen of Bridgnorth his heirs and assigns and here remains in the hands of the lord
Memorandum 2 April 1684
Roger Walford & Grace his wife came to the court at the home of Sir William Whitmore called Apley and surrendered (Roger in the right of his wife and Grace in her own right) one part of a nook of land customary to be divided into 3 in Winscott to the use of William Bridgen of Bridgnorth his heirs and assigns and here remains in the hands of the lord
15 Oct 1685
John Crudgington and Ann his wife at Apley before Wm Whitmore surrendered a parcel of customary land called The Nedge and another parcel of land customary called the Woodcroft extending to a nook of land in the possession of Francis Haslewood with appurtenances in Newton to the use of William Bridgen of Bridgnorth his heirs and assigns and here remains in the hands of the lord
6 March 1689
Court Baron. To this court came Thomas Crudgington of Bridgnorth, feltmaker a customary tenant of this manor and surrendered into the hands of the lord the reversion after the death of his mother, Frances, one cottage and a yard called a backside and a customary parcel of land in Newton, in Beggar Hill, in estimation, an acre and half an acre of land to the use of William Bridgen of Bridgnorth his heirs and assigns and thus remains in the hands of the lord (subject to the payment of a £10 bond
29 April 1697
William Sadler surrendered a nook of land in Stableford, a messuage, an ancient messuage in the possession of Richard Haslewood to his use and that of his wife, Dorothy. 5s ingoing
Richard Haselwood and Dorothea surrender (she examined separately) a messuage, toft and land pertaining to use of William Bridgen 30s ingoing
Memo: this surrender was taken in the name of Mr William Bridgen for the use of Sir William Whitmore present Lord of the Manor his heirs and assigns and he is to resurrender the same as the said lord and his heirs shall direct it

E Mr Davenport's Lands in Worfield 1719 (1190/1/276) (Shropshire Archives)
1. The Ancient Messuage at Hallon
2. One toft late Wermotts
3. One toft Late Lollysticks
4. Half one toft late Catstrees
5. One toft late Barker's Demesne in Hallon
6. One messuage late Barretts

Chapter 5 Eighteenth Century

     Demesne in Hallon late Barretts
7. One messuage late Hackletts
     The Ruddings in Catstree
8. One messuage in Hallon late Eggingtons
     late Warters land in Hallon
     late Walkers land in Hallon
     late Preice's -half a nook demesne except 20th part
                -half a nook customary except 20th part
9. One messuage late Harrieys in Hallon
     An edifice in Cranmere
     Cottage called Winter's Yard late Warters
     Cottage and late late Pertons
     Cottage, place and close of land late Barkers
     2 doles of meadow in Half Meadow and Pillingshall
     Harris Meadow
     Bishton Dole adjoining Half Meadow
     Marsh and Bullerges Yard in Hallon
     2 cottages late Barretts in Worfield
     3 sellions in Hallon
     One cottage late Peries in Worfield
10. One toft and ~~fulling mill~~ in Ewke
     One fulling mill in Ewke
     Newton Meadow
     One parrock or moor called Eggingtons
     2 acres and a half and 6 perches late Hackletts
     Oscott Meadow
11. A messuage in Hallon) Mr Billingsley
12. A toft   )
13. A toft. Fletchers
     A parcel of land called the Moyelyss containing 1 acre
[there is no 14 or 15]
16. 3 messuages in Hallon
     Hallons Yard Allscroft Harris
     Little Meadow
     Bromley Meadow
     Millcroft
     Land in Hallon
     A wear
     5 selions
     1 dole
     1 half yard dole
     1 cottage croft
     1 nook dole
     Great Dole in Half Meadow
     Little Dole sometimes in Half Meadow sometimes in Pillingshall
17. A messuage & land in Rowley
     A fulling mill place

Chapter 5 — Eighteenth Century

    A toft & half a yard land in Sond
    3 cottages in Sond
    One nook land in Ewke
    One wear in Ewke called Ewke Wear
[Note: there is no 18]
19. One messuage and a yardland in ?Bradney
    Mutlands Meadow
    2 doles in Newton Meadow late Rowleys
    About an acre in White Furlong
    3 parcels of land lying between Rowley Ford and Hallon More of 2 acres and 10 perches
    Three eighths of a nook
    2 nooks and half of demesne in Hallon
    Half a nook and the 80th part of a nook customary
        Demesne in Hallon
    Broad Bridge alias Plate Meadow in Hallon
    Aston Moors in Ewke
    2 cottages with a curtilage called Worfield Yard and a parcel of land called
    Allscroft Harris
20. One toft and a nook of land late Warters in Ewke
    2 parcels of land called Dogdale, Parkhill and meadow called The Stockins and a wear place in Ewke
 A cottage and curtilage at Farhills Gate in Hallon and Catstre

Barn at Lower Burcote in 2016

Chapter 6   Nineteenth Century

Birthplace of William Hardwicke 1772 in Allscott, formerly the home of the Ouseley family. Photograph by T. C. Bromwich in 'A Short Memoir of the late ... William Hardwicke' by Hubert Smith, 1879

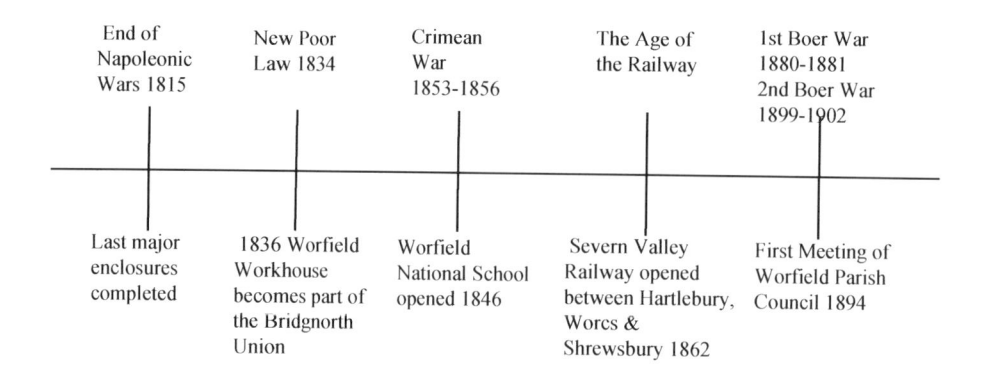

Timeline:

- End of Napoleonic Wars 1815
- Last major enclosures completed
- New Poor Law 1834
- 1836 Worfield Workhouse becomes part of the Bridgnorth Union
- Crimean War 1853-1856
- Worfield National School opened 1846
- The Age of the Railway
- Severn Valley Railway opened between Hartlebury, Worcs & Shrewsbury 1862
- 1st Boer War 1880-1881
- 2nd Boer War 1899-1902
- First Meeting of Worfield Parish Council 1894

Chapter 6 Nineteenth Century

Farmhouse at Allscott built in 1804. Photo taken 2015

As the agricultural revolution gave way to the industrial revolution, economic power shifted from the countryside to urban areas. This was the era of new technology, of steam power and mechanisation, of factories replacing workshops, the movement of people from rural areas into towns, improvements in transport, and the widening of people's horizons. It was a time of cultural revival and educational reform; indeed of social reform in general. Novelists, such as Dickens and Mrs Gaskell, astute observers of contemporary life, recorded the new order, and poets, such as Wordsworth and John Clare, mourned the loss of a rural life prior to enclosures. In Worfield, non-fiction writers such as John Randall and William Hardwicke began to record local history, and later in the century, through photographs, we start to see the landscape as it was and it begins to feel familiar.

Chapter 6   Nineteenth Century

Worfield in the early Twentieth Century

Worfield Mills

The new technology of the industrial revolution would not trouble Worfield until late in the nineteenth century when agriculture began to be mechanised. Until then it was the power of the River Worfe which ground the corn, fulled the wool (cleansed & compacted the fibres), sawed timber, extracted oil, processed wash leather and pumped water. The versatility of the mills meant that they could change their function; at one time they might be a corn mill, then a fulling mill, for example, and later used for extracting oil.

Rowley had an ancient mill which was in the hands of William de Rowlowe when he died in 1331. In the late fifteenth century, Giles Duckwell and Agnes Romsall were indicted for theft from the mill of John Theyn called Rolow Walk Mill,[1] so we know that it was then a fulling mill, as it was in 1611 when John Gould surrendered it to his son Simon[2]. By 1719 Rowley Mill was no more and is referred to as a *fulling mill place* (see page 98). There is little left on the ground to indicate where the mill stood, except tracks leading to the possible location and large sandstone blocks in the Worfe, which may be old bridges or the site of a mill. Upstream from Rowley Mill, permission was granted in 1365 to build another mill, Ewyke Mill, as long as it did not interfere with the lord's mill downstream[3]. Ewyke[App. 2] still had a mill in 1719. (See page 98.)

Chapter 6   Nineteenth Century

Chesterton Mill was initially a fulling mill. In 1369, Roger de Kyngeslowe was permitted to erect a mill on the waste,[4] and in the sixteenth century the parish registers have references to the shearmen and clothworkers 'of the walk mill.' In a court roll of 1607-1608, Sherrington Talbot surrenders a parcel of land called Crawston in Kingslow with a fulling mill upon it, but in the early part of the eighteenth century, Chesterton Mill became a paper mill. The paper was made out of rags which were pulped and then put into moulds which had horse hair mesh at the bottom to allow the water to drain away. One can imagine that the piles of rotting rags would have been very offensive, indeed, the whole process sounds pretty unpleasant. Richard Adams of Chesterton, is recorded in the parish registers of 1728/9 as a paper-maker. In 1747 Richard Cowell and Hester Millingchamp *both living at ye paper-mill at Chesterton* were married. On 24 January 1753 the burial is recorded of Thomas Phillips, *apprentice to Richard Cowel of Chesterton, paper-maker*. After that there are no further references to the paper mill or to paper makers, suggesting that it may have become a corn mill. William Wier of Chesterton Mill, who died in 1817, is buried in the churchyard and we know that the mill was in operation probably until the early 1920s. Again, little remains, if anything, of the old mill building and today we only know from the name, Chesterton Mill Farm, that an ancient mill once stood here.

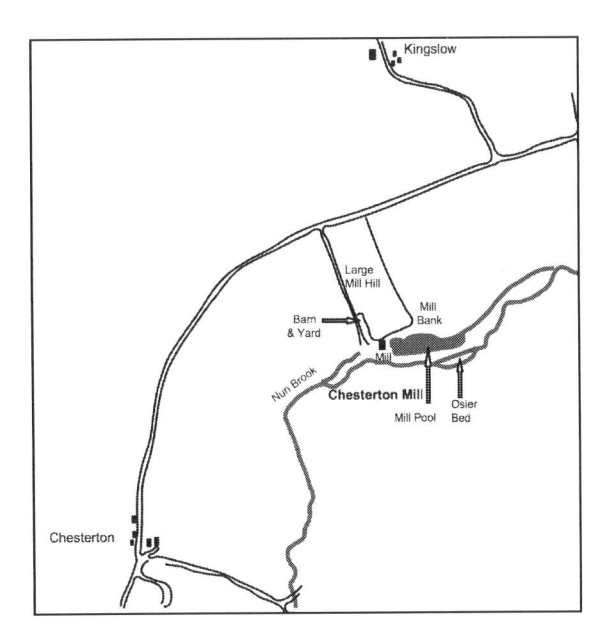

Site of Chesterton Mill taken from the 1839 Tithe Map
Scale: 1inch to 1 mile

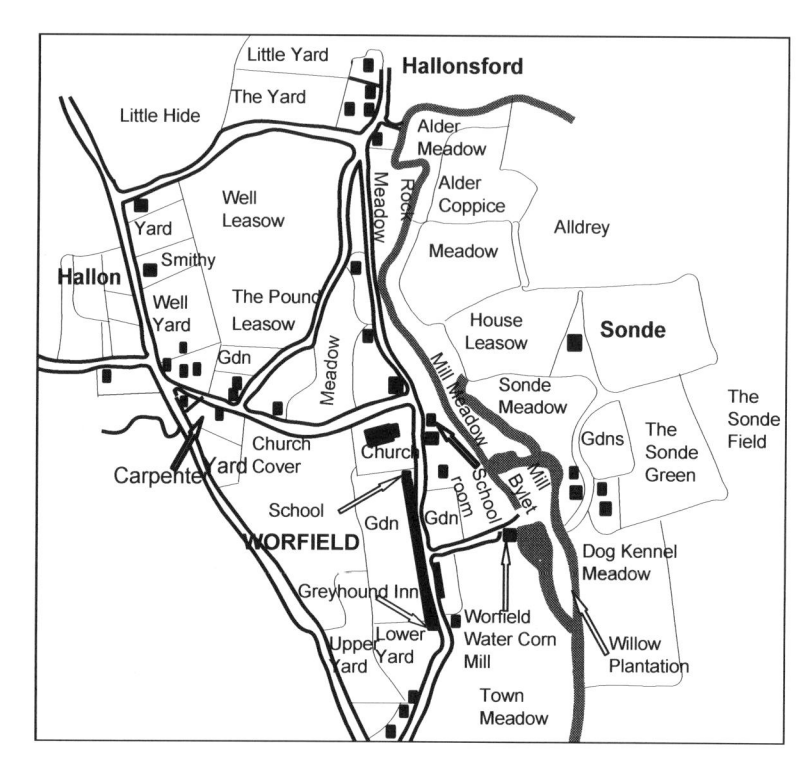

Chapter 6 Nineteenth Century

Worfield Mill taken from the 1839 Tithe Map. Scale: 1 inch to 200 yards

Worfield Mill was one of three mentioned in the Domesday Book as belonging to Worfield. The other two were, according to Randall, Rindleford and Badger. Worfield Mill was initially a corn mill, but the only obvious evidence there was once a mill in the village is from the road name, 'Mill Close.' The large expanse of water in Lower Hall gardens and the area behind Mill Close bungalows were once part of the mill pond. In 1666, William Whitmore of Apley leased[5]

Two water corn mills at Worfield and Mill House in Worfield together with the mill ponds, water courses, stankings, bayes, dams, floodgates, fishings and all other commodities belonging and a plot of ground called the mill bylet of half an acre adjoining the mill dam to Roger Rowley of Rowley for an annual rent of £20 paid twice a year at the Feast of St Mary and St Michael the Archangel

Inventory: a pair of millstones, the runner 6 inches thick and the under stone 3 inches thick, one iron crowe, one corn shoft and one sledge hammer

Worfield Mill was demolished in the 1930s on the instructions of Sir Oliver Leese.

Chapter 6   Nineteenth Century

At Wyken there was a fulling mill at Churleford which was built by the Chapel of the Blessed Virgin Mary. By 1365,[A] the mill had fallen into disrepair and was leased to William de Asterhull as long as it was rebuilt or repaired. The mill was also recognised in 1802[6], in the field name Mill Parock or Bridge Meadow, at Churle. The Churle ran from Hilton to the confluence with the Worfe at Wyken.

Rindleford Mill 2017

Rindleford Mill is the only mill still standing in the parish. At various times it has been a corn mill, rapeseed oil mill and a wash leather mill[7]. The present building dates from the eighteenth and nineteenth centuries. In the late nineteenth century, Randall, wrote that:

... its covered wagons may constantly be seen along the lanes and highways for half a score of miles around

Just a short distance upstream from Rindleford is Burcote Mill which was a fulling mill and sometimes a corn mill. Over the centuries there were complaints about this mill because of the effect it had on Rindleford Mill downstream and because it caused local flooding. In 1518, the people of Roughton and Barnsley complained that Roger Walker, the miller, had built up the banks so much that there was flooding to the danger of those crossing the bridge[8].

Chapter 6 　　　　　　　Nineteenth Century

Former Packhorse Bridge at Rindleford. Above: 2017 Below: circa 1950s

Chapter 6   Nineteenth Century

In spite of the poor siting of Burcote Mill it continued to operate into the nineteenth century. In 1799 it was bought from Thomas Boycott by a consortium of William Macmichael, Joseph Macmichael and Jeremiah Baker. In 1804, William and Joseph Macmichael were granted permission from the Bishop of Lichfield and Coventry to use Burcott Mill as a Protestant Meeting House[9]. The Macmichael family were part of the carpet making factory in Bridgnorth and here, in this remote valley, was built a three storey spinning mill for spinning worsted yarn. It was known simply as, 'The Factory,' and contained carding engines, drawing frames and 256 spindles for spinning yarn. About twenty eight people were employed, four or five adults and the rest were children aged 12-15. In 1814 the mill complex, consisting of the spinning mill, two cottages and a stable, were put on the market. The advertisement[10] read:

This mill is capable of great improvement, the stream being sufficient for a much larger number of spindles

Robinson, in 'The Wandering Worfe', says that the mill was bought by Mr Davenport who sold it to Mr Hardwicke. In 1838 it was converted into a corn mill and became known as Hardwicke's Mill or Burcote Mill.

Burcote Bridge and Burcote Mill Cottages 2017

Social Change in the Nineteenth Century

Immediately after the end of the Parliamentary Enclosures, optimism about the future of farming could be seen in the new farmhouses and farm buildings which appeared across the parish. Allscott was one such farmhouse, built in 1804. The landowners had reason to be optimistic, not least because the government was working on their behalf. The threat of cheap imports from Europe at

Chapter 6   Nineteenth Century

the end of the Napoleonic Wars was countered by Corn Laws which restricted imports and protected the price of home-grown produce.

Protection of one sector of society was bound to adversely affect another. Preference given to rural areas was at the expense of wealth from industry. In the 1830s, Bridgnorth sent two MPs to Parliament, while newly industrialised towns such as Birmingham, Manchester, and Leeds, had no MP to represent them at all. The middle classes wanted representation, the poor simply asked for the necessities of life. Reform was long overdue, but while the Reformers fought for change, the Tories resisted. The struggle was bitter, vocal and often violent. A Worfield man wrote about Thomas Whitmore Esq. of Apley via the Shrewsbury Chronicle (27 October 1837) under the name Crito. (His real name, according to another correspondent, was Captain Fitz Williams.) Crito's opinion was that Whitmore had encouraged Mr Piggott, a Tory, to stand as MP to prevent Henry Tracy, a Reformer, from taking the second Bridgnorth seat. Williams warned Apley tenants that Whitmore had served notice on those who voted for Tracy. Another Worfield man wrote to the same paper on the 13 October 1837 on the subject of 'Tales of my Landlord'. He criticised not only Thomas Whitmore, but the clergy and landed gentry of Worfield. The vicar and landowners, as trustees of a Worfield charity, had, according to this letter, given notice to one of their tenants to quit the property he rented from them because he had voted for Mr Tracy.

Even fifty years later it could be dangerous to vote according to one's conscience. In 1885 an Ackleton farm worker was dismissed because he voted for the 'wrong' candidate[11].

Henry Curran, aged 53, a labourer of Ackleton, committed suicide on Wednesday morning by drowning himself in Badger Pool. The deceased had been employed by Mr Piper of Ackleton. He recorded his vote at Worfield on the 2nd December in favour of Mr More, the successful Liberal candidate and on meeting his employer told him he had done so, contrary to his wishes. An assault took place and the deceased was dismissed by Mr Piper against whom the deceased obtained a summons. The case was compromised [ie the parties came to an agreement]. *The deceased did in fact get another position with Mr Meredith of Rowley but for some reason didn't take the post. On the day of his death he left his home at one in the morning and was found at half past nine in the morning, in Badger Pool, with his hat still on his head and showing through the ice. The deceased leaves a widow.*

Perhaps it was the possibility of social upheaval which caused William Farmer of Brockton Court to emigrate to Canada in 1834. William Farmer, his wife, and seven children, set off for Liverpool in June 1834 in a stage coach drawn by four grey horses. Farmer took another ten families with him, forty five people in all, and some of his livestock, namely: a Clydesdale mare and stallion, another mare, two Durham bulls, two Hereford bulls, six cows - Durham, Hereford and Highland, two Southdown rams, fourteen Southdown ewes, a Leicester ram and thirteen Leicester ewes, a Berkshire boar and a Shropshire boar, nine sows, game cocks and hens and ten

Chapter 6   Nineteenth Century

dogs - pointers, bull terriers and a fox terrier. All arrived safely in Canada to start a new life and the place where they settled is still called, 'Farmer's Rapids'[12].

Care of the Poor
Emigration to the New World was not an option for most of the poor of the parish. For them, enclosures had only negative effects, fewer opportunities for work, high prices for food and low wages. Care of the poor was the responsibility of the parish one lived in or were born in, as it had been since Elizabethan times. In 1601, an Act for the Relief of the Poor, was passed which recognised three groups of poor - a)the elderly, sick, infirm and disabled, b)those able to work but unable to find any and c)those who wouldn't work but were able.

In 1723, an Act was passed to allow the setting up of parish workhouses providing indoor relief for the elderly. In return for their shelter and keep, the inmates were expected to work. The Worfield Workhouse, now numbers 4 and 5, Main Street, was provided in 1729 to house 12 inmates. The law did not allow help to the labouring poor until 1782, when Gilbert's Act was passed which provided outdoor relief so that the able-bodied poor could stay in their own homes. While this was a lifeline to many, the stigma of their impoverishment was visible to all. The workhouse poor, in receipt of indoor relief, had to wear a WP on their upper garment and those in receipt of outdoor relief the letter P. The system reduced hard working parishioners to paupers and benefitted employers who were not similarly stigmatised for keeping wages low. William Taylor, living at The Folly, was a labourer, when his child was baptised in 1779. By 1785, he was officially a pauper[B].

Under the old poor law system, a weekly amount was sometimes paid, mainly to widows and young children. Other poor people were allowed according to their needs; clothing, food, coal, rent and sometimes the tools of one's trade. Examples of both types of allowance are shown below.

Allowances for the Poor [13]
1804
that Widow Bennit of Madeley Wood be allowed to buy a shirt for her husband 2s 6d
that Richard Baker of the Fen Gate having 6 children and lately lost his wife and buried her at his own expense be allowed £1 1s
Widow Gittos towards buying a second hand pair of shoes 2s 6d
Charles Robinson of Brosely being lame with the rheumatism 2s 6d
Thomas Haynes of Worfield allowed 2s 6d
Mary Felton of Madely be discontinued after Aug 5th being 7 year old 2s
that Mrs Sherwood buy for Ann Bishton's child a pair of slip shoes
1805
that Elizabeth Guest be allowed to buy a shift for her daughter 3s and also 2s 6d for some coals 5s 6d

Chapter 6   Nineteenth Century

that Prudence Wilson be allowed 2s 6d
that Elizabeth Law be allowed to buy some clothing for Richard Meredith 5s
that Mrs Sherwood buy a petticoat and a pair of shoes for Sarah Richards that she is also allowed 2s
that Elizabeth Robinson be allowed towards buying a pair of shoes 3s
that Thomas Mattocks be allowed for coals he being presented by particular misfortunes in his family firm purchased by himself £1 1s
that Elizabeth Nicholas is allowed to repair her spinning wheel 2s.
1817
Mr Hardwick be paid the rent of William Nicholls ... at the Factory
1819
that John Colley be allowed to buy a bag of potatoes
John Painter be allowed 10s 6d on account of the death of his pig which died a short time ago

Worfield Workhouse. 4 & 5 Main Street 2017

Chapter 6 Nineteenth Century

Payments to the Poor. 1833 Weekly pay list to the poor of the Parish of Worfield[14]

Auden, Elizabeth 1s
Anson, Mary, child 1s 6d
Baker, Joseph 1/6
Bishton, Thomas 2s
Booth, widow 1/6
Beetlestone, Widow 1/6
Burton, Jane, child 1/6
Bishton, Julian, child 1/6
Barratt, George 1/-
Blunt, widow 1/6
Barratt George and Family 4/6
Clewett, Widow 1/6
Clewett Widow, Tettenhall 1/6
Cartwright, Mary, child 2/-
Child, widow, children, Broseley 3/-
Child, Ann, Broseley 1/6
Cockram, John, Lodging 1/-
Doughty and wife 3/-
Edwards, Benjamin 3/-
Fowler, Hannah, child 2/-
Felton, Sarah, child 2/-
Fowler, Sarah, child 2/-
Hand, Margaret 1/6
Harris, Widow, 1/6
Higgins, Widow 1/0
Hoccom, Mary, child 2/-
Harper, Widow 1/6
Hill, Mary child, Tettenhall 3/-
Hall, Elizabeth, child 1/6
Lewis, Widow 1/6
Lawley, Elizabeth, children 4/-
Loy, Edward 2/-
Phillips, Joseph 1/6
Piper, Widow 2/-
Pooler, Mary child 1/3
Painter, Thomas 1/-
Painter, Susan child 1/6
Pateman, blind child 2/-
Price, Jane child 2/-
Rowley, Widow 1/6
Rogers, Widow, Tipton 1/6
Southwell, Hannah child 2/-
Taylor, Samuel lame child 2/-
Tooth, Maria child 1/6

The poor were paid for out of a rate levied on property owners and occupiers[14], a system which was never popular but became much less so as the bills escalated. With a population of stable size the old system was sustainable, but by the late eighteenth century a big rise in population meant that a new system was needed. In 1834, a new Poor Law was passed which grouped parishes into unions to make provision for the poor. In 1836, the Vestry Minutes[13 & 15] recorded that:

The rents due from the outdoor paupers be paid up to the 29th and notice be given to the several landlords that the parish will be giving up possession of the workhouse and the several tenements concerned at Lady day next.

The Worfield Workhouse continued until the twentieth century as part of the Bridgnorth Poor Law Union.

The able-bodied who were seeking work were apprenticed to employers, a system which went back a long way, certainly to the sixteenth century and probably before that. In 1674 John Billingsley was apprenticed to John Brodburne until he was twenty four[16]. By the nineteenth century apprentices were often used as cheap labour. Most of the girls went into service and the boys into farming. Children as young as seven were apprenticed, usually until the age of 21, but in some cases to the age of 24. In 1842, William Higgs, a deaf and dumb boy, was apprenticed to William Mc Clellan, a tailor. Thomas Rogers, a shoemaker, had a child by Mary Valentine in 1807

Chapter 6   Nineteenth Century

and decided to take the child himself as an apprentice, but in the main children were balloted for by eligible parishioners. Neither side in the arrangement had any choice in the matter and in 1805 William Pratt of the Old Lodge refused to take his apprentice, William Wilde, who then had to be cared for at the cost of the parish. In another case the parish was not impressed at having to keep Thomas Pinches' daughter in the workhouse, *on account of a complaint of ill treatment*[13].

Enclosures also had an effect on those who wandered from place to place. Before enclosure, vagrants, hawkers and gipsies were able to camp on open ground, but afterwards, with much of the open land gone, travellers could only camp on the verges of roads. Even this was denied them when a law was passed in 1835 which stopped all hawkers, higglers and gipsies camping on roads and lighting fires at night. Contravention of the law meant a 40s fine or three months imprisonment. In 1855 eight people in Worfield were brought before the bench to answer charges under this law. Job Holland, Henry Neale and James Hodgkins were charged with camping and lighting fires in a lane near Stanmore Grove the previous Friday. The men were vagrants and said they did not know they were in breach of the law and that this was their first offence. The bench dealt leniently with the men and each was fined 6d with costs of 8s 6d: in total 9s. Major Lovell and James Lovell, who had camped and lit fires at the top of Burcott Lane, then approached the bar and made a similar plea of ignorance and that this was their first offence. They were also fined 9s.

Elijah Locke, Beaufoy Locke, his son and Unity Locke, his daughter, were accused of camping in Barnsley and having a fire burning at 1am. They were gipsies and Police Officer Lloyd from Claverley gave evidence that the three had been very abusive to him at different times when he had asked them to move from the area. The last time Beaufoy had threatened *to do for him*. Thankfully for the policeman Beaufoy's hand was bound up and swollen. The bench fined the group 9s or 14 days' imprisonment. The newspaper report[17] relates that the "Bamfylde Moore Carew" company *mustered some few dozen men, women and children of the Egyptian caste and the fines were duly paid*.

Roads
From medieval times to the seventeenth century, each parish had repaired and maintained their roads. While one parish did link up with the next, these were essentially roads designed to meet the needs of a local community. The roads between parishes probably received much less attention than the road to the mill or the common field. The nationwide problem in the eighteenth century was how to create a road system which would take people across the country as quickly, reliably and safely as possible. The solution was to set up toll roads also known as turnpike roads. Turnpike gates were put across the road at various points which were opened on payment of a toll. The main roads we now have through Worfield, the A454, A442 and A458 (Bridgnorth Turnpike Trust) and part of the B4176 (Madeley Trust) were all turnpiked[C].

Chapter 6   Nineteenth Century

Above: Former toll house on the A442 by the Worfe Bridge in 2017. Below: Postcard showing the now-demolished toll house opposite the Wheel Inn (postmarked 1907). The toll collectors were: 1841 James Lloyd, also a shoemaker, 1851 Edward Jones and in 1861 Mary Nicholls (census returns)

Chapter 6   Nineteenth Century

The only toll house which remains today is near the Worfe Bridge on the A442 on the corner of the road to Bromley. In 1821 a load of lime and turnpikes were delivered to improve the Worfe Bridge and William Powell was paid for laying the coping stones. Improvements were needed if carts and coaches were to be able to cross the Worfe in all weathers. Nearby was a milestone, another requirement of turnpikes, now lost, and presumed stolen.

The toll house on the A454, at the Wheel, has now disappeared. (The present wooden sign post may date from 1912 when the Wyken Farm Accounts show a payment to Mr Wood's executors for a sign post.) The toll house on the A458 was at the parish boundary between Worfield and Claverley, where the road from Roughton and Barnsley meets the Stourbridge Road, near to the Old Lodge. The Madeley Turnpike went from the Buck's Head to the New Inn. A newspaper report in 1867 records an income of £355 from the Madeley Toll Gates at Cuckoo Oak and Lawley Gates, £74 from Meadow Gate, Coalbrookdale, and £5 from Rudge Heath Gate, near the New Inn (Shrewsbury Chronicle 8 March 1867). The road went through Beckbury and I assume must have then joined the now B4176 and continued on this road to the New Inn (Boycott Arms). We cannot be sure of the location of the Rudge Heath Gate but at Littlegain there is a field called Gate Leasow which may relate to a turnpike gate. There is also a Gate Leasow by the Worfe Bridge toll house. The very low income of this Toll Gate may have given rise to the name of the hamlet, Littlegain.

In 1820, a Scottish engineer, John McAdam, developed a way of providing a smoother road surface by compacting stone and filling in gaps with powdered stone. Even without macademising Worfield roads might have been better than most, since gravel was readily available across the parish close to the surface. In 1815 the road from Sandy Valley (see page 115) to where it meets the Dudley to Enville Road was already good gravel road but in some places gradients were steep. When the Stourbridge Road was turnpiked in 1815, plans were included to reduce the summit of Gatacre Hill by six yards and use the gravel to infill Spring Valley on the other side by three yards[18].

Some of the road work was recorded in the Highway Surveyors' Accounts. The parish was divided into four quarters for managing the infrastructure of the area and two books of accounts, for the north west quarter and the east,[19] from 1770 -1840, have survived. The first thing which strikes one from these accounts[D] is how extensive the road building programme was. It wasn't just the turnpike roads which were improved, even the minor or bye roads were subject to the same treatment, resurfaced, widened, levelled, bounded by stone and fenced. (Stone edging can be seen at the sides of many footpaths which were formerly roads.) This was a mammoth community effort. The property owners paid for it and, in the main, the poor did the work and were rewarded; not handsomely, of course, but rewarded nonetheless. Two Irish workers, Conner Macnamara and James Ohara, were employed in 1826 for breaking stones when Worfield's street was macadamised. Quarries were opened up across the parish. There were so many gravel pits and so much removed that one wonders what the landscape looked like before quarrying began, or indeed what it was like at the time the pits were in use. The north west records show that, amongst many

Chapter 6   Nineteenth Century

others, gravel was taken from Hartlebury, Soudley (pit infilled 1829), Echoeshill and Meer Pit(in Stockton parish), where 677 loads of gravel were removed. As soon as one pit was filled in, another was opened. Allscott Pit was levelled in 1823 and Meare Bank opened in the same year. Pebbles were also gathered off the fields by men, women and children[20].

1814 Mrs Williams paid for 4 loads of pebbles put down on the Rindleford Rd
1825 A woman at Hilton for picking 5 loads of stones
1826 Molly Pugh, widow Harris, Toye's sons and several others for picking stone and Fowler & son for breaking them

The streams which criss-crossed the landscape were an impediment to travel, and were either forded, crossed by a foot or horse bridge or by a broad bridge suitable for carts. The broad bridges were at The Lowe, Wyken, Stableford and Rindleford. The earliest record we have of road works in the parish is from 1672, in Thomas Lowe's[19] accounts as Supervisor for the west of the parish:

Disbursed towards the mending of the Hermitage and keeping it in repair - 4s
Disbursed for Rindleford Bridge as followeth
For a boat and help to draw the bridge out 4s 6d
For timber and workmen's wages 8s 2d
for the mending of the bridges in Halfmeadow
Disbursed for stouckes and plancks and workmens wages 9s 6d

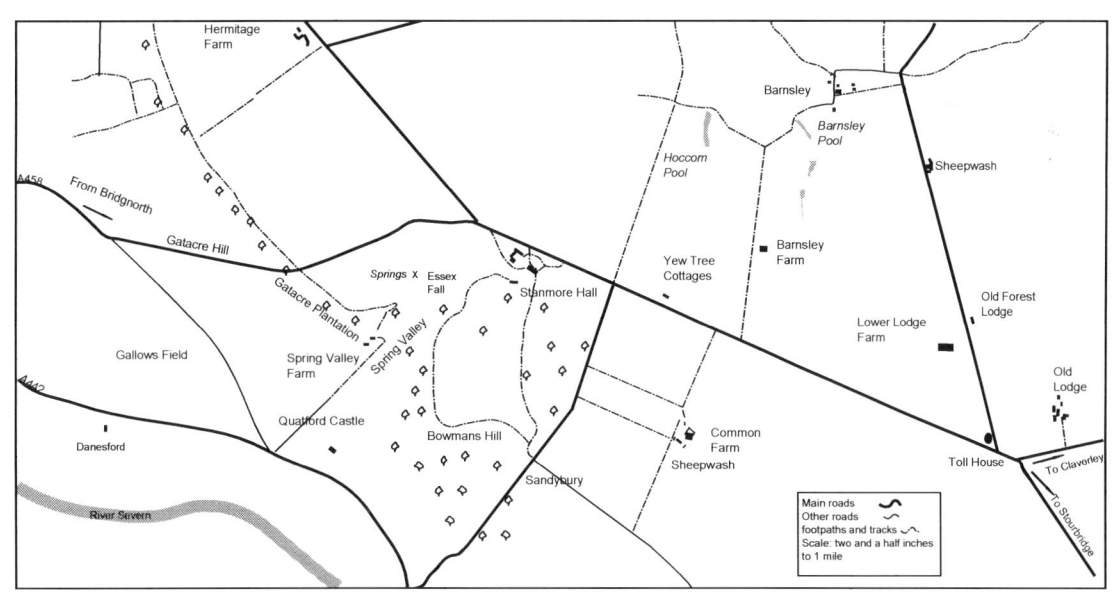

Part of the Turnpike Road between Bridgnorth and Stourbridge showing the toll house, Gatacre Hill and Spring Valley.

Chapter 6   Nineteenth Century

The B4176 in 1968 before this section near Littlegain was widened in the 1970s

John Kirkland seeing the last of the cows across the road. James Gilson is his indispensable helper

116

Chapter 6   Nineteenth Century

Wooden bridges became brick built and the Wood family, owners of brickyards at Hilton, Cranmere and Hartlebury, who we met in the previous chapter, benefitted from the increase in demand. Improvements to the bridges alone required many bricks - 600 bricks in 1780 for the Hilton Bridge[20], and between 1790 and 1792, 2,100 for the Wheel Bridge and 1,000 for the Broadbridge at the Lowe.

Stableford Broad Bridge, a three span bridge, planned in 1800 and designed, it is thought by Thomas Telford,[21] replaced a single span bridge which had fallen into disrepair. A wooden bridge had been built alongside which was washed away in the floods of 1795, thus necessitating the building of a new and more substantial bridge.

The Broad Bridge at Stableford built of Badger stone

In 1834, improvements to the Stableford Bridge[22] were again needed. Bridges needed frequent repair as natural wear and tear, damage by carts and swollen rivers took their toll. Sometimes vandalism was the cause of the damage. In 1838 payment was made firstly for repairing the Wheel & Lowe Bridges and again for repair after someone had pushed the upper bricks into the brook.

117

Chapter 6   Nineteenth Century

In 1843 the dangers of trying to cross the Hilton Brook when it was in flood were brought to the attention of the turnpike surveyor[23].

In August last the Brook was swollen with heavy rains to such an extent upon the turnpike road that the Mail Coach was detained upwards of six hours and was then drawn through the water with ropes - the Driver in the act of riding the horse through the water was thrown off and both nearly drowned

Several heavy laden waggons were detained from eight to ten hours and Pickfords waggons, heavy laden with goods of considerable value from the Bridgnorth Carpet Factories, were detained many hours at the Brook and the driver in attempting to ride the leader through was thrown off and carried by the stream to the Horse bridge where he clung to the parapet and remained there nearly an hour bellowing out for help and was then rescued by some casual stragler who happened to take refuge from the storm in a barn near the spot. The horses were with difficulty saved and the goods much endangered

The following day the Brook was nearly as high as on the one preceding and passengers were detained upwards of four hours.

The present Horse and foot bridge is so damaged that passengers cannot safely use it and its reparation is required with the hope that a proper bridge will be erected.

The travel upon the road above mentioned is now four times what it was a few years since in consequence of the new communication from Morville through Hopton and Corve Dale to Ludlow and other more distant places and of the railway station at Wolverhampton and diverse other causes.

Some roads became main thoroughfares and others became redundant. A road which has now fallen into disuse was that from Hartlebury through Newton to a ferry terminal on the River Severn. The new sections provided a ring road around Newton, presumably to prevent a succession of carts and gigs clattering through the village. The gradient of the road was also reduced by making a deep cutting and over it was built a bridge now known as Hunter's Bridge, dated 1804. It was built by Charles Head of Bridgnorth, a mason, and commissioned by Thomas Barnfield, occupier of Ewdness, agent for Thomas Whitmore.

In an agreement[24] between Thomas Barnfield on behalf of Thomas Whitmore and Charles Head, mason, of Bridgnorth, Charles Head agreed to erect a bridge over the Cave Holloway at Winscot Hills,

... at the summit of the said hills at the spot already marked out and where the centres are at present fixed for the erection thereof. The arch to be erected with blue brick and the parapet and other walls thereof with rough stones to be got upon the said hills near to the said bridge in a good and workmanlike manner to be approved of by John Webb of the cottage near Lichfield in the county of Stafford Esq, the person nominated by Thomas Barnfield and Charles Head. Whatever

Chapter 6   Nineteenth Century

sum John Webb shall say then Head should reasonably have for erecting the bridge. Head should complete in a reasonable time as soon as the brick, sand and lime may be conveniently found.

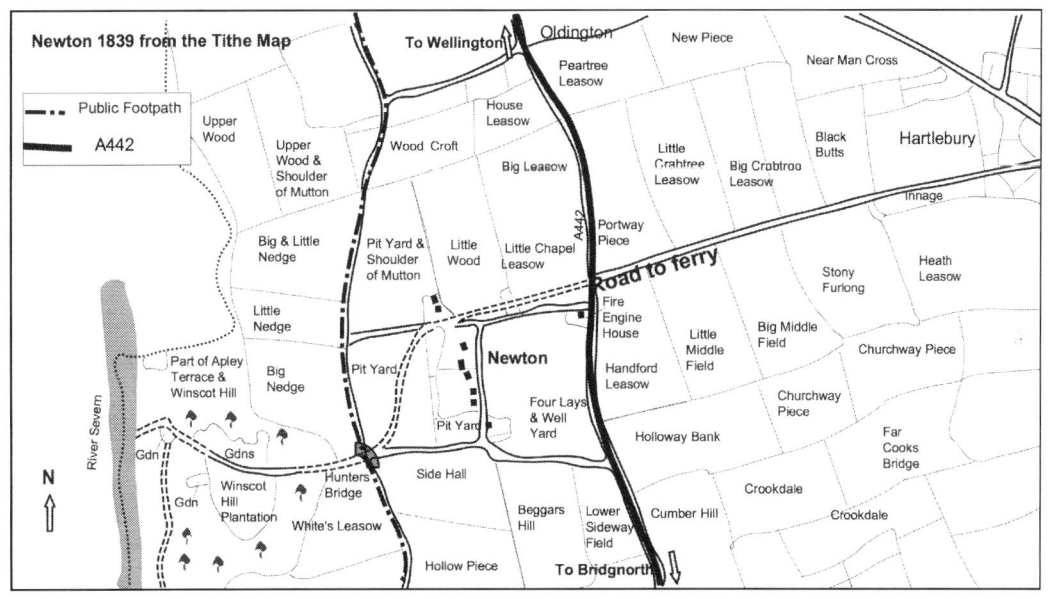

Newton showing the road to the ferry. Scale 2 inches to 1 mile

The road itself was not new. The ferry to Astley Abbotts had been there for many years and there may also have been a 'loade' for loading and unloading goods. Road improvements in the eighteenth century enabled people to travel across land more easily but Worfield had been fortunate in having the River Severn on its western edge to carry goods in and out of the parish. In the first forty years of the nineteenth century there was a dramatic shift from river to road and rail. For the carriage of all but heavy and bulky goods, Worfield began to look east to the railways of Wolverhampton, rather than west to the Severn, leaving the road shown in the picture overleaf a forgotten byway.

Chapter 6 Nineteenth Century

Cave Holloway from Newton to the River Severn in 2016 looking towards the bridge built in 1804. Ron Summers in the foreground

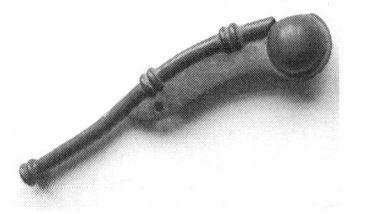

A find from the days of river trade. Believed to date from the late nineteenth century this bosun's whistle has the owners's name on it - Michael Worthington

Chapter 6   Nineteenth Century

Worfield School circa 1995

Education

In the centre of Worfield the National School was built in 1846, on what was formerly the Town Meadow. Now known as Worfield Endowed School, there have been some additions, such as the Infants School built in 1874 (on the left in the above photograph), and some units added in the twentieth century, but the original school buildings are little altered externally.

Before the Reformation, formal education in the parish was organised by the church through its chantry system. The school was in various places in the village. In 1523 it was in the house of Sir John Lye, the Chaplain, at Walstone and before that it was held in a gallery in the Lady Chapel of the Church. When the Chantry was dismantled in 1551 the school moved back into the Lady Chapel. The Churchwarden's Accounts record[26] a payment for repairing Thomas Garbett's irons for *bolling down the chapel now the school house*. By 1581 the same accounts[24] show that work was being done to convert the court house to a school.

1581
3 ton of square timber to board the court house and mend the penthouse 12s
150 saw boards to board the schoolhouse 18s

121

Chapter 6   Nineteenth Century

2 long planks to sit on 12d
Daubing the schoolhouse and making the hearth 2s 8d
1582-3
Timber for the court house
For Frances Barrett for helping Sheynton and making the hearth in the school house
Paid to Thomas Taylor for a key to the school house door

The church has always had a close connection with education, partly in its role as administrator of charities for the poor[27]. There were two main charities associated with education. In 1618, some of the wealthier members of the parish purchased the former chantry properties, five cottages and a barn in Worfield, one cottage in Bridgnorth and a croft in Quatford, through William Lloyd and Thomas Parker of London. Henceforth known as the Lloyd and Parker Charity it allowed for the maintenance of a school and schoolmaster to educate thirteen poor children. Any surplus funds were to be distributed to poor widows and the poorest inhabitants[28]. Worfield Grammar School was thus formally established and located in the old Court House, the half timbered building at the end of the church path. Lloyd and Parker funding meant that the school was financially separate from the church, although Lichfield had to approve appointments. In 1704, Theophilus Barney was recommended to Lichfield as Master to teach ten poor children, but in 1709 he was given notice because he had no licence. The licence was a requirement because this was a free school, a description which Robert Barrett from Worfield contested and suggested could be changed if necessary[E]. The second charity was the Brierley Charity, so called because properties were bought in Brierley Hill through Thomas Woolley's bequest in 1609 and James Hancox's gift in 1697.

In the nineteenth century, it was recognised that a much bigger school than the Grammar School was needed and one which would provide education for girls. Again, it was the church which helped in this regard. The Church of England promoted a national strategy for the building of new schools and the vicar of Worfield, the Reverend Cornelius Farnworth Broadbent, embraced the challenge to provide such a school in Worfield. Thanks to careful and fortuitous investment of bequests (the Brierley properties had a rich seam of gold beneath them in the form of the ten yard seam of coal) there was money available to build a school. In 1846, the Trustees of the Brierley Estate bought part of the Town Meadow from W. S. Davenport and then paid for the building of the school and two schoolhouses. Further provision was made for staff salaries, books, clothing and stationery.

The school was such a success that within six months it had 172 pupils, almost achieving the target of 200. In 1873, there were 102 boys and 103 girls attending, and to comply with the 1870 Education Act, fifty additional places were provided for infants[29]. The Brierley Charity once again funded the building. A good teacher was essential to the success of the school and the Boys Department was fortunate in having William Lloyd as teacher for forty seven years. Lloyd understood the difficulties of running a rural school. Sometimes pupils had to sit all day in wet

Chapter 6   Nineteenth Century

clothes having walked miles from their homes in snow or rain, but Lloyd allowed no excuses from his pupils. The Master expected 100% attendance and high academic attainment. The regime was hard, but there was a genuine interest in each child's progress even after they had left school. Gainful employment was arranged for pupils on leaving, apprenticeships for boys, mainly in farming, while the girls were found posts as servants. Some pupils fulfilled their potential outside the parish. Charles Tantram[30] became a teacher of music and Benjamin Lewis, as John Turnock records, *who had entered the School at the age of six in 1872, gained a First Class Queen's Scholarship to Battersea Training College*[31]. Sadly, the Girls School seems to have fared less well. The teacher, Miss Martindale, who had been the headmistress of the Girls School for seventeen years from 1873, was asked by the Vicar to resign her post and left in 1890 and Miss Evers resigned at the same time[31].

Church and Worfield School staff in 1887. Back Row l to r: Miss Gotley (Infants), ? Mr Ormerod (Organist), Edith Lloyd, Charles Tarrant, Heather Thatcher, Fred Lloyd (Pupil Teachers), Miss M. E. Evers
Front Row: Mr Willoughby (Curate), The Reverend E. P. Nicholas (Vicar), Mr William Lloyd (Boys Headmaster), Mrs C. Martindale (Girls Headmistress)

Chapter 6　　　　　　　　Nineteenth Century

In contrast to the success of the National School, the Grammar School was floundering. In 1842, the old Grammar School had shut its doors and the question was whether it had any role in educating the children of Worfield at all. As with the National School, its future would depend on the right curriculum (well taught), the correct location and adequate funding. The decision was made to have a practical curriculum suited to the needs of future farmers, with subjects such as surveying, mechanics, and agriculture. The school would stay in its existing building, and while it would continue to be funded by the Lloyd and Parker Charity, fees would be charged for attending. In February 1876, following the death of the headmaster, Isaac Hoppett, the future of the Grammar School was again in doubt. Parishioners met in the National School Room to determine the school's fate and the vote was unanimously in favour of the Grammar School continuing[32].

Changes were clearly needed. The current building was deemed unsuitable and new premises essential. The Lloyd and Parker funds were tied up in land and property, but the sale of some of their assets could go towards building a new grammar school. To further bolster assets, some Worfield charities, including the Lloyd and Parker and Worfield Brierley Charities, amalgamated to form the Worfield United Charity. A Lloyd and Parker map shows not only the occupants of its houses in the village of Worfield, including a former pigsty converted into a house for Sarah Hall, widow, but also the miller's house, and a watering place on the Worfe[G].

In 1879, a suitable property for the school came on the market in Roughton (Roughton Cottage), and in 1880, the new headmaster, the Reverend Thomas Turner, and his wife were installed in, what was to become, the new Worfield Grammar School. The old Grammar School was bought by Mr Davenport from the trustees, and became a library and reading room for a club of no more than twenty five members[33]. At last an explanation as to why it was known as the Old Club Room.

In 1883, three extra rooms were added to the Master's House adjoining the Grammar School so that it could house more than the eight boarders who could be currently accommodated, and in 1890 a playroom was added. However, after an initial flurry of interest, numbers at the school declined. Worfield Grammar School in Roughton was to have a brief flowering. In 1902 the school closed and, after nearly 300 years, Worfield Grammar School was no more. The property was sold in 1917 for £740.

The Reverend Turner, who by all accounts was a kind and gentle man, stayed on in Worfield as curate. Evans, in his book, 'A History of the Rectors and Vicars of Worfield,' recalls that the curate *used to cycle all round the parish visiting parishioners. When he got on his bicycle he was a changed man, he had only one pace and that was absolutely flat out...It must have been an astonishing, and indeed, surprising sight for a stranger to see this mild looking, white haired old clergyman dressed in the clothes of a previous generation negotiating hell for leather the down hill run of the China Bridge Hill. He had the most extraordinary method of mounting his cycle which necessitated climbing on a bank and jumping in a frog like manner over the back of the bicycle (on which was always strapped a box of sweets which he used to hand out to the children) and landing safely on the saddle.* Father Turner, as he like to be known, retired to Tabley in 1917.

Chapter 6 Nineteenth Century

ROUGHTON COTTAGE,

A pleasantly situated residential Property, in the parish of Worfield, County of Salop, 3 miles distant from Bridgnorth, on the Wolverhampton road, and near to the picturesque Village of Worfield, with its fine old Church.

PERRY AND PHILLIPS

Are favored with instructions to submit this desirable

PROPERTY

TO PUBLIC AUCTION,
AT THE
CROWN HOTEL, BRIDGNORTH,
ON TUESDAY, THE 27th DAY OF MAY, 1879,
At 4 o'clock in the Afternoon, subject to conditions which will then be read.

The House and Premises are substantially built, and with a small outlay may be made a most delightful Residence for a genteel family, surrounded by good roads, approached by a carriage drive, and contain Dining and Drawing Rooms, Domestic Offices, 4 Bedrooms, Two Closets, and Conservatory at end of house, Stable, Coachhouse, and Piggeries. The Land is pasture, of excellent quality, and comprises an area of 5a. 0r. 1p. or thereabouts. *The property is Copyhold of the Manor of Worfield*

The Auctioneers feel they cannot too strongly recommend this eligible Property to persons seeking a retired situation in a salubrious and picturesque neighbourhood. Its proximity to the villages of Wyken and Worfield, within easy distance of Bridgnorth, where is a first-class Station on the Severn Valley Railway, renders it an exceedingly good opportunity either for investment or occupation.

Further particulars may be had from Messrs. Robinson and Watts, Solicitors, Dudley; Messrs Combe and Wainwright, Solicitors, Staple Inn, London, W.C.; or the Auctioneers, Bridgnorth.

C. EDKINS, PRINTER, HIGH STREET, BRIDGNORTH.

Chapter 6   Nineteenth Century

WORFIELD GRAMMAR SCHOOL,
ROUGHTON, NEAR BRIDGNORTH.

FOUNDED 1605.

Head Master:
THE REV. T. W. TURNER, M.A.,
Trinity College, Dublin.
(Formerly Head Master of Ashley House School, Kingsdown, Bristol.)

The above School has been re-modelled under the Charity Commissioners, and now offers a thorough Education, including:—

RELIGIOUS INSTRUCTION, READING, WRITING AND ARITHMETIC; GEOGRAPHY, HISTORY; ENGLISH GRAMMAR; COMPOSITION AND LITERATURE; MATHEMATICS; LATIN, FRENCH; DRAWING AND NATURAL SCIENCE.

The Fee is £2 per quarter, which must be paid in advance to the Head Master.

The School Year is divided into Quarters of about Ten Weeks each. The next Quarter commences July 26th.

The Site of the new School Buildings and grounds comprises 5 acres in a healthy and pleasant spot, at Roughton, upon the high road between Bridgnorth and Wolverhampton, 2½ miles from the former, and 11 miles from the latter town.

BOARDERS.

Boys are received in the School-house upon the following terms, which are additional to the School Fee:—

Yearly Boarders...	£30 per annum.
Laundress and Repairs	£2 ,,
Weekly Boarders	£24 ,,

There are no extras for Books, Stationery, or other necessary to the School routine.

All Fees are to be pre-paid.

A Quarter's notice is required previous to the removal of a Pupil.

Each pupil has a separate sleeping apartment, and is to be provided with Fork, Spoon, 2 Table Napkins, 2 pairs of Sheets, and 4 Towels.

Application for admission should be made to the Head Master.

Chapter 6   Nineteenth Century

The Reverend T. W. Turner

The former Grammar School at Roughton as a private house, possibly in the 1920s

Chapter 6 Nineteenth Century

The Restoration of the Church

In 1830 a visitation by the Archdeacon of Stafford[34] revealed serious problems with the fabric of the Church. It was ordered:

1. That the state of the tower and walls, especially the wall on the south side be carefully examined by an architect and the necessary measures be taken for putting the whole into thorough and substantial repair.
2. The earth to be cleared away around the Church walls and chancel to the depth of the level of the Church floor and an open drain, two foot or more wide be made for carrying off the water from the foundations and keeping the Church dry internally
3. The buttresses to be repaired where needful and the walls pointed.
4. Spouting to be carried all round the roof and the water carried off by horizontal and perpendicular spouts to guard the walls against damp.
5. The iron to be prevented from injuring the walls and roof of the chancel.
6. An additional casement to be made on the south side and one in the chancel. The casements to be always kept open in dry weather and also the south door after the iron gates are put up in order to keep the church ventilated.
7. No graves to be allowed nearer than six feet to the walls
8. The ? on the north side behind the Bromley monuments to be restored
8. The register to be rebound and the bible in the Reading Room to be repaired
9. The quarries in the floor of the Church to be taken up and relaid even
And recommended
10. The building of a gallery in the north aisle or by an arrangement of the pews to provide much needed accommodation for the poor
11. The removal of the pulpit to the south side of the middle aisle.

By the time of a visitation in 1847[35] the tone is much more positive:

The improvements in the church are highly creditable to the ... and number of parishioners.
The Fabric itself. Nothing further seems wanting at present but the pointing of the tower and its buttresses which ought to be done as soon as convenient from top to bottom.
The new schools are the handsomest I have seen anywhere.

So it is something of a surprise to read that in 1861 the condition is described[34] as follows:

The greater part of the roofing of the church is in a very dilapidated state
A portion of the pewing is also in an unsound condition
There is a want of better accommodation within the church.

At a vestry meeting held on the 8 August 1861[36] it was advised that:

Chapter 6   Nineteenth Century

The north, south and nave roofs should be repaired immediately and a rate of seven and a half pence in the pound be levied to defray the expenses.
That the reseating of the church, the removal of the galleries, restoration of the porch and conversion of the ground floor of the tower area into a vestry be commenced as soon as a sufficient sum has been raised by voluntary contributions.

Application was made to the Bishop's Consistory Court for a faculty to authorise the vicar, the Reverend Cornelius Farnworth Broadbent, and the churchwardens, Alfred Blundell and Richard Eykyn, to reroof and repair the north, south and nave roofs, to take down the present pews, seats and sitting places, pulpit and reading desk and to restore and 'repew' the church, to remove all the galleries, to thoroughly repair and restore the porch of the church and to convert the ground floor of the tower into a vestry room. Commissioners were to be appointed to allocate the seats amongst the parishioners.

The faculty was granted in 1861, and work commenced, being completed a year later[37] giving us substantially the church we have today. Much of the old feel of the church has been lost, leaving us with a church which can only be described as, 'heavily victorianised.' According to Evans[38] we have lost:

- The old high-backed box pews
- A three decker pulpit
- The galleries
- All the old windows on the north and south side and the chancel.
- An altar piece of wood, inlaid with oak, walnut and holly in the centre of which was a star with eight points. Made by Richard Saddler it was burnt by William Davenport when the chancel was being restored.
- Plaster ceilings in all the aisles and the chancel
- The old porch, built in the classical style in 1796
- An ancient font which was in the chancel and in 1796 moved to the St Nicholas Chapel.
- An oak screen around the St Nicholas Chapel taken down in 1819 and sold to the Vicar of Atcham in 1866
- The old chancel which was extensively restored

There is probably much more which was destroyed at this time of which we have no record and we have acquired items which now seem without any great architectural or spiritual worth. Very noticeably the church has lost light, with the plain glass windows being replaced by stained glass.

The End of the Century
In 1875, when Edmund Henry Davenport returned from Australia with his Tasmanian-born wife, the parish was probably little changed from that which he had left. The third quarter of the nineteenth century would, however, prove to be a very difficult time for farmers. Extreme weather

Chapter 6   Nineteenth Century

in this country[F] led to reduced yields, and imports of grain from North America dramatically reduced prices. Farmers with mortgages struggled to pay them and sale prices for farms dropped, if there were any buyers at all[H].

Lost and Found

Three Russian Orthodox crosses found in a field in the parish. The first is from the nineteenth century and the third is the oldest. Were they trophies from the Napoleonic Wars? Were they linked in some way to the Prisoners of War held in Bridgnorth at that time who may have been working on the land or on the roads?
Finder: Frank Taylor

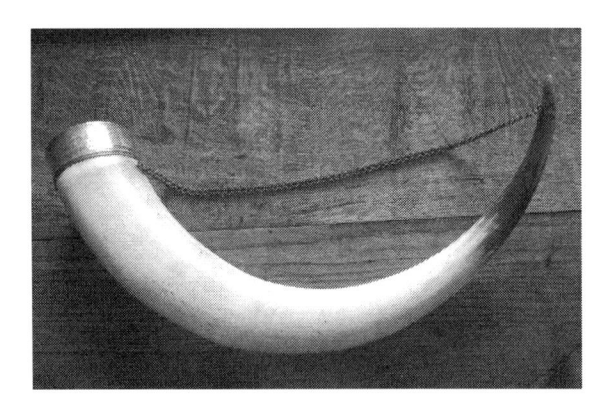

The inscription reads: "Bowman." Bred at Cranmere by Valentine Vickers. Slaughtered 1831 weight 1535lbs. Valentine Vickers was the agent for Apley and Davenport Estates, a banker and surveyor. He worked far beyond Worfield, as a surveyor during the Parliamentary Enclosures, and gained a national reputation for his work. He married a gipsy girl but the marriage was difficult. The couple moved to Newport and after his wife's death in a driving accident he married again.

News from the Parish
1824 Henry Good, a respectable-looking man of about 30 years of age was indicted for feloniously stealing on 10 August 1824, a bank post bill for the sum of £1,000, the property of Elizabeth Elcock, widow. Mr Justice Park remarked on the wretchedness of the prisoner in robbing a defenceless widow and sentenced him to 7 years transportation.

Chapter 6　　　　　　　　Nineteenth Century

1830. Thomas Morris stole a quantity of barley meal from his master, Valentine Vickers. Sentenced to six months hard labour.

1831 A brown hackney mare stolen from Roundabout Farm, the property of Michael Smith Stokes.

1835 Samuel Rowley convicted of stealing £20 belonging to Mr Gibbons, a farmer, at Worfield. The prisoner had been sent to Wolverhampton with a load of barley for which he received payment. He then absconded with the money but was found the next day. 12 months hard labour.

1843 William Askew, a strong built man aged about 35 pleaded guilty to breaking into Worfield and Morville Churches. He added in defence, *My Lord, I did it for want, being in great distress; and in one of the churches there was silver plate and other valuable things which I did not touch; neither did I break any locks. I was nearly naked and bought a shirt and waistcoat with part of the money.* His Lordship after a severe reprimand, sentenced him to 18 months hard labour and the man was grateful for such a light sentence. (Wolverhampton Chronicle 9 August)

A Day at the Races (Wolverhampton Chronicle 9 May 1898)

On Tuesday, Bridgnorth races were held and Wolverhampton spectators were there in force. Queen Square at 10 o'clock was full of brakes, waggonettes, char-a-bancs, every conceivable kind of vehicle. Off they went down Darlington Street and but for the dust the journey was A1. There were few cyclists but a constant stream of coaches, traps, landaus, gigs, waggonnettes, with every now and then, a smart trotter. Posthorns, hastily blown, gave warning of something special for which way had to be made.

The fair sex seemed quite at home. One gaily-decked lady was eating sandwiches and looking unconcerned, three miles out, and was measuring a wee dram of whisky at Trescott. Luncheon baskets were secured on top of buses, the rail preventing them falling off. Cases of bottle beer, stout and lemonade - very little of the last - were constantly being brought into view by their owners desiring to get on with the pleasures of the day.

The Fox Inn was surrounded with coaches and people. It looked like a fair, and inside it was difficult to get served. The ladies' needs were met by gallants who every now and then squeezed past the front door with trays of spirits. A short halt and we were behind a waggonnette where the occupants were constantly going 'nap.' When nap was got, a bottle was brought out, and the company's respective thirsts quenched.

At Hilton, flower girls offered their wares and in doing so were nearly run over. We threaded our way through carriages in front of the Wheel at Worfield and in another twenty minutes dismounted to walk down the hill. I hear there was a nasty accident in the morning. A cob was driving down and bolted. The sole occupant managed to jump out but the driver had to be taken to the Infirmary.

Then on through Low Town, up the steep hill and we arrived half an hour before the first race. It cost us 5s for our vehicle to be admitted, a black man entertained us with his banjo and did a comic turn. Other artistes, one a conjuror using guinea pigs, did likewise. Back home around 10.30 after an enjoyable day only marred by the coldness of the weather.

Chapter 6 Nineteenth Century

References

General
Robinson, D. H., The Wandering Worfe, (Waine Research Publications)
Turnock, J., A History Little Known (J. L. Turnock 1996)
Evans, R. M. H., A History of the Rectors and Vicars of Worfield 1205-1972
Randall, J., Worfield and its Townships
Worfield Manor Court Rolls.
1. P314/W/1/1/540 Rowley Mill. Court Roll (Shropshire Archives)
2. 5586/1/270 Court Roll (Shropshire Archives)
3. P314/W/1/1/61-62 Court Roll (Shropshire Archives)
4. Manor Court Roll 1369 (Edward III, 42) re permission to build a mill at Chesterton
5. 5586/2/1/375 Lease (Shropshire Archives)
6. 1190/1/448 & 449 Minute Book of the Manor of Wyken 1785-1850 (Shropshire Archives)
7. 99 year lease of Rindleford Mill 1691 5586/2/1/417 from Sir Thomas Whitmore of 2 mills at Rindleford, formerly corn mills to Thomas Blyth and his son, oil leather dressers
8. 5586/1/226 Court Roll (Shropshire Archives) Complaint against Roger Walker
9. Registration of Burcott Mill as a Protestant Meeting House B/A/12/ii/7(Lichfield Archives)
10. London Courier and Evening Gazette 4 February 1815, page 4 sale of spinning mill
11. Wellington Journal 26 December 1885. Henry Curran
12. Farmer's Rapids 1834-1934. 'Electrical News and Engineering Journal' Toronto, Canada, 15 June 1934
13. P314/C/1/2 Vestry Minutes & Committee Book 1804-1847 (Shropshire Archives)
14. P314/L/3/29 Weekly Pay List of the Poor of the Parish 1831-1836 (Shropshire Archives)
15. P314/L/2/1 Poor Rate Book 1834-1836 (Shropshire Archives)
16. P314/L/11/6 Apprenticeship Indenture (Shropshire Archives)
17. Justices Meeting 'Eddowes's Journal & General Advertiser for Shropshire & the Principality of Wales' 31 October 1855
18. 5586/1/214 Precedents of the Manor (Shropshire Archives) & DP268 Proposed Turnpike Road from Stourbridge to the Liberties of Bridgnorth (Shropshire Archives)
19. P314/N/1/1 Accounts of Thomas Lowe, supervisor of the west of the Parish (Shropshire Archives)
20. P314/N/1/2 Surveyors Accounts for the North West Quarter 1770-1847& P314/N/1/3 for the East 1777-1835 (Shropshire Archives)
21. DP173 Stableford Bridge drawings and specifications received by the Clerk of Peace on 2 Jan 1800 of a three arch stone bridge at Stableford. Unsigned but thought to be by Thomas Telford.

Chapter 6					Nineteenth Century

22. P20/N/2/1 Rebuilding of Stableford Bridge (Shropshire Archives)
23. DP72 Letters from turnpike surveyors re Hilton Bridge (Shropshire Archives)
24. 5586/5/13/1 Agreement between Thomas Head and Thomas Barnfield acting for Thomas Whitmore (Shropshire Archives)
25. Walters, H. B., 'Churchwardens' Accounts of the Parish in Worfield 1549-1572,' in Transactions of the Shropshire Archaeological Society 3rd Series Vol IX, 1909, pages 113-140
26. Walters, H. B., 'Churchwardens' Accounts of the Parish in Worfield 1572-1603,' in Transactions of the Shropshire Archaeological Society 3rd Series Vol X, 1910, pages 59-86
27. Benefaction Boards, Worfield Church
28. P 314/Q/1/4/2 Lloyd & Parker Charity (Shropshire Archives)
29. Worfield Parish Magazine July 1874
30. Turnock, J., A History Little Known (J. L. Turnock 1996) p68
31. Turnock, J., A History Little Known (J. L. Turnock 1996) p69
32. Worfield Parish Magazine April 1876
33. Worfield Parish Magazine November 1882
34. P314/B/7/1 Archdeacon's Visitation 1830 (Shropshire Archives)
35. P314/B/7/3 Archdeacon's Visitation 1847 (Shropshire Archives)
36. P314/B/4/4 The Vicar & Churchwardens of the Parish of Worfield against all & singular the Parishioners and Inhabitants of the said Parish (Shropshire Archives)
37. Reopening of Worfield Church. Eddowes's Journal 22 October 1862
38. Evans, R. M. H., A History of the Rectors and Vicars of Worfield 1205-1972 P. 35

Notes
A Worfield Court Roll P314/W/1/1/61 (1365)
Roger of Cattestre, perpetual chaplain of the Blessed Virgin Mary at the Church at Worfeld gave to William of Asterhull a certain fulling mill with appurtenances at Cherleford on condition that between himself and the rector of the Church of Worfeld they regulate and arrange the mill and the pond without nuisance to the church mill aforesaid. And William is given the right to build or rebuild the mill which has fallen into disrepair and which belongs to the Chapel of the Blessed Virgin Mary and valuing the ancient and customary weir. And on this William came and received the aforesaid mill on the conditions aforesaid, paid 12d fine and made fealty

B Extracts from Worfield Parish Registers showing pauperisation post 1783
Occupations Pre 1783
Thomas Bache, hemp dresser, married 1754
Timothy Barney, blacksmith, married 1754
William Baker, labourer, married 1754
William Hill, shoemaker, father at baptism 1765
Samuel Smith, nailer, Rudge Heath, father at baptism 1765
Richard Rowley, labourer, Bentley, father at baptism 1766
John Meredith, tailor, Hilton, father at baptism 1766
Matthew Haywood, labourer, father at baptism 1767

Chapter 6   Nineteenth Century

Thomas Perry, wheelwright, Winscot, father at baptism 1768
Thomas Bentley, labourer, Rudge Heath father at baptism 1768
Thomas Tedstill, labourer, Roughton, father at baptism 1768
William Trumper, labourer, father at baptism 1771
Henry Bromwich, vicar, father at baptism 1772
Thomas Broadhurst, travelling chimney sweep, father at baptism 1778
Thomas Billingsley, tailor, Stableford, father at baptism 1778
Jonas Barney, blacksmith, Ackleton, father at baptism 1778
Thomas Pace, carpenter, Stableford, father at baptism 1778
Isaac Mason, labourer, Ackleton, father at baptism 1778
James Shaw, labourer, Oldington, father at baptism 1778
John Pugh, gardener, Mere, father at baptism 1778
John Williams, soldier, The Batch, father at baptism 1778
John Painter, labourer, Woodside, father at baptism 1778
Thomas Bishton, labourer, Hilton, father at baptism 1778
Edward Sherwood, mole catcher, Hartlebury, father at baptism 1778
Thomas Bentley, labourer, Hilton, father at baptism 1778
Richard Fox, labourer, Oldington, father at baptism 1778
John Cluet, labourer, Roughton, father at baptism 1778
John Pearce, tailor, Roughton, father at baptism 1779
Samuel Page, labourer, Ackleton, father at baptism 1778
William Fazey, labourer, Stanlow, father at baptism 1779
Richard Walker, labourer, Burcott, father at baptism 1779
William Taylor, labourer, The Folley, father at baptism 1779
Richard Bill, labourer, Hartlebury, father at baptism 1779
John Reynolds, labourer, Winscott, father at baptism 1778
James Shaw, labourer, Oldington, father at baptism 1778
William Bentley, labourer, Allscott, father at baptism 1778
Benjamin Malpas, labourer, The Folly, father at baptism 1778
John Barney, blacksmith, Hallon, father at baptism 1778
Thomas Hemus, labourer, Roughton, father at baptism 1778
John Piper, blacksmith, Stableford, father at baptism 1778
John Baddesley, vicar, father at baptism 1779
Charles Stokes, schoolmaster, father at baptism 1783
Richard Walker, labourer, Burcott, father at baptism 1783
Sarah Laurence, pauper, mother at baptism 1783
Richard Rowley, labourer, Hilton, father at baptism 1783
John Jones, labourer, father at baptism 1783
Thomas Bentley, labourer, father at baptism 1783
Occupations/Status Post 1783
William Nichols, pauper, father at baptism 1784
Thomas Pinches, pauper, father at baptism 1784
John Littleford, pauper, father at baptism 1784
William Cooksey, pauper, father at baptism 1784
William Kirkham, pauper, father at baptism 1784
Thomas Cartwright, pauper, father at baptism 1784
Thomas Rowley, pauper, father at baptism 1784

Chapter 6   Nineteenth Century

John Lawrence, pauper, father at baptism 1785
John Bishton, pauper, father at baptism 1785
George James, pauper, father at baptism 1785
Ann Morris, pauper, mother at baptism 1785
William Taylor, pauper, Ackleton, father at baptism 1785
John Richards, shoemaker, father at baptism 1785
Thomas Simpson, pauper, father at baptism 1785
Elizabeth Powell, pauper, mother at baptism 1786
John Cluet, pauper, father at baptism 1786
Mary Hand, pauper mother at baptism 1786
Mary Bennet, pauper mother at baptism 1786
John Billingsley, pauper, father at baptism 1786
Thomas Pinches, pauper, father at baptism 1786
Thomas Hayns, pauper, father at baptism 1786
Thomas Rowley, pauper, father at baptism 1786
William Cooksey, pauper, father at baptism 1787
William Nichols, pauper, father at baptism 1787
Thomas Rowley, pauper, father at baptism 1787
Elizabeth Powell, pauper, mother at baptism 1787
Thomas Pinches, pauper, father at baptism 1788
John Jones, pauper, father at baptism 1787
Jane Morgan, pauper, mother at baptism 1788
Elizabeth Billingsley, pauper mother at baptism 1788
Christian Power, pauper, mother at baptism 1788
Sarah Stevenson, pauper, mother at baptism 1789
Elizabeth Powell, pauper, mother at baptism 1789
Richard Ebrey, pauper, father at baptism 1789
Edward Millichip, pauper, father at baptism 1789
John Billingsley, pauper, father at baptism 1789
John Baxter, pauper, father at baptism 1789
Robert Bishton, pauper, father at baptism 1789
John Hemmings, pauper, father at baptism 1790

C Improvement Act In 1725, the first turnpike roads appeared in Shropshire and in 1752, an Improvement Act was passed regarding the roads around Bridgnorth. In 1816 an Act approved the turnpiking of the road from Stourbridge to Bridgnorth.

D Extracts from the Surveyors' accounts.
Surveyor's Accounts for the East Side of the Parish
1780 Paid Samuel Wood for 1100L of brick [What the L denoted isn't known]
for lugging brick to Broadbridge, three quarters of lime for repairing bridge, 600 of brick from Hilton
Brickel to repair Hilton Bridge, paid William Amiss the mason for mending the bridge
John Dulson for composition to turnpike road to Madeley
1809 By Roads. For stoking in ruts and loosing water, levelling and screening gravel. 6 days for stoking in ruts on Hilton Turnpike Road. Wm. Meads for getting gravel
for stocking up the rock in Stratford Holloway
1811 By Roads
paid James Oakley and John Timmins for work done in Stratford Lane
post and rails to fence the roads from the brook

Chapter 6   Nineteenth Century

1812 paid Timins for widening Brasset Lane, for gravel and finding same
paid Mr Davis for repairing Hilton Bridge
paid William Lye for mending the Church Road
paid Barcklam for getting gravel
George Wheeler for getting and leveling gravel
Thomas Binsley for 60 loads of gravel at Rudge Heath
William Lye for putting piles to hold up a bank
George Wheeler for filling up a gravel pit and stocking in ruts
paid the turnpike surveyor two thirds of the composition for the turnpike roads
overpayment on the (Black Brook) Turnpike Road. [The road went east across Rudge Heath through Shipley, over Shipley Common to the Black Brook where it met the Wolverhampton and Bridgnorth Turnpike]
Mr. J. G. Smythe refuses to pay his levy on account of his land not being paid for which is thrown into Turn Road
1813 Wharton for getting gravel out of pit and his boy for getting water out of gravel pit
Cartwright for widening the road and stocking in ruts
for letting water off and making a ditch
3 load of stone

Surveyor's Accounts for the North West of the Parish
paid for getting stone to mend the Church ill
1783 for leaveling ruts, laying a suff, for getting stone
1784 for cutting rock in the back of the Church Holloway
for setting posts and rails on the Church Hill
for repairing the wall up the Church Hill
1788 journey to Bridgnorth to advise about making the building of the Worfe Bridge a county expense and asking for an allowance towards the cost of rebuilding the bridge which has been done
1810 paid John Jones for throwing in and forming the road through the shoulder of mutton.
paid William Reynolds for widening and forming the road through Mr Vickers' land
paid for scraping dirt
paid for 8 posts to secure the footpath near Catstree
widening the road near the china bridge. Richard Pinches 6 days work
2 loads of posts and rails from Apley Park to fence with the road being widened
73 pair of oak rails to fence with near Oldington where the road was widened
for stocking, lowering and widening Cranmere Heath road
1812 for repairing the footpath down to the bridge at Rindleford
15 days stocking rock at St Peter's Well
for getting and screening 210 loads of gravel from the pit
Thos Littleford for getting and carrying large rock stones
1828 repaired road below Chinese Bridge injured by the negligence of a waggoner

E Appointment of Theophilus Barney B/A/11/3/134/1 (Lichfield Archives)
1704 Theophilus Barney appointed to teach
For Mr Ryder, with care
We the Minister, Trustees and others of the inhabitants of the parish of Worfield do by these presents certify that we do nominate and appoint Theophilus Barney our schoolmaster in Worfield to learn and to instruct children in reading English and learning Latin and teaching to write; whom we judge very fit and qualified for this imployment both on the account of his ability and his conformity to Ecclesiastical Law and the Canons and constitutions of the Church. In testimony hereof we have put our hands this twentieth day of June AD 1704. (signed: James Hancox, Minister)

Chapter 6　　　　　　　　　Nineteenth Century

1709 letter to Mr Ryder
I would desire you to show … Theophilus Barney what kindness you can for he tells me that the Apparator has given him notice that he must have a licence because he keeps a free school. It is such a free school as we …pay him for to teach ten poor children but when ?we think think fit we can dispose of it other wayes and it is not otherwayes a free school so no more at present but my greetings to you and … at your command. Robert Barrett
Agreed a licence for Theophilus Barney to teach scholars in a free school in Worfield. W. Walmsley
F The Reverend Nicholas records in the Parish Magazine that January 1895 was a month of hard weather but July one of drought, the worst since 1868 *when some of us can remember the weary months of heat and dryness, the constant expectation of rain, the constant disappointment.* And then it did rain, a glorious thunderstorm, as Mr Nicholas recalls. In 1896 the summer was again dry, the fourth in succession.
G. (see next page)

H Agricultural Depression
A meeting of local farmers was held in Bridgnorth to discuss the agricultural depression and to consider the setting up of a Union. George Broughall from Oldington was one of those who attended. The meeting was chaired by R. Jasper Moore and W. L. Dodgson, land agent for Lord Boyne, gave his account of the meeting. It was the unanimous decision of the 2,500 who attended, that an agricultural union should be formed. Mr Dodgson, who had been the farmers' delegate to a conference on the agricultural depression, was to act as chairman and secretary of the local farmers group and obtain the names of those who wanted to join the union. (Wolverhampton Chronicle 21st December 1892)
[W. L. Dodgson was the brother of Charles Dodgson, Lewis Carroll, author of 'Alice in Wonderland.']

Derelict Building at The Batch

Chapter 6   Nineteenth Century

G Lloyd and Parker map of Worfield village showing the occupants of the Worfield charity estate with details of premises. Undated. Date estd circa 1850. P314/Q/1/2/23(Shropshire Archives)
Scale: 1 inches to 200 yards

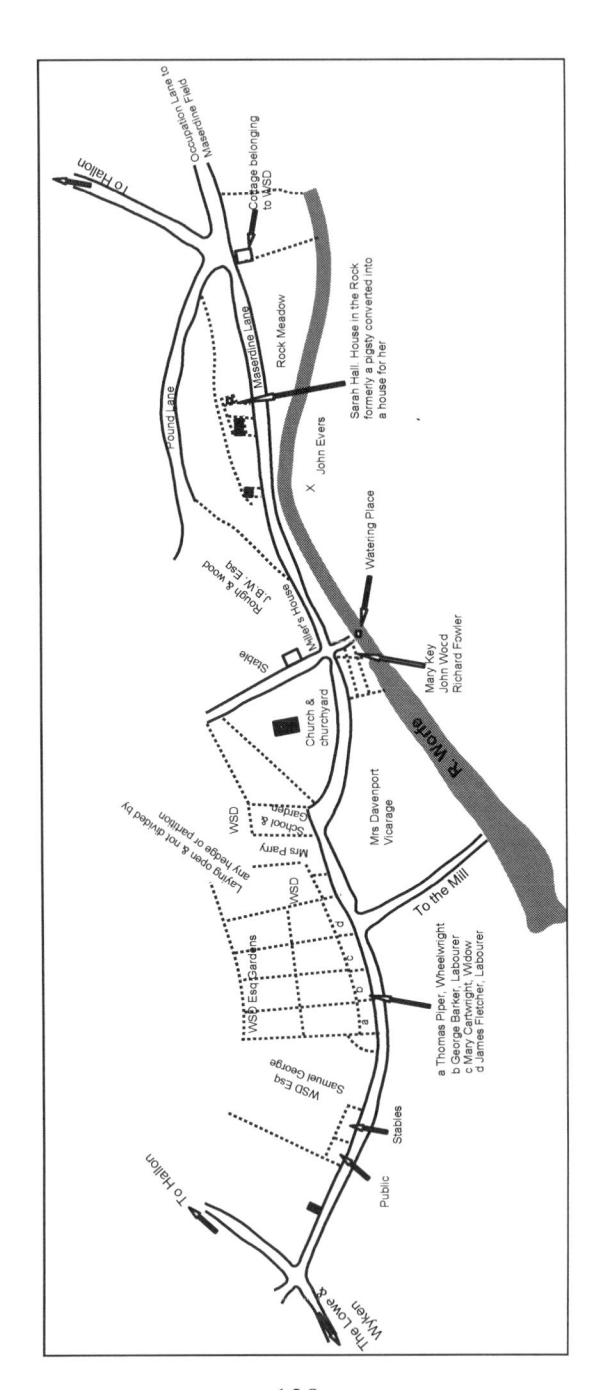

Chapter 7   Twentieth Century

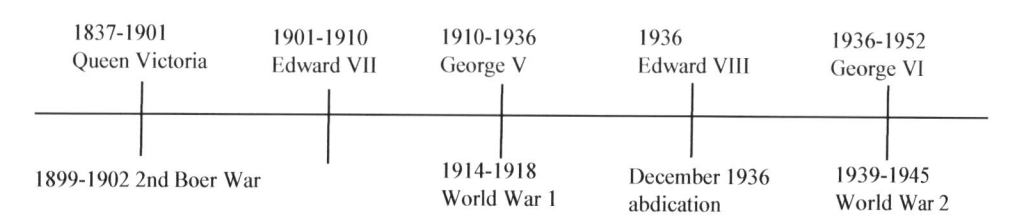

1837-1901	1901-1910	1910-1936	1936	1936-1952
Queen Victoria	Edward VII	George V	Edward VIII	George VI

| 1899-1902 2nd Boer War | | 1914-1918 World War 1 | December 1936 abdication | 1939-1945 World War 2 |

The Old Blacksmith's Shop in Hallon at the beginning of the twentieth century

At the start of the century Queen Victoria was still on the throne and, on her death on January 22 1901, she was succeeded by Edward VII. The talk abroad was of the Boer War which raised the question of how we were to defend our Empire. As yet there was no sign of the conflict which would destroy so many lives in the Great War of 1914-1918. The focus in the St James's Gazette of January 1901 was on economic development and the need for new inventions. These would come in abundance, the motor car, electricity, the telephone, water piped to homes, and by the latter part of the century, computers. The nineteenth century had seen the rise in the middle classes but the task for the new century was how to empower all classes. This change was still to come as Worfield greeted the new century.

Chapter 7   Twentieth Century

Wheel Inn, Worfield - Shropshire.

"Meet" of Albrighton Hounds at Worfield 1909

Chapter 7   Twentieth Century

Worfield at the Beginning of the Twentieth Century
In the Summer of 1898, the Reverend Wellesley Wesley became the Vicar of Worfield. He tried hard to understand his wayward parishioners, talking to them about the evils of drink, the wickedness of adultery and the need to live prayerful lives. It was from the heart that he said, *a priest's life, even at Worfield, is by no means a bed of roses without thorns.* Poor Mr Wellesley Wesley; how he despaired when his system for providing alcohol to the poor and needy was abused. Appealing as the scheme did to a wide audience, restrictions had to be put in place[1].

I gladly provide wine, whiskey, brandy etc for sick and needy people, but in future I can only give it by the Doctor's order. People must ask the Doctor for a note, specifying exactly what wine is needed, how much is to be given, and for how long.

Nor would his parishioners come to church. The times of the services were changed to make it easier for working people to attend, but to no avail. There was, however, one service which the parishioners had no difficulty finding the time nor the inclination to attend, Dole Sunday. In January 1902 the vicar noted that *even the bitter cold and wet could not keep them away*[2].

At Hallon, in 1903, Mr Turner the blacksmith was looking for an assistant, *a good shoer*, to live in[3]. The Old Lodge Farm, the Old Forest Lodge and the Roundabout were up for sale, as they would be again in 1915, and in 1902, there was a farm sale at Rowley Farm, on behalf of Mr Alfred Meredith, who was leaving England. Petty crimes were as much a fact of life as they are now. Bicycles, tools, and in this case, clothing, were all fair game. Thomas Towner, from Wolverhampton, was accused of stealing a pair of boots from Arthur Kilvert, a farm hand from Roughton, and leaving his old ones in their place[4]. The number of farm fires was causing unease, six in five months in 1901[5], one of which, at B. Hallam's Farm in Wyken, destroyed two ricks of straw[6]. At Roundabout Farm in 1908, four ricks of barley and oats were saved by the efforts of the Bridgnorth Fire Brigade[7].

On the the 21st July 1904, the marriage of Marguerite Davenport, only child of Edmund Henry and Margaret Davenport, and Cuthbert Leicester-Warren, of Tabley in Cheshire, took place at St Peter's Church, Worfield. Mrs Davenport entertained 200 children and 50 parents to a sumptuous tea, musicians from Bridgnorth performed, and there was dancing and games. *All went as merry as the wedding ball,* the reporter noted. The newly-weds left Davenport for their new home in Cheshire, and while they would be frequent visitors tonWorfield, from now on this would be their second home.

Social change was slow to come to a rural area such as Worfield. Isabel Baseley was only three when she moved with her family from London in 1907. Her father had a job at Chyknell and the family lived at Woundale, a hamlet of four houses, very much off the beaten track. No-one would speak to the family, as they were outsiders, and Mrs Baseley didn't help matters by refusing to show the same deference to her employers as the other servants did. If the master or mistress

Chapter 7 Twentieth Century

passed by when a servant was carrying a bucket of water it was the custom for the bucket to be put down and for the servant to curtsey. Mrs Baseley simply refused to do that; it didn't happen in London and she wasn't going to start it in Chyknell. In 1910 the family moved to Hilton where there were plenty of horses and carts passing, although rarely did they see a car[8].

Farming was more profitable early in the twentieth century than it had been towards the end of the nineteenth. Hunting, shooting and fishing were pastimes of the privileged and for those with no legitimate means of participating, poaching was their pastime, as it always had been. There were otters in the Worfe, foxes aplenty, rabbits and hares in abundance and the Worfe teemed with trout and eels.

The Boer War

Overshadowed by the Great War of 1914-1918, the Boer War is often forgotten today, but in 1900 the War was very much at the forefront of people's minds. Prayers were offered in Worfield each week[9] for all serving soldiers and sailors. There are two plaques in St Peter's Church remembering those who died in this conflict. One is in memory of the boys of the Grammar School who died in action, William Lomas, Charles Meredith, Jeremiah Mapp, and Harry Wadlow. The other is in memory of those from Worfield who died and did not attend the Grammar School, namely, Walter Bishop and Driver William Fincher, who died of fever in 1900. Gunner Alfred Thatcher, who died in the Egyptian Campaign in 1885, is mentioned on the same memorial.

Walter Bishop

Jeremiah Mapp

Chapter 7   Twentieth Century

Walter George Bishop of the 10th Royal Hussars died on 19 June 1900 of wounds received at Diamond Hill. In a letter home[A], he described a cavalry charge over four miles, galloping all the way under gunfire from the Boers. Many men were killed or had their horses killed under them, but Bishop was lucky on this occasion. His horse had a bullet straight through its thigh but still carried its rider to safety and miraculously recovered. Dead horses provided food for the native population but the diet of the soldiers seemed to consist mainly of hard biscuits and a very limited amount of water. Because there was so little water, the biscuits were hard to swallow. Bishop wrote that he could only eat one a day.

Jeremiah Mapp was born in 1873 at the Old Park Farm, Norton, the second son of Richard and Jane Mapp, and attended Worfield Grammar School at Roughton. Jeremiah served in South Africa in the Imperial Yeomanry of the Staffordshire Regiment, and after a year's service joined the Johannesburg Police. He was injured in an ambush at Florida and died the next day of his injuries. Jeremiah was buried in South Africa, a memorial service being held for him in Stockton Church. The Mapp family would later farm at Bromley, Catstree, Burcote and Fenn Gate.

Another Boer War casualty with Worfield connections is buried in the Churchyard. Lieutenant Talbot Neville Fawcett Davenport[10] served in South Africa in the Royal Irish Rifles and returned to England in 1904. He died at his London home on 3rd March 1905, having accidentally swallowed carbolic acid instead of medicine. Davenport had contracted blood poisoning while he was on active service and was being cared for at home by his wife at the time of his death. It was thought that his wife, being her husband's sole carer, was worn out by her duties, and by mistake put carbolic acid for her husband to take instead of the medicine as she had intended. The Coroner returned a verdict of death by misadventure. Davenport's body came by train to Bridgnorth Station and was then taken by hearse to Worfield Church for burial in the churchyard.

Two Worfield Families
An advertisement appeared in the Wellington Journal on Saturday 9th December 1905 for the sale of household effects of the Old House at Stableford. Messrs Perry and Phillips had been ordered to sell furniture, china, books and pictures. The vendor was Mr H. E. Wodehouse who was leaving the neighbourhood. Even now we might pass over this event as simply another house sale. On the other hand, we might think that the name Wodehouse has a familiar ring to it relating to a certain author of that name, and you would be correct. H. E. Wodehouse was the father of the author, P. G. Wodehouse. In 1901 the census records the occupants of The Old House as:
Henry Ernest Wodehouse, aged 55, Ex Official Colonial Civil Service
Eleanor Wodehouse, aged 48, wife
Ernest Armine Wodehouse, aged 21, Scholar Oxford University
Pelham Grenville Wodehouse, aged 19, Bank Assistant
Mary Parton, aged 24, Cook
Mary Mason aged 22, Housemaid

Chapter 7 — Twentieth Century

Wodehouse's father had retired from the Hong Kong Civil Service on health grounds. On his return to England, he first took a house in Dulwich for a few months, and then moved in 1895 to the Old House at Stableford. The two Wodehouse boys were at boarding school but came home in the holidays. Armine, P. G. Wodehouse's brother, then went on to Oxford, and it was thought that P. G. or 'Plum,' as he was called, would follow in his footsteps. Instead, Plum went to work in a bank, writing novels in his spare time.

It seemed unlikely at first that Mr and Mrs Wodehouse would take the lease on the Old House. As they drove away after their first visit, Mrs Wodehouse expressed her relief that she wouldn't have to see *that awful house* again. But the deed was already done. *Didn't I tell you,* said Mr Wodehouse, *I have signed a twenty year lease on the house.* In the latter part of the nineteenth century, Stableford was an idyllic, remote hamlet with no amenities and Mrs Wodehouse found her new home very lonely. Plum, on the other hand, found it the perfect place to write - *I have never found better*, he wrote[11].

The Shropshire landscape, *miles of smiling countryside*, and its villages, found their way into Wodehouse's books. Local place names appear throughout the novels, for example, Badgwick (Badger), Rutton (Ryton), Worbury (Worfield) and Eckleton (Ackleton). The holy grail everyone seeks is the identity of Blandings Castle. Apley, Weston, Patshull, Dudmaston and Chillington have all been suggested as possible contenders.

N.T. P. Murphy, who wrote 'In Search of Blandings,'[12] is sure that Weston Park is Blandings, but perhaps the fictional castle is a blend of several of the local country houses to which Wodehouse was often invited for the weekend. Being inarticulate and clumsy, these visits were a torture to the young Wodehouse. He felt that he was only invited because his brother, Armine, was a highly desirable guest and one brother couldn't be invited without the other.

It is hard to imagine that an author who could write such beautiful dialogue could also be inarticulate but perhaps this meant that he observed more. Guy Bolton asked Wodehouse if they had any neighbours in Stableford[11].

One family, about a mile away. We quarrelled with them two days after we arrived and never spoke to them again. It was milk that caused the rift. At least they said it was milk ... and we said it was skim-milk. Harsh words and dirty looks passed to and fro ...

Father sorts out his things, has a wash and brush-up, and looks in on Mother. "All set?" he asks. "All set," says Mother. "Fine" says Father. "Then let's go and beat the stuffing out of those swindling crooks down the road who've been selling us that so-called milk." And off they go, Father with his Roget's Thesaurus under his arm in case he runs short of adjectives.'

Some of the local people must have had their fictional counterparts but remain anonymous, probably for good reasons. Sibell Corbett from Stableford was one of the few mentioned by name in the author's notes to be woven into a story. I am grateful to N. T. P. Murphy for this snippet.

Chapter 7   Twentieth Century

Sibell reared ducks for shooting but Wodehouse noted that she treated them so well that when they were sold they would come towards their would-be assassins for food rather than flying away in fear. It is a sweet story telling much about Sibell's love for her animals.

The Corbetts, a family of four girls and two boys, lived at Stableford Hall, just down the road from the Wodehouses. One of the boys, Major F. H. Corbett, was killed in action in 1918, and in the Church there is a beautifully decorated cross in his memory. The inscription reads:

In loving memory of Major F. H. Corbett R.F.A. Battery 75th Bde Guards Div. Killed in action May 5th 1918 'Rest in Peace'. Erected in gratitude by men he led so well. This cross removed from the Military Cemetery at Bienvillers-au-Bois, France, is placed here in proud and loving memory of Major Frank Harvey Corbett M.C. born 26 November 1882 second son of Richard Cecil and Susan Horatio Corbett of Stableford.

Sibell Corbett at Stableford

Chapter 7   Twentieth Century

Two of the Corbett girls, Helen and Sibill, epitomised the social change affecting the role of women at the beginning of the twentieth century. Both took up careers and lived very independent lives. Sibill, as we have seen, was a farmer and Helen became a nurse.

Sibell Corbett took over the running of the Home Farm, Stableford Farm in March 1906 when Mr Dowman, the tenant, moved to Ewdness. There was a lot of correspondence with the agent about the state in which the farm had been left. Poor fences led to Dowman's bull getting in to the Corbett's cows, good hay and muck were carted off to Ewdness leaving behind rubbish and land and buildings were in a shocking state. The complaints went on and on for months. Actually, Mr Corbett went on and on and Mr Dowman tried rather lamely to defend his position which probably was indefensible[13].

Sibell and Helen left Stableford to live near Bath, Sibell to continue farming and Helen to pursue her nursing career. She later took on civic duties as a J.P. and Conservative Councillor.

The Recreation Room

The upper classes in the nineteenth century indulged in hare coursing, hunting, shooting and fishing. Worfield had its own racecourse by the Hobbins until the beginning of the nineteenth century. Prize fighting at the Wheel was the entertainment for the masses and quoits and football the sport of the working man. What was lacking was a place where working men could meet and relax after work, a sort of Working Men's Club. One family had a determination to provide such a facility but there were obstacles to overcome. Here is the explanation provided by Mr Evans. [Note: At the time of writing there is talk of changing the name from the Recreation (Rec) Room to Worfield Village Hall.]

When I came to Worfield in 1903 the only place for general assembly was the school and the only place for a parish club for men was what is still called, "the Old Club Room." ...Neither place was exactly ideal. I was very anxious to be able to provide a Room which would serve the double purpose of Club Room and Concert Hall.

I approached Mrs Davenport ... with an offer to provide the funds to build such a Room if she could offer a site in the village. She sympathised with my aims, but was unable unfortunately to provide a site. She however suggested that it might be possible to build the room elsewhere. This was of course possible but rather altered ...things. Somehow the room did not seem quite so parochial if it had to be built outside the village. So very regretfully I let the matter drop for a time. But the need for such a room seemed to increase. Then Mrs Morrison most generously offered not only a site but the expense of building and furnishing it. Thus the Recreation Room came into being. Circumstances had tended to make it a private concern and it seemed more satisfactory to keep it so. We therefore placed it at the disposal of the parish, reserving a certain very limited control. ...The Men's Club paid for heating and lighting. We had one season before 1914 and it was most successful[14].

Chapter 7   Twentieth Century

A recreation room of similar construction was built at Ackleton by Mrs Morrison as a thank-offering for her grand-daughter. It was difficult to find a site and was built on leased land which was not bought until 1918. The original intention was that it should be a recreation room and during the winter months would be used for cottage services and holy communion and so it has continued. Today the room is used for social gatherings and sometimes for church services[14]. Kate Morrison was a great benefactor to the parish. She came to live at Wyken in 1901with her husband and was widowed shortly afterwards. She died in 1933[15].

The First World War 1914-1918
In 1914 the worst fears of the country were realised and we went to war with Germany. Hopes were high that the war would be over by Christmas; we would have been successful, of course, and life could get back to normal. What a cruel deception this was. Led to believe that it was a young man's duty to go to war, the Church and the upper classes encouraged those who needed persuasion to sign up. Some of the recruits rode their horses to Bridgnorth station to be loaded on to the train for the front, others walked to Bridgnorth to join up. In view of what they were to face, the picture of cheerful innocence is chilling.

Contingency plans for war were being made several years before the First World War actually started. In 1909 the War Office in England was wrestling with the vulnerability of England in the event of invasion from Europe. The solution was a territorial army which would be a last line of home defence, and a network of first aid detachments to deal with the sick and wounded. The Scheme for the Organisation of Voluntary Aid in England and Wales, as it was known, was to be set up as part of the Territorial Force, but to operate under the British Red Cross Society with the help of the St John's Ambulance Service. The word 'aid' today has connotations of food and support for the poor, but at the beginning of the twentieth century it meant first aid. The Voluntary Aid Scheme was introduced locally in 1911 at a public meeting in Bridgnorth. The chairman was W. H. Foster of Apley,[16] and Worfield was represented by Mrs Davenport and Mr and Mrs Cunliffe.

The government scheme for first aid met with an enthusiastic response as people joined training classes. The scheme's adoption was greatly helped by the upper echelons of society who were in charge of the organisations involved , namely, the Territorial Force, the Red Cross and the County. In Staffordshire, for example, Lord Dartmouth was the Lord Lieutenant of the County and his wife was the President of the Staffordshire Red Cross Society. So when Lord Dartmouth introduced the Voluntary Aid scheme, his wife was almost bound to support it, and where the upper classes led, their staff and tenants followed. By 1911, 24,000 people had joined the VAD scheme.The participants took their work seriously, encouraging others to join them by giving demonstrations, for example, at Trentham Park in 1912. The Territorial Army gave similar displays and in lanes all over the country, battles were played out to enact possible invasion.

The VAD (Voluntary Aided Detachment) scheme was ambitious to say the least. To succesfully treat injured soldiers implied transport to take them from the battlefield back to this country, a

Chapter 7   Twentieth Century

hospital within which they could recover and staff to nurse them. No-one could envisage the scale of the task created by the First World War but at least contingency plans had been put in place.

Interior of Recreation Room 1915-1918 when used as a VAD hospital

And so it was that eleven casualties arrived from the Front in February 1915 from various regiments. They were in the care of the Honorary Surgeons, Dr L'Oste Brown of Shifnal and Dr Hewitt (Capt R.A.M.C. Reserve), of Claverley. Mrs Eykyn of Ackleton was the matron, Helen Corbett of Stableford was the commandant and Mrs W. O. Wilson of Norton, quartermaster. There were four day nurses, two night nurses and two cooks.

Staff from Wyken House joined the team, as did local girls such as Annie Chester and Catherine Rochelle. For some this was the start of a new career, others found the love of their lives. Catherine Rochelle met William Cornes of Alveley while she was nursing. The couple were married at Worfield Church and went on to have five children. Patients who were able could wander in the grounds of Davenport House and Wyken House and trips farther afield were offered in the Wyken House car[17].

It is hard to know how many Worfield men served in World War 1 because, if they returned safely, there may be no public record remaining of their service. It is only through family history, for example, that we know that Arthur Seedhouse was a farrier in the South Staffordshire Regiment. John Bowen's service in France in 1918 was recorded in an arrangement made by Edward Humphrey Bowen to surrender the land of John Bowen, late of Chesterton, to Daniel Jones

Chapter 7   Twentieth Century

of Cranmere[18]. The service of Richard Sidney Wilson, Major Wilson, might have gone unnoticed had he not gone bankrupt. Before the war, Richard Sidney Wilson had been part of the firm of Wilson and Son, maltsters, a profitable business based around a malthouse in Ackleton. Wilson enlisted and put his business affairs in the hands of the bank. When he returned from war, the business was in ruins. He blamed the bank for its demise and restarted his business but then went bankrupt again. Wilson was forced to sell everything he owned, including the entire Kingslow Estate[19]. Major Wilson lived for the remainder of his life at 'The Elms,' in Pattingham, a sad end to a man who had been another generous benefactor to the parish.

Many servicemen would not return, of course. Mrs Fryer was a mother who received the letter

Nursing staff at Worfield VAD Hospital. Believed to be Mrs Morrison in the centre

every mother dreaded, that her son had been killed on the 30th September 1915. He was just seventeen years old.

Dear Mrs Fryer, I expect you have heard before this reaches you the very sad news that Private W. E. Yates No 17367 1st King's Shropshire Light Infantry was killed in action on September 30th. I am writing to tell you how deeply I sympathise with you in your sadness. I went up to take the

Chapter 7	Twentieth Century

funeral just behind the Trenches near ---------- but it was a very noisy night and they could not get the body out of the trenches before I was obliged to return. He was laid to rest by -------- on the following morning in ---------- cemetery. I can only hope and pray that God will comfort your heart and you will feel proud to know that he has done a very fine thing in giving his life for such a splendid cause.
Yours faithfully SMW Chaplain to 1st KSLI[20]

The roll call of those who died is shockingly long. Some families lost more than one son and some wives were widowed soon after getting married. A brass plaque in St Peter's Church records the following dead:

T. Bishop, T. H. R. Bomford, A. E. Boucher, W. J. Brown, P. H. Chapple, F. Christy, E. C. Clarke, H. Cooke, F. H. Corbett, S.T. Elcock, W. Elcock, W. Gardiner, G. Gill, R. Harley, J. Jones, J. T. Jones, H. Langford, J. Lewis, C. Lloyd Acton, H. G. Lloyd, H. Lockett, A.E. Morris, J. H. Morris, J. H. Onions, T. Pace, H. Price, W. N. Price, E. Pugh, W. Pursehouse, E. Rogers J. S. Sargeant, R.T. Sargeant, E. H. Starkey, E. Teague, S. Thomas, R. Turner, R. H. Wainwright, F. Wall, T. Welsby, E. Yates.

The Wyken House car taking patients for an outing.

Chapter 7   Twentieth Century

In spite of the War, work on the land had to carry on. At Allscott Farm in February, apart from livestock to be fed, there were swedes to be carted, manure to be taken to the fields, hedge brushing to be done and wheat to be delivered. One week all the workers were involved with threshing. In March, apart from shepherding, there were mangolds to be cleaned, hurdles to be moved. gapping to be done, and rye to be sown. Kale stalks were cleared in April, mangolds were carted, and scutch [couch grass] cleared. How relieved the farmer must have been when May arrived and some serious money was made - bullocks £51, £44 5s, £42, sheep 5 @ 102/-, 98/- and 95/-, 5 pigs 86/-. By August, apple picking started, barley was *sticked* and *rakings* got and *cocked*. In September, damson picking and taking occupied a whole week and thatching of ricks began[21].

Sister Oulton and patients harvesting at Wyken Farm.

Worfield Between the Wars
Those who had suffered during the war might have hoped that its conclusion would have brought a better life, but rural society was slow to change. In 1919, there was a meeting to decide on a memorial to be erected to those who fell in the War[22]. The committee was divided into three groups, land owners, farmers, and the working classes. Why this division by class, you may ask? The answer lay in the past; it was the way Worfield had always worked and even a World War wasn't going to change things.

Chapter 7   Twentieth Century

Farming did change, but not for the better. After 1918, farm incomes were so low that many tenants resorted to paying their rents by selling rabbits. Even in 1933, the Cricket Club was suffering from the poverty of its members. Many of the players *are only fitfully at work and can scarcely afford to bear the whole cost of travelling to away matches or entertaining visiting teams to tea*[23].

In spite of difficult economic circumstances, parishioners found time to enjoy themselves. Concerts took place in the school, and later in the Recreation Room. In 1920, the Worfield Flower Show, begun in 1908 by Frank Turner, the Headmaster, restarted after the War as did the scouts and guides. There were clubs and groups aplenty, friendly societies, a working men's club, the Women's Institute, Mother's Union, football club, cricket club, tennis club, quoits. For the musically minded there was a brass band and the choir. The choir's annual outing was a highlight of the year. Edward Driver, aged 11, described the 1932 trip.

On the morning of the fifteenth of July I awoke at five o'clock. I did not have much sleep on the night of the fourteenth but lay awake thinking of the trip.
I was a bit disheartened at first because it was raining but it soon gave over.
At exactly twenty minutes to seven I started out from home to the cross-roads where I was to be picked up.
After I waited for about ten minutes the char-a-banc came and I got in.
All went well for quite a long time and then we came to a drove of cows and Tom Welsby got out and drove them up a side turning.
We stayed in Llangollen for twenty minutes and while some of them went and had a cup of tea I went to the fruiterers and bought some cherries...
At about twelve o'clock we arrived at Llandudno and met Mr Lunt outside the Red Garage. We stopped at the fruit shop and Mr Lunt bought a basket of strawberries which we ate on the beach. After we had eaten all the strawberries we bathed and Mr Lunt paddled.
When we had finished bathing we went half way up the Great Orme for lunch in a tram. While we were having lunch the sea gulls came and Wilfred Elcock took a snap of them. For the whole of the afternoon we could do what we liked, so I went round the town and into Woolworths. At half past three we bathed again and till five o'clock I sat on the shore. At five o'clock we went and had tea at Summers and had salad and trifle. When we had finished tea we went to the char-a-banc and two boys got lost. We went to look for them and they came back at twenty past six.
We had several breakdowns on the way back, the first was on Madley Hill. The petrol would not reach the engine. I arrived back at a quarter to one, very sorry it was all over[24].

Transport was definitely changing and opening up the countryside. The nineteenth century had been the golden age of the railway and in 1845 a rail link was proposed between Wolverhampton and Bridgnorth. Various routes were suggested, one via Pattingham and Hartlebury, another through Tettenhall and Compton. Agreement on the route took so long to be reached that it was

Chapter 7   Twentieth Century

1925 before the first 12 miles of track were laid from Dunstall Park to Brettell Lane. By this time, the age of the motor car had dawned, and branch lines couldn't give a return on the investment required. GWR had already recognised that a connection between Wolverhampton and Bridgnorth could just as well be met by road transport as by rail, and in August 1904 it ran a steam motor car[25] along the A454 proudly bearing the GWR logo. The motorised omnibus service started in November 1904, the terminus being outside GWR's Wolverhampton Low Level Station. Wolverhampton Corporation took over the route in 1923, but Low level Station continued to be the terminus for the Bridgnorth bus throughout the 1960s, a nice reminder of the origins of this bus route.

Fred Taft and Rebecca Turner, wife of Frank Turner, the headmaster of Worfield School. The Taft family ran the Worfruna Garage at Wyken. The car is believed to be a Castle Three cyclecar made between 1919-1922 at the Castle Mill Works, New Road, Kidderminster. About 350 were made, and two are known to have survived.

Chapter 7   Twentieth Century

Enterprising Worfield people realised that there was a business to be made out of servicing motor vehicles. A cluster of garages appleared, two in Wyken and one in Roughton. In the 1920s,[26] the Worfruna Garage was owned by Mr Taft who invented an early device to measure a gallon of fuel. Just down the road, also in Wyken, was Wyken Garage, which was set up in 1920 by John Whitefoot Wilcox and later run by his sons, George and Bill Wilcox. According to John Wilcox, the Americans rented Wyken Garage while they were at Camp Davenport in the Second World War. The Worfruna Garage in the Second World War also served as the Fire Station. Harry Taft had converted a 'gentleman's car,' for the purpose of carrying the firemen and towing the water pump. The fire engine was to be used as a contingency in the event of Bridgnorth's fire engine being required to assist in Birmingham and the Black Country. Bert Bentley ran the fire station and, according to Bob Adams, the team of firemen prided themselves on maintaining a very professional standard. Only a mile towards Bridgnorth, in the village of Roughton was a petrol station and cafe. Bought in 1946 by Bernard Turvey from Mr Lawrence, the garage was on the opposite side of the road from the Worfruna and Wyken Garages.

The Worfruna Garage next to the Wheel Inn, Wyken. Advertisement 1920s. Photograph estd 1950s

Chapter 7   Twentieth Century

Above: Wyken Garage. Below: the same scene circa 1912

Chapter 7   Twentieth Century

1910 Thomas & Sarah Botley at Hartlebury Farm. with two of their children, Esther & John[B].

The future might be with the internal combustion engine, but until well into the twentieth century horses did most of the farm work, and personal transport was mainly by horse, bicycle, or pony and trap. Wagon and implement repairs were carried out by blacksmiths and wheelwrights, and horses were shod by farriers. Before cars and tractors were in general use, almost every village in the parish had a farrier, blacksmith or wheelwright; now there is only one blacksmith left in the parish, at Hallon. Mike Seedhouse describes how, as a child, he was mesmerised as he watched his father and grandfather mend wheels, *making the iron hoop the exact size then getting it red hot, fitting it to the wheel then cooling it with water so that it contracted and held firm against the wheel.* Skills such as these went from person to person down the generations, and in most cases this continuity has been lost. This was not so in the Seedhouse family. Arthur Seedhouse arrived at Hallon in 1911, aged 20, to work with Henry Tarrant, who was then the blacksmith, at Hallon Forge. In 1921, Arthur Seedhouse bought the business, and in 1936, his son, Henry, joined him as apprentice. Even in the 1950s there were still heavy horses to shoe and Henry's son, Mike, describes watching his father and grandfather shoe these horses. He remembers the men, *a breed on their own,* such as, Tommy Hirons, Harry Davies and Bill Griffiths, and the talk as to who had the best team. I, too,

Chapter 7   Twentieth Century

remember Henry Seedhouse as a farrier - quiet and gentle. Horses seemed to understand instinctively they were in safe hands. In 1961, Arthur Seedhouse died and Mike Seedhouse joined his father in the business. Not interested in horse work, Mike specialised in welding and metal fabrication and a new workshop was built where the company is now. In 2002, Mike's son, Iain, joined the business as the fourth generation of the Seedhouse family at Hallon.[27]

Memorial marking the site of RAF Station, Bridgnorth. 2017

Worfield in the Second World War
In 1939 the new vicar, Stanley Moore, and his wife moved in to the vicarage, and in July he wrote in the Parish Magazine, *We all feel that we are living on the edge of a volcano.* The volcano was the inevitability of war, and in September the inevitable happened - Britain declared war on Germany. The Reverend Moore had already signed up to become a chaplain in the army and on September 12th 1939 he wrote his letter for the Parish Magazine from Aldershot. He was then padre to a casualty clearing station which received the wounded from field ambulances. It would be 1945 before Stanley Moore would return to Worfield as vicar. Meanwhile, throughout the war, Worfield Parish was cared for by the Vicar of Quatt, the Reverend John Robinson.

In June 1939, plans were afoot to create an RAF training school on land at Stanmore, part of Stanmore Grove estate owned by the Hamilton Russell family. The intention was to house 2,000 trainees in wooden huts at a total cost of £300,000,[28] and in November 1939, No. 4 Recruit Centre

Chapter 7   Twentieth Century

was built to train RAF recruits. In 1940, this was a transit camp for a short while, and in 1941 the Camp was taken over by the W.A.A.T and renamed No. 1 Women's Auxiliary Air Force Depot. In September 1942, there was a further change when it became the No. 1 Air Navigation School and the School of Flying Control. Air gunners and wireless operators were trained here but there was no airfield. There is very little left today of RAF Bridgnorth. The houses at the Hobbins, which were married airmen's quarters and those at Russell Close, which were married officers' quarters, are now private homes. On what is now Stanmore Industrial Estate, Helga's Cafe and a few other original buildings are all that remain. In Stanmore Country Park the road layouts are visible and one remnant of the Camp has been kept as a memorial, the cookhouse chimney of No 3 Wing.

More building work took place in 1943, in Davenport Park, for soldiers of the US Third Army. Work began on Davenport camp in November and by March it was ready to be occupied. Twenty-nine officers, three warrant officers and six hundred and three men were the new arrivals and nissen huts and tents the accommodation. The troops, who were destined for the Normandy beaches as part of the D-Day landings, were to spend their time at Davenport, training and adjusting to European conditions. At the end of the month's training, the men went to Sennybridge for target practice and then briefly back to Davenport before going to France. Some of those stationed at Davenport wrote about their first impressions of the area, the beauty of Davenport Park, the green rolling hills, the fields surrounded by hedges, the ancient village. One wrote that this was the most beautiful place he had ever seen. Another soldier recalled how he and his friends walked down Church Avenue, through a clump of trees, until they came to an open area and looked down over the Lower Churchyard. They went into the Church, walked towards the altar, and were overwhelmed by the age and beauty of the building, and the peace it evoked. He mused that surely God must have been well-pleased with this place[29].

Once installed in Davenport Park, training began. Tanks were seen in the lanes of Worfield and there was one fatality when a tank driver was killed. At the Sonde, the Fincher's dog was run over, and some of the farm ducks shot. Strange accents were heard in the village, some local girls fell head over heels in love, and there was a lot less room at the bars of the local hostelries. Apart from that, there was little disruption to the rhythm of everyday life.

Tabley also became an American camp and the photograph opposite shows Margaret Davenport with General Patton. Before the troops left for Normandy they were visited by Generals Patton and Bradley as a boost to morale. General Patton even took the trouble to visit Mrs Wilcox at Wyken Garage and thank her for her help.

After the Americans left, Camp Davenport was used by Italian and German prisoners of war. They were taken out daily by the WARAG (War Agricultural Executive Committee) to work on farms. In their spare time the prisoners of war made craft items such as boxes and slippers, and entertained themselves by singing. Bob Adams described how you could hear them singing in the evenings, making a sound as rich as any male voice choir.

Chapter 7   Twentieth Century

General Patton and Margaret Davenport at Tabley

British troops also trained in the parish. Chippine Breeze nee Hartley described their arrival in Ackleton as follows[30]:

As far as I know there was no warning that the men were coming. They arrived one day, soldiers returning from the Battle of Dunkirk, and many, including one prisoner of war, were billeted in the new malthouse. Others were billeted in houses throughout the village as temporary accommodation. We had eight soldiers in our house. One morning my father arrived home after a night shift with the Air Ministry Police at Cosford, to find a stranger shaving in our kitchen. 'Who are you,' said the stranger. Father replied, 'more to the point, who the hell are you'. After a while more permanent living quarters were sorted out. Nissen huts were erected in the field next to the telegraph exchange and the telephone box and the field became known as Soldiers' Field. How they arrived in Ackleton I don't know. Perhaps they came by train to Albrighton or Bridgnorth and then walked, or were brought by vehicles. The women of the village ran a canteen for the soldiers in part of the old malthouse which was still standing, an area with a lovely tiled floor. I can only suppose that the army supplied the food, but the women of Ackleton made sandwiches and baked cakes. For us children all this activity was very exciting. The soldiers trained by marching up and down the road and I remember sitting on our doorstep watching them. The fuschia bush was in

Chapter 7   Twentieth Century

Top: circa 1905. Photo below the old cottages have been replaced. Date estd 1910^C.

Chapter 7 Twentieth Century

bloom and I kept popping the buds until mother caught me and stopped my fun.

I said there was one prisoner of war in Ackleton. Why he was there I don't know. He was housed in a room above a reservoir in the malthouse. One day he walked across the loading bay going towards the main building and fell through a trap door. He fell a great height and broke his ankle.

There were German and Italian prisoners of war in Worfield and they came to work on the farms. On Mr Neale's farm in Ackleton there were three German POWs, Helmut, Billy and Dieter. One was a fisherman by trade, one a farm boy far from home and the third was one of the ruling classes.

The government made regular appeals for housing for evacuees, and the vicar had the thankless task of going round the parish to get billets. Apart from a natural reluctance to having strangers living in one's house, most of the houses were small farm cottages with scarcely enough room for the current occupants. Somehow the evacuees squeezed in and settled down to an unfamiliar life in the country, where water had to be pumped from a well, and produce came from a farm rather than the shop down the road. Empty cottages were spruced up and large houses with spare capacity received new visitors. Miss Cunliffe from Bradeney House took in two evacuees, and Davenport House became the temporary home of John Groome's orphanage at Clacton-on-Sea with its own classroom in the Club Room.

The Recreation Room was once more brought into commission as a VAD hospital for the wounded. The following letter, appealing for gifts, was sent in January 1941 by the Commandant, Salop 28[31] from Wyken House.

The Worfield Convalescent Home under the Red Cross may be opened very soon. When patients arrive we shall be very grateful for any gifts our friends can send. Rationing will make catering difficult, so we should be very thankful for presents of potatoes, vegetables, fruit, rabbits, boiling fowls, cakes, jam, eggs, puddings, or any other food. Magazines would be most welcome and, of course, cigarettes.

I remember vividly the great generosity shown to this hospital in the last war and this has given me the courage to send this appeal.

Mrs and Miss Evans of Wyken House and Mrs and Miss Cunliffe of Bradeney House were staunch supporters of the hospital. Mrs Mapp and Lennie Perkins were trained nurses and Miss Lee and Mrs Fee lent a hand. Mrs Stinton was the cook. It would be lovely to have photographs from this period, but photographic film was in short supply.

The Land Army arrived in Worfield as girls came to replace the farm workers who had gone to war. At first they must have seemed like a mixed blessing or no blessing at all. *What the hell am I going to do with you?* was Bill Mapp's reaction when he collected his two sixteen year-old land girls from Shrewsbury. The girls stayed at a hostel on the Stourbridge Road in Bridgnorth and shared a bicycle to get them to Bromley. In spite of Bill's initial misgvings they became a great asset on the farm and much-loved members of the Mapp family.

Chapter 7   Twentieth Century

Some of the men who remained in the parish joined the Home Guard. The Worfield section met in The Granary Loft at Catstree House Farm where John Taylor farmed. There was a rifle range at Mere Pool and the old gravel pit at Rudge Heath was used for grenade practice. There were three or four old cars in the gravel pit which acted as targets. Sunday morning was practice time, and afterwards the men adjourned to the local pub for target practice of the darts variety. Others, including Bill Mapp, joined the ARP (Air Raid Precautions) and were issued with a navy uniform and tin hat. Their equipment was rudimentary to say the least - a whistle, stirrup pump and a bucket. The ARP ensured that blackouts were observed and reported air raids. Some incendiary devices were dropped over Worfield and on one occasion they fell in Rowley Wood. The schoolchildren were warned to avoid them which inevitably had exactly the opposite effect; off the children went on a 'treasure hunt' to find some of the offending objects.

Worfield Home Guard. Seated: centre, George Ridley (Major), extreme left, John Taylor. (rest unknown) Standing :..., H. F. Parker, ..., W. Taylor, ..., ..., ...

Chapter 7   Twentieth Century

Sir Oliver Leese
Worfield had many war heroes, but Sir Oliver Leese[32], who married Margaret Leicester-Warren and made his home in Worfield, was of national renown. Although Leese's war achievements were exceptional, in both the First and Second World War, it was his last appointment, in East Asia, which brought about the end of his active service. It is never easy to make the transition from army to civilian life but Oliver Leese was the man to do it.

Born in 1894, Oliver Leese was the eldest of four children. Educated at Ludgrove from the age of nine, Oliver did well both academically and on the sporting field. From Ludgrove he went to Eton where he again threw himself enthusiastically into school life. Cricket was one of his loves and he played well. Academically he had the ability to excel but didn't apply himself. At the age of fourteen, Oliver joined the Eton Officer Training Corps. His intention on leaving school was to go to France for a period, learn how to speak French fluently, and then to work in the City. The First World War changed that idea and, as so often happens, it was a conversation with a friend whose father was Colonel of the Coldstream Guards which was to set the course of his life. Oliver joined as a reservist in the Guards and in 1914 was sent to Ypres. Luckily for him he was wounded and thus survived this dreadful battle which took so many lives. The injury left him with a slight stoop for the rest of his life.

In July 1915 Oliver was wounded in the face but was able to continue and in September was at the Battle of Loos, after which he was promoted to Lieutenant. In 1916, he was in Paris on leave when he heard about attacks and heavy losses in the area of the Somme. In order to get to his men as quickly as possible, he commandeered a vehicle and drove to his battalion. Leese faced a court of enquiry about the incident but it was reported that he had been killed in action. The report was incorrect although he had been shot in the stomach. The bullet was deflected off Oliver's whisky flask (a 21st birthday present from his mother) or it would have gone straight through his heart. Corporal Jack Lambert witnessed the incident, shot the German officer dead, and carried Leese on his shoulders for 150 yards. Realising the danger he was in from loss of blood, Leese stopped a convoy taking German prisoners and asked them to get a stretcher and take him with them. Thankfully, the Corporal did as he was asked, and was certainly responsible for Leese's survival. The whisky flask was found in 1920 and returned to its original owner.

There was no doubting Oliver's bravery, and on the 15th September 1916, Leese was awarded the DSO. The citation reads:

For conspicuous gallantry in action. He led the assault against a strongly held part of the enemy's line, which was stopping the whole attack. He personally accounted for many of the enemy and enabled the attack to proceed. He was wounded during the fight.

It was 1917 when he was again fit for duty. He was assigned to training duties and then put in charge of the OTC at Eton. Returning to his regiment in 1925, at a time of great hardship in the

Chapter 7   Twentieth Century

country, he was given the job of protecting meat supplies in London. The soldiers arrived in battledress and wore steel helmets. The women in the streets booed and shouted and then they, too, marched down the street in fours with tin jerries (chamber pots) on their heads. Everyone laughed, and within no time at all, the soldiers were playing soccer with the strikers in Victoria Park. That was the nature of the man - he could diffuse tricky situations because he could get on with anyone.

Margaret and Oliver Leese cutting the wedding cake at Tabley

In 1933, Oliver Leese married Margaret Leicester-Warren, who was such a beauty that the artist Philip de Laszlo asked for no fee for the privilege of painting her portrait. The de Laszlo experience inspired Margaret to write about artists, and in 1927, she had several books published. Oliver

Chapter 7   Twentieth Century

Leese's introduction to the family came through Margaret's brother, John Leicester-Warren, who invited him to his sister's coming-out ball. Eventually, after some prompting from Margaret, the couple became engaged. Cuthbert Leicester-Warren was not impressed with Oliver's prospects and quizzed him on how he was going to support his daughter. Oliver's brave reply was, W*ell, sir, I'm going to be a great man.*

A honeymoon in Paris and Madeira followed the wedding, and on their return, the couple split their time between a house in London and Lower Hall in Worfield, the latter having been given to them by Margaret's mother, Hilda Leicester-Warren. After various army posts and travel on the continent, Oliver and Margaret sold their flat in Wilton Place in 1938, and made Worfield their home. Central heating, hot water and electricity were installed in Lower Hall, and Worfield Mill was demolished because Oliver thought it spoilt the view from the Hall. In this alone one might have wished that the man had been less decisive. Had he reflected even for a short while he would have been called away to take up his next posting in Quetta, Baluchistan, and Worfield Mill might have survived a little longer.

Worfield Mill on the right and Mrs Robinson's house straight ahead

Chapter 7   Twentieth Century

Throughout their many separations, the love Margaret and Oliver had for each other never wavered. They took every opportunity to be together, and if that wasn't possible, their correspondence filled the gap and gave them strength.

On 13 May 1940 Margaret (or Margie as she was known) wrote from Worfield.

Oh it's so lovely here today. The woods are just coming out into bluebells. I'm sitting in the garden and the blossom is out and the birds are singing
14 May *The cottage is now prepared for the evacuees if they ever come. It's such a glorious day and the garden looks lovely and full of promise. I am sitting on our future verandah writing - perhaps I ought to get on with the packing ... I wish the evacuees would start arriving and one would feel one was doing something. Tomorrow I go to Tabley by train to Alderley Edge. It's horrid leaving here, but I shall try and get back soon - at the same time I don't think it would be easy to stay on alone here just now, and better for one to do something rather hectic.*
15 May *…Darling I do so love you more and more - and look forward passionately to our little house! How lovely and peaceful it is.*
17 May *Worfield is making great preparations if Wolverhampton gets bombed*
27 May *I think of our Lower Hall and the garden and the view and all the people of the village which is our England and it seems like a lovely world of its own.*

Meanwhile Oliver was having a much less tranquil time serving with the British Expeditionary Force as Deputy Chief of Staff under Lord Gort. He was sent on the 15th May to Arras and on the 18th May, seeing the hopelessness of the situation, he prepared a plan of evacuation of the troops to Dunkirk. The decision to retreat was, however, outside Gort's control. Oliver's letters to his wife reveal his deep concern. For once, even Margie doesn't know what to say. She writes:

25 May *Tabley. Just one word. I don't know quite what to say except I am thinking and thinking of you, and love you more than all the world.*

Eventually, the necessity of retreat became apparent to Gort's superiors, but the chances of it being successful seemed slim. The escape had to be made through a narrow corridor about twenty miles wide. *A depressing thing, a retreat,* Oliver said, *and soon men will be fighting for boats and food.* Whatever his personal views, Sir Oliver's job as an officer was to get his men to the Dunkirk Beaches and keep their morale up as they waited, sitting targets, to be taken home.

James Carne, who was later to excel himself in the Korean War judged Leese's abilities as follows:

He appeared to me a superb leader. He had a tremendous grasp of detail and imaginative ideas.

Chapter 7   Twentieth Century

Others noted that Leese's dress was casual to say the least. The higher up the army ladder he climbed, the worse his dress became. If he was expected to dress a certain way you could guarantee that he would dress another. On one occasion he was reminded to dress properly when inspecting the Grenadier Guards and wear field boots. Leese didn't answer but promptly threw his field boots out of the window and turned up for inspection in khaki plus fours and stockings.

Whenever Oliver had a new posting, Stanley Moore (Vicar of Worfield) was asked to go and celebrate holy communion with him. Worfield seemed to be one of the realities of life he clung to in the surreal conditions of war. Postings came, first to North Africa to head 30 Corps of the Eighth Army, where he played an important part in the Battle of El Alamein, then to Sicily and Italy. Assignments such as these came not by being adequate but by showing exceptional qualities. Inevitably this meant conflict with his superiors. Leese observed that Montgomery was easier to work under, rather than in parallel with, and when Mountbatten became Supreme Allied Commander in South Asia, Leese wrote to his wife that this may be a good appointment but the man himself is very forceful and appears overbearingly conceited. Of an ill-conceived plan in Sicily he wrote to Margaret:

The chances of bringing off this plan are none-too good ... I'd like to shoot the ... who chose this plan and send his head on a pitcher back to Mountbatten and his useless racket

Leese was a man of action with a desire to achieve. *Never frig about on a low level*, he told his young staff officers. How did he cope with the pressures of the job? On one occasion when he was about to be given news of casualties he was standing in a field of cornflowers. The officer bringing news of the casualties approached but Leese put his hand up and said, *Stop, let's pick some cornflowers*. And so they did until their arms were full. Then he said, R*ight! Now tell me about casualties*.

The Italian campaign was a battle against weather, terrain and poor morale. Leese took over a tired 8th Army, denuded by Monty of his personal and senior staff but in the end the campaign was successful. Leese wrote to his wife:

I don't feel that I could be civil to the war Office or to O and all I feel is, 'Thank god we've got Worfield.'

In July 1944, Leese was knighted by King George VI, and in September of that year was appointed Commander Allied Forces, South East Asia, under Mountbatten, replacing General Gifford whom Mountbatten had sacked. Gifford's predecessor, Irwin, had in turn been sacked by Allenbroke. Lieutenant General Slim, who had fought for three years against the Japanese, thought he would be Gifford's replacement, so it was always going to be difficult for Leese to work with

Chapter 7 Twentieth Century

him. On the other hand, Leese and his Eighth Army entourage could have given Slim more credit for his achievements in this theatre of war, rather than emphasising their achievements elsewhere. Slim said that they came with too much sand in their shoes. Leese found Mountbatten difficult, lacking in self confidence, a leader who didn't trust his subordinates and seemed always trying to undermine their authority. The geographical difficulties of managing such a vast area also made the job almost impossible.

At first all went well, Mandalay was taken, and then Rangoon was captured from the Japanese. Malaya was the next target, but Leese felt that Slim was tired and the assault should be carried out with Christison in charge of the Fourteenth Army, with Slim having a supportive role. Slim was incensed and insulted. There was no-one to sort out the three-way disagreement between Leese, Mountbatten and Slim. Someone had to go. Leese told Christison that it happened in this way:

Brookie went to Churchill and told him the Indian Army wouldn't fight without Slim. 'Who sacked Slim?' said Churchill. 'Leese,' said Alanbrooke. 'Well, sack Leese.' I gather I am carrying the can for Dickie over this.

On the 1st July 1945, Sir Oliver Leese received a letter from Mountbatten saying that his services were no longer required by him; a sad end to a lifetime of active service. Oliver's next appointment was as GOC Eastern Command in Hounslow and in 1946 he retired from the army and returned to life in Worfield. He had some of his army colleagues to help him adjust - Bill Buck, his driver, Ernie Bishop, a Worfield man, who had been at El Alamein, and Gordon Davey, an orderly to Oliver, who married Margie's maid, Crowe.

On his retirement, Sir Oliver Leese approached civilian life with the same gusto he had applied to his army career. He and Margaret started a market garden, then they tried mushroom growing. Finally, inspired by Sir Oliver's desert experience, they turned their hands, very successfully, to growing cacti. Worfield Gardens gained a considerable reputation locally and nationally for cacti and succulents and Sir Oliver was recognised as an accomplished horticulturalist.

In their spare time, Sir Oliver and Lady Leese enjoyed entertaining, when at home, and visiting friends abroad. Class, wealth and status meant nothing to them, everyone was treated the same. Although they had no children of their own the couple loved children. There were Christmas parties, a trip to the pantomime and wherever they went in the world each child in the village received a postcard. Sir Oliver's love of cricket continued throughout his life. He became President of the MCC, and no less important locally, of Worfield Cricket Club.

Lady Leese died in 1964 and Sir Oliver in 1978, aged 83. Both are buried in Worfield Churchyard, two people who loved Worfield and whom Worfield loved in return. In 1990, the Wolverhampton branch of the Eighth Army Veterans handed over their flag to St Peter's Worfield for safe keeping. It was a touching reminder of Sir Oliver Leese's contribution to keeping the country safe in some very dark days of war.

Chapter 7   Twentieth Century

Conclusion
At this point this history of Worfield must end, although there is much more to tell. As I said at the beginning, this is very much a work in progress but a line has to be drawn and the end of the Second World War seems a fitting place to finish.

Sir Oliver Leese at home at Lower Hall

Chapter 7   Twentieth Century

Lost

Stone lion from Worfield Churchyard
I think it was in the 1980s that it went missing. One Sunday I went to Church and the much-weathered medieval lion had disappeared. It had lain by the wall and next to the gate. Perhaps it isn't far away. If you see it in a garden somewhere, Worfield Church would love to have it back.

Sundial
In the churchyard there was a sundial which had the inscription, "Jerusalem, Mexico, Worfield."
Auden, J. E. 'Shropshire' (Methuen & Co 1912)
The presence of the sundial was noted more recently in the magazine, 'Country Quest,' December 1972, in an article entitled, Wandering by the Worfe, by C. W. Daniels. So where is this sundial now?

Worfield Mill
Water mills were under threat even in the late nineteenth century. Rollers replaced stones for grinding corn and diesel and electricity replaced water as the power source. Worfield Mill was one of many across the country which bowed to these developments. Jack Rochelle was the last miller and before that, Jack Burrows. Mrs Burrows recalled a time when Worfield flour was milled by the ton and was well known for miles around. It used to be sold in shops in the local towns all along the Severn. Then came the big milling concerns and demand disappeared. (1939)

Clarke's Bakery
Next to Clarke's Stores (now the Post Office) was Worfield's bakery which, by all acounts, baked superb bread.

News From the Parish

Her Majesty the Queen passed by from Bridgnorth to Dallicott to visit her nephew the Earl of Eltham . The town was decorated and thousands lined the streets(Aberdeen Press and Journal 19 August 1927)

The Vicarage, October 28 1935
My Dear Friends,
    Easily the most exciting event recently was the fire which gutted all the old part of the Ackleton Malt Houses, on Saturday evening, October 12th. It started just before 5pm and was not really subdued till 11pm. At one time it seemed that nothing short of a miracle could save the cottages down the road, or the two above. The difficulty was to get any water. The Bridgnorth engine got bogged in the field near Broadbridge, but Shifnal, after trying to get to Badger Dingle, at last were successful in pumping water from Royal Pool through 1200yds of hose pipe to the malt house. Meanwhile all the furniture had been got out from the cottages and carried down to Mrs Wainwright's yard. Hundreds of sightseers in rows of cars had came from all the countryside round as the blaze was visible from Wolverhampton in the east and from all the high ground in the Wheatland country between here and the Clee Hills. It was a week-end which will not soon be forgotten in Ackleton.
    Of an entirely different nature but no less memorable to me, was the party given to all the able-bodied inmates of the workhouse in the Recreation Room on Oct. 7th, by the generosity of two of our parishioners. Foxalls brought them out in two char-a-bancs and after tea the Women's Institute performed an amusing play. Then some of the old men, a little wheezy perhaps and more than a little nervous, sang us songs of fifty years ago- The Farmer's Boy and The Old Arm Chair.

Chapter 7 Twentieth Century

The first dance of the season in the room was a great success since, owing to the generosity of a former pupil of the School, a band from Walsall came and gave their servicess entirely free of charge. The Boot and Shoe Club made over £11 profit. So we are hoping that after two or three years of depression, Worfield dances will now stage a come-back.

On the opening of the Mens'Club, Mr Stinton was presented with an armchair as some token of his services to the Club as secretary and caretaker ever since 1913. Though ill health prevents him from regular attendance we are glad still to have him as a member.

The first sharp frost came on Oct 18th-20th and cut down the dahlias and brought down a carpet of leaves beneath the chestnut trees. We have had several gales which brought down branches but nothing worse. Sugar beet harvest is in full swing. Wheat is being drilled and at least one field is up already. Hilton has had its bridge broadened and the corner widened. It has made a better road but taken away some of the picturesqueness of the village. The Lowe bridge is still with us and so are the potholes on the road down to Rindleford but the road across from the Hermitage to Stanmore has been much widened. Hallon farmhouse is most attractive with its cream washed walls and fresh brown paint. We are rather disturbed by rumours of Wolverhampton Corporation Pumping Stations threatened in our midst, and with it the jerry builder. But otherwise we remain unchanged and the rooks still go home to roost at Apley, and just when you think you've counted the last one another party of stragglers appears in the dusk
Yours sincerely,
Cyril M. Lee
(Worfield Parish Magazine 1935)

References

1. Worfield Parish Magazine January 1900
2. Worfield Parish Magazine January 1902
3. Wellington Journal 8 August 1903
4. Wellington Journal 11 April 1903
5. Wellington Journal 27 April 1901
6. Wellington Journal 19 January 1901
7. Wellington Journal 28 November 1908
8. Shropshire Star in 1999 or 2000 [Apologies for the vagueness of this reference. the article had been cut out of the newspaper & time prevented me from identifying the exact issue JAS]
9. Worfield Parish Magazine April 1900 has a list of those prayed for
10. Pall Mall Gazette 1905 & Hastings and St Leonards Observer 18 March 1905
11. Wodehouse, P. G., Bolton, G., Bring on the Girls in Wodehouse on Wodehouse (Penguin 1981)
12. Murphy, N. T. P., In Search of Blandings (Viking Press 1987)
13. D-NAJ/C/1/204 Nock and Joseland Papers (Wolverhampton Archives)
14. Worfield Parish Magazine 1935
15. Worfield Parish Magazine March 1933
16. Bridgnorth Journal February 4 1911
17. Bridgnorth Journal February 13 1915
18. Deeds in private hands - Barnsley
19. Birmingham Mail 17 July 1917

Chapter 7   Twentieth Century

20. Bridgnorth Journal 1915
21. 5586/5/17/38 Account Book, Allscott Farm (Shropshire Archives)
22. Minutes of War Memorial Committee Meetings. Booklet in private hands
23. Worfield Parish Magazine 1933
24. Worfield Parish Magazine August 1932
25. Wellington Journal and Shrewsbury News 27 August 1904
26. Worfield Parish Magazine 1925
27. Seedhouse, Michael, Worfield's Blacksmiths from 1911 to the Present Day, 2014 (unpublished)
28. Birmingham Gazette 10 June 1939
29. Turley A. & N., The US Army in South East Shropshire, (Adrian and Neil Turley, 2004)
30. Breese, Chippine, (unpublished autobiographical notes)
31. Worfield Parish Magazine 1941
32. Ryder, R., Oliver Leese, Hamish Hamilton 1987

Notes

A Letter from Walter Bishop. Thanks are due to Walter Bishop's great niece, Madeleine Farbrother nee Devey for permitting the inclusion of this letter.

Monday Feb 21st 1900

My Dear Father & Mother, You will be pleased to hear I am safe & sound at Kimberley. In my last I told you we were making a quick move somewhere. Well we started due south from Modder, did about 25 miles & halted at a farm for the night, next day we marched about 15 miles. These two days we were rather badly off for water, but as the Doctor pronounced the pool water alright we were only too glad to drink with our horses. I cannot tell you the particulars, so well as the papers will, for I almost lost count of the days.

    We had a sharp skirmish with the Boers at Modder River but when they saw our number they made off like the wind leaving several loaded wagons behind. We stayed here for rest - 24 hours & as each man carried his own rations we were glad to look around for something to eat, they had left some flour behind so we got a sack of that in the lines & each tried his hand at making cakes. I had a tin of Treacle in my wallet so made a dumpling in my mess tin with that. It didn't rise much but was a change from biscuit, being thirsty the biscuits wouldn't go down at all, one would last me all day. By this time we were within a days march of Kimberley, expecting a big fight, & we were not mistaken, for soon 6 Boer guns were banging into our Artillery, ours soon began to slacken their fire & now came the move that astonished the Boers. The dash had to be done & Gen. French meant to do it.

    The two Cavalry Brigades moved forward & made across the open country between the Boer positions - we had to gallop over four miles most of the way under rifle fire & didn't the bullets whizz about, we (the 10th) were in the centre. Its wonderful that none of us were hit but several horses were hit including mine. I heard the bullet hit, but thought it was in my saddle pack. She carried me well out of danger & then I found it had gone clean through her one thigh. We halted for the night just outside Kimberley. Then the two brigades moved off after the Boers up the Free State. I had to stay here, as it was not safe to take the horse, though it is quite healed up again & she is not lame. I was lucky wasn't I? Those whose horses fell had to run leaving everything. I haven't heard the casualties, but don't think they were heavy. I believe the Kimberley people could not believe their own eyes when they saw us coming over the Veldt, there was great rejoicing when it became known who we were.

Chapter 7   Twentieth Century

They expect the railway will be open today so hope to post this. They couldn't have held out much longer. It's a sight to see the blacks come round the camps for dead horses, they had one of ours this morning that died in the night & they carried it all off. One said he didn't mind it, for it was just like beef. Yesterday we had a heavy thunderstorm & having no tents everything was soon wet through, that made it rather a miserable night for us.

The town sent out a wagon laden with tanks of soup for us, goodness knows what it was made of but we had our fill of it, for it tasted very nice. It is a hard matter to say when we shall see our regiment again, for they must be some way up the States by this (sic). I shall not be able to stamp this letter for those you sent me are in my kit bag at Modder River, the bit of paper I've carried in my haversack about 100 miles. I am very glad I brought it. Please let Brothers and Sisters know I am well. I hope yourselves keep quite well.

B. The Botley family might have come to Worfield to be toll collectors. In the 1861 census, at the Worfe Turnpike Gate is Thomas Botley (30), Eliza (30) a toll collector and their son, William (11).

C. Houses built by the Wilson family. The new cottages in Ackleton may have been built by the Wilson family who owned the Ackleton Malthouse. The mock tudor style was something of a trademark of Richard Sidney Wilson seen in three houses at Kingslow and one at Chesterton. the Kingslow houses bear the following inscriptions; RSW 1904, 1908, RSW 1913. These houses are all slightly different, as indeed are the Ackleton houses. Perhaps it was houses such as that shown below which inspired the design of the new houses.

A substantial half timbered house at Wyken now known as Rookery Cottages

Chapter 8   Walks

Early History

This walk takes you around the Iron Age Hillfort of The Walls. Time: retracing one's steps to Chesterton the walk will take about 20 minutes. Easy walking and no stiles. If you wish to descend to Littlegain the steps are steep and not so easy.

1. Start at the Telephone Box in Chesterton and walk south past the last house in the village on your left.
2. Turn left following the signpost and at the end of the track turn right.
3. Continue and The Walls hillfort is straight ahead. The footpath takes you to the left and you can follow it down to Littlegain.
4. Before you leave Chesterton, walk north through the village. The cottage facing you, at the point where a footpath on your right goes into a valley, is the former St John's Chapel. Following the footpath will take you to the Nun Brook. You can then continue across the stream to Nunfields and across two roads to Rudge. On the opposite side of the road is the old pound where stray animals were penned. Turn left and you will see Rudge Hall and on its left an old building believed to have been a monastery. Retrace your steps to Chesterton.

St. John's Chapel Chesterton in 1982. (PH/W/33/120 Shropshire Archives)

Chapter 8   Walks

Early Medieval

This walk is in Worfield village. From the A454 take the turn to Worfield opposite the Wheel Inn and Worfield Garage. Bear left where the road forks, past the Recreation Room on your left and take the first turn right into Worfield. Parking is difficult when the school is open but out of school hours there is ample parking in the school car park opposite the Dog Inn. Walk down Main Street towards the church to view the oldest surviving man-made features in the parish, the church itself and the Picture Doors which, at the time of writing, hang in the gallery of the church. Allow an hour and a half. Walking time 30 minutes. All road walking but fairly steep in parts.

1. At the beginning of the church path on your left is a black and white building known as the Old Club Room. Formerly this was the Grammar School and where the manor courts were held.
2. As you walk up the path, note the medieval preaching cross on your right, the cross itself is a later addition by the Rev Nicholas, and the medieval stone coffin on your right immediately in front of the church.
3. Before entering the church, turn left and go to the back of the church. The first window is a type of Kentish tracery. Note the lovely old door to the Bell Tower. Retrace your steps towards the main door and you will see an old window just before the porch. The interior of the church has been much restored but note the two arches over the chancel of different ages, and the old pillar at the junction of the nave which may indicate a former transept. You will also see old stonework at the west end of the church near and in the Madeley Room.
4. Climb the stairs to the gallery and hanging on the wall you will see a pair of Picture Doors; early examples of medieval decorative ironwork and a Davenport hatchment representing the death of a member of the family.
5. On going back to ground level, turn left towards the chapel at the north east end, the Saint Mary's Chapel. Pass the Bromley memorials and on the first you come to, Edward Bromley's, note the graffiti on the pillars. In front of St Mary's Chapel you will see the sixteenth century tombstone of John Lye ,1542, a chantry priest and within the chapel a medieval chest.
6. Walk across in front of the pulpit and behind it is a cross in memory of Major Frank Corbett. The chancel itself was improved by the Davenport family in the late nineteenth century and the plaques on the walls commemorate various family members. Adjacent to the chapel on the south east side, St Nicholas Chapel, is a small memorial to Thomas Berkeley of Ewdness.
7. Walk down the church path, stop at the church gates and look across towards Lower Hall on the opposite side of the road. The entrance gate probably dates from when the Rectory (or Lower Hall as it is now known) was built in 1549 by Sir John Talbot.
8. Turn left at the church gates and take the road straight on round the churchyard. Note the half-timbered building adjacent to Lower Hall which was once the vicarage and on your left, exactly opposite, the small gateway in the churchyard wall, now bricked up, which I assume was used by the vicars as they went to and from church. On your right, alongside the last bungalow in the village, you will see a footpath. This led to a watering place on the Worfe.

Chapter 8   Walks

9. Walk straight on, ignoring the road to your left. From this point we are in Hallonsford. It is now seen as part of Worfield but in medieval times would have been part of Hallon. Just past a stone cottage on your left, are a number of caves and the site of St Peter's Well both in an area known as Walstone. Walk on, and as the tarmac road gives way to a dirt track, you will see in front of you two of the common fields of Hallon - Mazerdine Field and Wheat Furlong. The township of Hallon in medieval times included a much bigger area of land than the village itself, on which the inhabitants depended.
10. Retrace your steps and at the junction of the first road up the hill, note a grass track which leads diagonally up to Hallon. This path can get very overgrown so instead take the lane up the hill also towards Hallon. The meeting of three tracks is indicative of how busy this area once was.
11. Turn left at the junction and walk past the modern graveyard. Note on your left the Old Vicarage Hotel which was built in the early years of the twentieth century as the vicarage.
12. Turn left at the next junction and go down the hill. Half way down, on the left, is a public road, Pound Lane, which once led to the Pound and may have been the site of Hallon Castle. It may even have been the site of an earlier Iron Age hill fort because of its strategic vantage point.
13. From the church, walk back down Main Street, surely one of the prettiest of village scenes. Hardwicke writing in the late nineteenth century had a different opinion and thought the houses a disgrace - *They are neither to the taste of the day nor to the comforts expected from the march of intellect.*

Sixteenth Century

Burcote, Bromely and Rindleford. Can be wet in places otherwise easy walking. 2 hours.
1. On the A454 Wolverhampton to Bridgnorth road, at the roundabout at the top of the Hermitage, take the turn for Bromley. From Wolverhampton this is the right turn. Take the next turn right for Burcote and look for a footpath sign on the left hand side of the road.
2. Follow the footpath down into the valley and almost immediately the path splits. The more obvious path goes down into the valley but don't be tempted. You want the path which goes left up the slope. This will take you across fields to a cottage in the hamlet of Fenn Gate, a place of some antiquity. Note the stonework of the cottage. Sandstone is an easily worked building material but weathers badly.
3. Turn right at the road and walk along for a short distance. Look out for a footpath sign on the left hand side. This will take you across fields which were once the Common Fields of Bromley. The field is bounded on the western side by woodland, replanted perhaps in the nineteenth century.
4. Into the second field and you will see the village of Bromley in front of you. Note the raised areas descibed as an *earthwork field system and possible settlement remains of probable medieval to post medieval date* (Shropshire HER Record 21467). Note also the huge oak trees, remnants of the Forest of Morfe which Bromley was within.

Chapter 8   Walks

5. Where the footpath meets the road you are now in Bromley. On the opposite side of the road is a group of beautiful sandstone and brick farm buildings.
6. Turn right at the road and on your right you will see a timber frame building - Baker's Cottage. On the left are other cottages. Note the chimneys which indicate how the houses have been extended. This is a village worth pausing in to admire, houses, farm buildings and views.
7. Follow the road round until you are facing a stone cottage. Take the lane to the left marked Rindleford. You will go down an ancient track, a hollow way. As you descend, the scene is of twentieth century chalets. Only the cottage on the right indicates that Rindleford extended to this side of the stream.
8. Walk across the bridge over the Worfe which was laid on earlier stone and rubble foundations of a pack horse bridge. Note the stone abutments at the ends and cutwaters on the south side. On the bridge look across to the pond in front of you. This was once the mill pond and much bigger than it is now. You will see brickwork in the stream, further indications of one of Worfield's most important mills.
9. Cross the bridge and you will see the mill on your right and the Miller's House in front of you. Turn right in front of the Miller's House and almost immediately take a right turn down a narrow path alongside a vegetable garden. This will take you back across the River Worfe.
10. Over the River the path turns left. Note the glaciated valley carved out by a force much greater than the present Worfe. On your right is exposed sandstone showing masons' marks, evidence of stone taken for building.
11. The path forks at this point. Take the path to the right, not the one straight on which follows the River. As you walk up the valley you will see signs that the original track was to the left of the one you are on. There are fenceposts showing where it was and on the one side a stone wall. This was once a main way to Rindleford, wide enough for carts going to and from the mill.
12. On your right you will see the first signs that there was once a settlement in this valley. Walking in winter gives you a better view of these houses and the terraces on which their occupants grew their crops. The history of these is unknown. Were they remnants of cave dwellings which were extended with brickwork much later? Were they quarrymen's houses? Did the occupants work in the mills of Rindleford and Burcote? The terracing appears nowhere else, as far as I know, in the parish.
13. Continue up the hill until you are back at the start.

Seventeenth Century

This walk takes you through Davenport Park which in the seventeenth century was part of the three field system of Hallon. It is a circular walk taking in Burcote, Rindleford and Hallon and observing all that remains of Davenport House's predecessor, Hallon Hall/House.

1. Park in the village of Worfield. If you park in the School car park opposite the Dog (outside school hours only), turn left on Main Street and walk to the T junction by the War Memorial.

Chapter 8 Walks

Cross over the road and bear slightly left to take the footpath. Over the stile then bear right over a second stile and follow a diagonal line over rising ground and down to the footbridge crossing the Worfe.

2. Note the remains of an early nineteenth century wheel which raised water up to Davenport House.
3. Cross the footbridge and continue over fields until you see a barn on your left. The footpath goes between the barn and a cottage. This is part of Lower Burcote.
4. Turn right on the track down into the valley. You will see stones, evidence of building. When you reach the bottom of the hill, before you cross the stream, this area was the site of a spinning mill in the nineteenth century known as The Factory.
5. In the stream to your right you will see evidence of mill workings. This was Burcote Mill which was in operation as early as the 1600s. It was this mill which powered the spinning mill.
6. The path takes you past Burcote Mill Cottage. Head towards the bridge but before you walk on, turn back to the cottage. High on the wall you will see a fireback with the inscription 'Richard Lea of Newton begs to offer his services as a founder 1636.'
7. Over the bridge at Burcote. If the weather is fair it is worth stopping at this spot to enjoy the peace (it certainly wouldn't have been as peaceful when the mill was in operation.) In 1300 there were eight fisheries or stakings at Burcote. Exactly where they were isn't known. They must have been in this area but I leave you to speculate.
8. The wood immediately in front of you is Soudley Wood which provided fodder for a large number of pigs in medieval times.
9. Follow the track towards Rindleford and, in the village, go past a cottage on the right. The house on the corner was the miller's house. Note a mill wheel on your left and Rindleford Mill, which you can't miss, also on your left. The mill is now flats and each one has some of the mill workings in it. If you walk to the side of the mill you will see one of the original doors.
10. Turn right then keep to the right at a dog's leg of a road by barn conversions. Go up the hill and at the top of the hill turn right at the cross roads. Ahead of you is Catstree.
11. Continue down into a dip with a cottage on the left and alongside a pool known as Mere Pool. In 1935 there was a drought and Mere Pool dried up. The Vicar wrote that, *hundreds of eels lay dead, some as thick as a man's wrist.*
12. Just past Mere Pool you will begin to see, on your right, a stone wall and a culvert, the only evidence on the ground that there was once a house here. Hallon House, which was the home of the Barker family and then the Bromley family, stood on an eminence on the right with a parterre on the far side. Where was the entrance to the house? I leave you to decide. Also on the right, now sadly covered over, is the Ice House.
13. At the road junction in Hallon is Hallon House or Hallon Farmhouse. In 1727 Mr Fletcher was the occupant. Either go straight across towards the church and then turn right down Main Street back to the car park or turn right down the hill. This is a busy road with fast traffic. The hill is

Chapter 8   Walks

known as China Bank, so named because there was a wooden bridge across the road in the Chinese style. Turn left at the War Memorial to the car park.

Eighteenth Century

This walk takes you from Ackleton through Badger and Stableford and back. It passes through Badger Dingle which was landscaped in the eighteenth century. Ackleton was partly in Badger Manor and partly in Worfield. Land transactions were dealt with in the small courts or courts baron of Badger Manor and transgressions within the Frankpledge or Great Courts of Worfield Manor.

1. Start at the Red Cow in Ackleton
2. Take the track at the side of the Red Cow shown by a bridleway sign. This will take you through a small gate, across a field and into Badger Dingle.
3. Follow the path down and you will come to a lake and stream. The lake is part of landscaping done around 1780 by William Emes who was a pupil of Capability Brown. Emes also landscaped Dudmaston. There was a mill at Badger from the thirteenth century and probably before that which was in the Dingle, *alongside the Ackleton Road,* This mill had gone by 1811 when Badger Heath Mill was described as the only mill in the parish. (See: A History of the County of Shropshire: Volume 10, Munslow Hundred (Part), the Liberty and Borough of Wenlock)
4. Cross over the bridge and take the path straight ahead. Note the cave on the right - was it just part of the landscaping? I don't know. On the left you will see a metal grill blocking off the ice house. Shine a torch in and you will see that this is a brick built, egg-shaped structure of considerable depth (7.5 metres in fact).
5. Walk up to the road and turn right which will take you into the delightful village of Badger. Turn left at the pond. You will pass Badger Church on your right. Ackleton people often came to this church rather than Worfield because it was so much nearer. Walk on until you come to Badger Hall on your right. This was built on a site north of the church in 1719 and replaced a moated house just west of the church.(If you wish to see all the village and Badger Heath Mill, turn right at the pond. The mill is quite a walk from the bridge at the end of the village, perhaps more than a mile, but worth it as the mill workings have been excavated.)
6. Take the path to the left. It will take you through a beech wood with evidence of quarrying. Continue until you reach the road. Turn right and walk on towards the bridge over the River Worfe. This river is the boundary between Worfield and Badger. Over the bridge and you are now in Stableford, originally called Stapulford, the post by the ford.
7. Note the two timber framed houses on the left. On your right is Stableford Hall, once the home of the Corbett family. Walk on a little farther and you will see Stableford House, formerly Stableford Farm, which is where Sibell Corbett lived and farmed. The house is a nice example of a Regency type house built in the early nineteenth century. If you walk up the side of the house, between the boundary wall and the hedge, you will come to a track. Turn left and the

Chapter 8   Walks

house on the right (which is in private hands) was where P. G. Wodehouse lived for 6 years. Retrace your steps back to the road.
8. Turn left and just past the houses on your right you will see a footpath sign. Follow this path but when you get into the next field the footpath is not at all obvious and one can be led into a very boggy area. To avoid wet feet, look ahead of you to the top of the hill and you will see a stile. This is the point you are aiming for. The best way at the time of writing is to bear slightly left and then across until you are out of the damp area.
9. Over the stile and carry on until you get to the road.
10. Either: turn right and then left following the footpath to Ackleton. Parts of this path were very overgrown in 2017 so not for the faint-hearted! On reaching Ackleton the last part of the walk has a wall on the right hand side, once part of the Maltings which were burnt down in the 1930s. Turn left at the road and note Maltings Close built on part of the Maltings site. On the right-hand side of the road is Ackleton Manor. Carry on to the junction and the Red Cow is opposite .
11. Or turn left and return to the Red Cow by road and walk up Folley Road to view the Manor House on the left and the Maltings farther up the road on the right.

Nineteenth Century

This is a walk west of the A442 which is now cut off from the rest of the parish. Traffic now moves in a north south direction rather than east to west as it did when Worfield looked to the River Severn for the movement of goods of all kinds. This walk is now the only way open to see this part of the parish.
1. The walk starts at Grid Reference S0739976. From Bridgnorth take the A442 to Telford. Pass two roads on the right and a track on the right. The walk starts at the second track on the left after this, at Ewdness. Unfortunately there are no obvious landmarks and the road is very busy. There is also no easy place to park a car. Verges are the only option. This is a walk which takes you to and fro on the same path.
2. Follow the track up the lane and at the farmyard (Ewdness Farm) take the track to the left not over the cattle grid. On your left are some lovely old farm buildings and on the right is Ewdness. In the seventeenth century it was second only to Hallon House in size. In the Civil War, Thomas Berkeley had a troop of horse here.
3. At the white cottage, 'Talbott Cottages,' turn left towards some farm buildings. Were the cottages so named because of a connection with the Talbot family who were the Earls of Shrewsbury or Sir John Talbot who built Lower Hall in Worfield.
4. The path goes to the right of Oldington, another very ancient house, once the home of a member of the Purton family.

Chapter 8   Walks

5. The next village you pass is Newton, a larger village through which the road to the ferry once passed.
6. At the corner of the field where there is a dip, you will meet the road which was cut through the rock to join the Severn at a ferry point across to Astley Abbotts. This was presumably also a loading and unloading point for goods. You will also see the bridge now known as Hunter's Bridge, which dates from 1804.
7. You can either walk on until the end of this path where it goes through Winscote and then joins the A442 or you can turn round now and retrace your steps.
8. If you have retraced your steps, as you approach Ewdness, note the pond which is now ornamental. In earlier times, ponds such as this would have been an important source of food.
9. Look up and you will see Ewdness and you will get an idea of the size of the township before this and the townships of Newton and Oldington shrank in size. They became more remote and cut off from the rest of the parish as Worfield turned east to the railways rather than west to the Severn.

Twentieth century

This is a walk around Stanmore Country Park. From Wolverhampton, take the A454 to Wolverhampton and turn left at the top of the Hermitage. Take the second turning on your left to Stanmore Industrial Estate and the car park is on the right. Follow the paths and information boards will tell you more about the history of RAF Bridgnorth. Easy walking, all off-road.

Appendix 1

Lists of Inhabitants

1327 Lay Subsidy Inhabitants of Worfield mentioned

Richard of Eudenas 3s 7d halfpenny
Roger of Eudenas 5s
Benigna of Eudenas 18d
Stephen Atte Sonde 18d
Waler Bolloke 12d
Roger of Hill 12d
Thomas Wylkyn 12d
Roger Gold 18d
Thomas Gerald 12d
Robert Owyn 12d
Robert Coke 12d
William of Kyngeslowe 3s
John of Stanlowe 2s
Thomas Bolloc 12d
Roger of Chesterton 2s
Agnes of Chesterton 6d
William Aldith 18d
Reginald Wychet 12d
Thomas Heynen 9d
Walter Heyne 12d
Thomas of Ewyke 5s 2d halfpenny
William of Roulowe 18d
Thomas Colet 2s
Richard of Bradeney 12d
Robert of Bradeney 12
Thomas Byrd 18d
Thomas atte Yate 12d
Adam of Oldynton 9d
Agnes atte Broke 6d
Roger of Swancote 3s

William of Swancot 2s 6d
Roger of Hoccombe 12d
John Gerbode 2s
Adam of Burcote 12d
William Gyll 18d
Thomas Simond 12d
Robert Edith 9d
Thomas Young 6d
Henry Aleyn 9d
Roger Walker 3s
Peter Jones 9d
Henry Dodemo 6d
Roger Weremod 12d
Henry atte Pyrie 12d
John of Hill 18d
Robert Mathew 9d
Roger Howe 12d
Stephen Adam 6d
Robert of Alvescote 2s
Alexander of Alvescote 12d
Robert Mercer 6d
Stephen Wylle 9d
William Massi 12d
Roger Louestycke 9d
Stephen Rose 12d
Stephen Kynge 6d
Thomas Freemon 18d
Richard of Roughton 18d
Stephen Henry 18d
William Weoremod 18d

1327 The subsidy (or tax) was granted by the Parliament of King Edward III to meet the expenses of the war against the Scots. The tax was a twentieth part of all moveable goods levied on all citizens although there were exemptions for the upper classes because they paid other feudal dues.

1524 The Lay Subsidy

This was a tax levied by Henry VIII and is an example of how comprehensive such taxes were. Property, goods and wages over a certain amount were all subject to tax, either land or goods not both. Where the wages were those of a live-in servant, the master would pay the tax but could pass it on to the servant in the following year. The first figure is the amount taxable, the second is the tax.

Appendix 1

Worfield with Members John Underhyll goods £4 tax 2s, John Underhill, fletcher, £4 2s William Taylor goods £3 18d, Richard Barrett £8 4s, Thomas Hasylwod £5 6d, George Underhyll 40s 12d, Thomas Weyver £4 2s John Byssheton, in wages 20s 4d

Stapleford John Warter goods £6 4s, William Warter 40s 12d, Thomas Merwall 40s 12d, John Barker goods 40s 12d, John Newton £4 2s, Richard Golde £4 2s

Stanlowe Thomas Austen £10 5s, John Yate 40s 12d

Kyngeslowe Rauff Graunger goods 40s 12d, William Frodesley £8 4s, John Gyldon £8 4s, Henry Jones wages 20^{tis} 4s

Chesterton William Adams goods £4 2s, William Rowlowe £3 18d, Thomas Garbott & John his son £3 18d, William Baker wages 20s 4d, Richard Newe goods £1 2s, John Hychecockes land £3. Thomas Barbor goods £3 18d

Bradeney William Golde goods £4 2s, William Bradeney senior £3 18d, William Bradeney junior 40s 12d, Roger Bradeney wages 20s 4d, John Yate goods £4 2

Rowloe George Rowley goods £4 18d, William Sonde goods £4 2s, George Sounde wages 20s 4d

Wyken William Sadler & Thomas his son goods £3 18d, Joan Sadler £4 2s, William Rowlowe £8 4s, John Garbott 40s 12d, Thomas Byrde land 26s 7d, Roger Stevyns wages 20s 4d, Hugh Tomky in like 20s 4d, Richard Baker in lyke 20s 4d, William Cattecham in lyke 4d

Hilton John Bruggend senior goods £4 2s, John Bruggend junior £4 2s, John Foxall 40s 12d, Thomas Foxall 40s 12d, John Bradeney wages 20s 4d, Humphrey Rudge wages 20s 4d, William Merwall wages 20s 4d, Thomas Jaimes/Jannes land £4 4s

Ewdenes Richard Felton goods £10 5s

Oldyngton Richard Haslewood land 20s 12d, Thomas Garbott goods 40s 12d, John Purton £4 2s, Humphrey Crudgington £4 2s, Roger Hasylwod & William his son goods £8 4s, John Pryste 40s 12d, William Rowlowe £3 18d

Cattystre Roger Cattystre goods £6 3s, Richard Rowlowe wages 20s 4d

Allescote William Townsend goods £3 18d, John Felton 40s 12d, Geffrey Down £4 18d, John Townsend wages 20s 4d, Roger Townsend wages 20s 4d

Roughton John Yate goods £9, John Walker land £4 4s, John Broke goods £10 5s, Richard Graunger £4 2s, Richard Broke wages 20s 4d, Margaret Hyll land 26s 8d - 16d, Richard Townsend goods 40s 12d, (m 3d) John Cattystre goods £4 2s, Joan Garbott widow land 20s 12d

Burcotte Thomas Valence goods 40s 12d, William Walker 40s 12d, Thomas Parton £3 18d, Thomas Rykthorne 36 3s, Elsbeth Hoggettes 40s 12d

Swancote & Ryndelford John Mylner 40s 12d, Richard Wever wages 20s 4d, Roger Walker wages 20s 4d, Richard Jaimes goods £3 18d, John Jaimes £7, John Walton land 40s 2s

Hoccombe William Mathewe goods £8 4s, Roger Russell £3 18d, John Pytte £3 18d

Halon Roger Barker goods £5 2s 6d, William Gravenor £4 2s, George Barrett wages 20s 4d, Richard Barker, weaver £3 18d, George Rowlowe wages 20s 4d, Joan Rowloe land 20s 12d, John Taylor goods 40s 12d, Richard Barker 40s 12d, Richard Holygreve wages 20s 4d, Richard Pryste wages 20s 4d, George Barker goods £7 3s 6d, Thomas Taylor wages 20s 4d

Bromley Richard Byllyngsley goods £6 3s, Roger Baker goods £10, John Baker wages 20s 4d, John Barrett wages 20s 4d, Joyes Barrett widow goods 40s 12d, Roger Hychecokes wages 20s 4d, Thomas Bolton wages 20s 4d, William Bradeney 20s 4d, Thomas Glover 20s 4d, Richard Collynge 20s 4d, Roger Barrett goods £6 3s

Sum £9 5s 10d

Appendix 1

1573-1574 Those from the townships of Worfield (Worveld Home) who lopped or cropped in the Forest of Morfe in 1573-1574 (Regarders Accounts E32/149 held at the National Archives)

Thomas Smithe
Humphrey Pyke
Thomas Whitmore
William Freckleton
John Rudge
Christopher Potter
Peter Potter
William Pyke
Thomas Palmer
William Wrighte
-
William Hockam
William Jannes
William Rowlowe
Roger Barrette
William Bickardine
John Oldberie
Richard Bradneye
William Billingsley

John Baker
John Barbor
Roger Jannes
Richard Billingsley
Henry Marrall
John Brooke
Richard Weaver
John Mathewe
Richard Yate
Humphrey Dovie
Thomas Smythe
John Bradney
John Billingsley
Humphrey Potter
Roger Rowley
William Billingsley
William Goolde
Richard Torner
Thomas Barbor

Appendix 1

1583 A list of the Quenes tennants within the manor and the Forest of Morfe. 21st January in the 15th year of the reign of Queen Elizabeth
(Regarders Accounts E32/149 held at the National Archives.

Worfeld Home
Bromley:
John Baker - 3s
John Barber - 3s
Roger Jannes 3s
Richard Billingsley 3s
Burcott:
H… Marrall - 3s
Richard Felton - 3s
William Felton - 3s
John Walker - 3s
Swancott:
John Jannes - 3s
Elizabeth Jannes widow- 3s
Occom:
William Occom - 3s
William Wryght - 3s
William Marrall - 1s
Barnesley:
Joyce Beche widow 1s
Roughton:
Richard Yate - 3s
Humphrey Devy - 3s
Walter Leihe - 3s
John Mathewe - 3s
John Broke - 3s
William R … Pr… 3s
John Shepherd - 3s

Roger Barret - 3s
Richard Bradney 3s
William Buccardine 3s
John Wolberey 3s
Thomas Marrall 3s
Hylton
Thomas Smyth 3s
John Marrall 3s
John Billingsley 3s
William Stocke
William Foxall the younger 3s
William Billingsley 3s
Richard Barker 3s
Richard Wever 3s
[First 2 letters smudged. Could it be **Swancote**]
Richard ?Tornor for like 3s
John Survound 3s
Rowley & Bradleye
Roger Rowley for like 3s
Humphrey Potter 3s
Walter Billingsley 3s
Chesterton
Roger Gould 3s
John Hitchox 3s
Richard Barbor 3s
William Newe 3s
Roger Garbett 3s
Thomas Webbe 3s (in the margin) the forester for Quatford

Appendix 1

1600 Presentment and valuation of Worfield inhabitants of the Hundred of Brimstree (National Archives)
A list of those presented before a jury for a minor offence

Worveld
Dame Jane Bromley in land £5 -20s
Thomas Barkeley, gent, in land £3 -12s
Edward Kynnersley in goods £4 -10s 8d
Roger Rowley in land 20s 4s
John Walker in land 20s 4s
John Barrett in land 20s - 4s
John Yeate in land 40s - 8s
John Brooke in land 20s - 4s
Thomas Gyldon in land 20s - 4s
Walter Beeche in land 20s - 4s
Richard Bradney in land 20s 4s
Roger Catstrey in land 20s 4s
Richard Rowley in land 20s 4s
Roger Jannes in land 20s - 4s
John Walker in land 20s - 4s
John Catstrey in land 20s - 4s
John Baker in land 20s - 4s
John Garbett in land 20s - 4s

1672 Hearth Tax

The Hearth Tax, or Fire Tax as it was sometimes known, began in 1662 to support the restored monarchy of Charles II. It continued until 1689 but not all the records have survived. The 1672 tax gives an insight into the composition of each hamlet within the parish and the comparitive wealth of the occupants.

Appendix 1

1672 Hearth Tax

Hallon   (hearths)
Lettice Davenport (13)
William New (1)
Benedicta Perton, wid.(1)
John Steventon (2)
John Barnett (1)
John Hitchcock (4)
Richard Shepard (1)
Margery Fibbs, widow (1)
Edward Purslow (1)
William Gold (1)
William Clarke (1)
Francis Burne (1)
James Hancox, vicar (4)
John Barnes (1)
Griffith Morris (1)
Robert Barrett (2)
George Barrett (2)
William Warter (3)
William Dovey
Kingslow & Stanlow
William Poten (1)
Widow Batch (2)
John Batch (4)
Widow Thomason (2)
Roger Barber (2)
Stephen Smith (2)
Joshua Hitchcock (1)
John New senior (1)
John New junior (1)
Swancott & Hoccom
John Warter
Thomas Lowe
Thomas Shepard
(about 9 names missing)
**Allscott, Winscott
& Rindleford**
William Beech, gent (6)
Thomas Weaver (1)
John Stringer (1)
Robert Barrett (1)
John Rowley (1)
Jane Walker, widow (2)

Nathaniel Garmeston (1)
Jonathon Felton (1)
George Bradborne (1)
Humphrey Bradney (1)
Margaret Bradney widow(1)
Katherine Bradney widow(1)
Bradney & Sond
Richard Billingsley (4)
Widow Annes (1)
Henry Mason (1)
George Sond (3)
Jonas Groome (1)
Rowley
Roger Rowley esq (10)
Widow Piper (1)
Accleton
Richard Jones jnr (1)
John Blakeman (1)
Thomas Tyrer (2)
William Perry (2)
John Felton (1)
Evan Leueillin (1)
Francis Bradborne (1)
William Bradney (1)
William Bradney & tenant (1)
Thomas Willis (2)
Richard Eakin (1)
Thomas Barrett (1)
John Bradborne (1)
Richard Clempson (3)
Stapleford
William Warter (2)
Richard Haslewood (3)
John Warter (2)
Roger Foxall (3)
Thomas Hubbold (1)
Thomas Gibbons (1)
John Preston (1)
John Sturmy (1)
Barneley & Roughton
(about 10 names missing)
Hilton
William Beech (2)

William Foxall (1)
John Merewall (1)
John Hubbold (1)
Thomas Lilly (5)
John Rowley (1)
Widow Norton (2)
Richard Billingsley & Henry
Mason (1)
William Okeley (1)
John Bradney (1)
John Smith (1)
Newton
John Crudgington (1)
Alice Warter widow (1)
William Taylor (2)
John Rowley (1)
Richard Snead (1)
Thomas Taylor (1)
Burcott
John Sadler (3)
Joseph Shelton (2)
Enoch Walker (1)
John Mills (1)
Bromley
John Richards (2)
John Cureton (1)
John Bates (?)
3 illegible
William Alc (1)
Ewdness & Oldington
Thomas Jobber (10)
John Yates (1)
William Gold (1)
Richard Slater (4)
John Hitchcock (2)
Francis Haslewood (1)
John Haslewood (1)
Wyken
William Palmer
Joseph Littleford
John Thomason
Matthew Walford
7 names missing

Appendix 1

Owners and Occupiers in Worfield in 1788 showing areas of land held. Taken from A Valuation of the buildings, lands, tithes and premises made and proportioned for a poor's rate 1788 by John Bishton and Daniel Banton. Ref: 5586/1/214 (Shropshire Archives)

Occupier & Residence	Proprietors	Acres-Rods-Perches
Ackleton		
Richard Adams & John Rowley	Jonah Barney	0-0-0
Bartley Baker		
Jonah Barney	Bartley Baker	2-1-37
John Bradney	Jonah Barney	4-1-37
J.H. Browne Esq	Joseph Willis	0-0-0
William Butcher	J.H. Browne Esq	11-0-5
Isaac Clarke	Miss Fletcher	160-3-28
ditto	Isaac Clarke	143-3-7
Phebe Dalloway	Richard Rushton	3-1-4
Mary Eykyn		0-0-0
Miss Eykyn	Mary Eykyn	285-2-1
John Gibbons	Miss Eykyn	11-3-5
Richard Harper	Richard Slater	1-0-0
Isaac Mason	Mary Eykyn	0-0-0
Susannah Mills	Susannah Mills	
Daniel Onions	William Taylor Esq	0-3-39
Edward Pearce	George Bennet	16-3-33
Purchase, William	Isaac Clarke	0-0-0
ditto	Miss Fletcher	0-2-33
John Richards	Joshua Badger	
ditto	John Richards	5-2-15
John Richards shoemaker	John Richards shoemaker	0-2-36
Richard Rushton	Richard Rushton	0-3-37
John Summers	Mary Eykyn	3-3-16
Thomas Roberts	Thomas Roberts	0-2-27
William Skett	William Skett	0-1-8
Ham Ford		
William Butcher	Miss Fletcher	5-1-22

Appendix 1

		ARP
Allscott		
Elizabeth Andrews	Thomas Whitmore	6-1-0
John Jenkins	John Jenkins	-2-39
Samuel George		1-10-0
John Hines	William Baker	-3-
John Jenkins	Richard Slater	174-2-4
Richard Slater	Richard Slater	73-0-28
Barnsley		
John Bell	William Beech	39-3-19
Thomas Baxter	Miss Bradbourn	1-3-
Widow Paine	William Guest	37-2-34
Bentley		
Richard Bowdler	Richard Bowdler	6-0-22
Bradney		
Thomas Bowen	William May of	154-0-34
Margaret Congreave	Compton	33-2-23
Bromley		
Samuel Bowdler	ditto	101-3-7
Isaac Clarke	John Parker	7—
Joseph Corbett	T. Whitmore Esq	115-3-17
Joseph Corbett	ditto	2-1-12
Coalbrook Dale Co.	Joseph Corbett	3-0-7
Richard Elcock	William Baker	65-1-3
ditto	ditto	60-0-28
John Hemming	John Jenkins	1-0-0
John Jones	John Jones	-2-0
Burcott		
Richard Allerton	Miss Bradburne	60-1-12
John Bache	John Bache	83-0-19
Richard	Thomas Elcock	20-3-2
William Hardwick	William Hardwick	39-3-13
Edward Pratt	Richard Boycott Esq	21-2-28
Robert Sadler	Robert Sadler	9-2-6
Samuel Walker	William Hardwick	1-2-21
Catstree		
Charles Bowen	Alan Pollock Esq	149-0-11
Benjamin Nicholls	T. Whitmore Esq	113-1-33
Chesterton		
Thomas Bache	Thomas Bache	213-0-38
Miss Bradbourn	Miss Bradbourn	15-2-11

Appendix 1

	Brought over	ARP
Chesterton		
Thomas Bache	Thomas Bache	213-0-38
Miss Bradbourn	Miss Bradbourn	15-2-11
Thomas Owen	John Owen	- - -
John Skett	John Skett	76-1-37
Elizabeth Skett		- - -
Thomas Grainer	Miss Bradbourne	207-0-6
John Trumper		
Nathaniel Nicholls	Thomas Bache	- - -
Francis Wiggin		-
Cranmere		
John Butcher	W.J. Davenport	3-1-0
Nathaniel Nicholls	W.J. Davenport	221-0-13
Cranmere Heath		
John Morris	T. Whitmore Esq	6-0-28
Ewdness		
Thomas Barnfield	T. Whitmore Esq	1303-1-32
Folley		
William Spencer	William Spencer	69-1-4
Hallon		
John Barney	Timothy Barney	-
Davenport Esq	Davenport Esq	1137-2-20
John Powell	Timothy Barney	-
Jon Tongue	Davenport Esq	237-1-34
Mrs Williams	Mrs Williams	1-1-5
Hilton		
Richard Allerton	Mrs Congreave	14-2-7
Thomas Rushton	William Bennett	- - -
George Whitby	ditto	-
John Billingsley	Ann Granger &	-
Ann Baylis	Mary Billingsley	-
John Bradney	John Bradney	- - 30
Isaac Clarke	Isaac Clarke	- 3-3-7
Davies James		
Miss Fletcher	Isaac Clarke	-1-30
Ann Edward	Edward Hill	12-2-20
James Meredith	James Meredith	1-2-10
James Meredith	James Meredith	-1-
John Meredith	John Meredith	-1-
John Poyner	Mary Congreve	103-2-23
T. Sond Pool	T. Sond Pool	-2-
Thos Smith Esq	T. Smith Esq	133-0-2
William Spencer	T. Smith Esq	226-2-8
William Stringer	John Bradney	42-3-2
William Stringer	John Bradney	38-1-16
Hoccom		
Widow Hoccom	Mrs Hoccom	14.2.0
Edward Pratt	Miss Bradbourne	189-3-36
Edward Pratt	Edward Pratt	1-3-4
Reynolds	C.F. Taylor Esq	1-3-8
John Sing	John Sing	260-0-39

Appendix 1

		ARP
Hopes		
Benjamin Thomason	T. Whitmore Esq	53-3-8
Kingslow		
Thomas Bache	J. Bache	10-1-1
Thomas Devey	J. Devey	236-2-3
ditto	T. Whitmore Esq	4-2-4
Newton		
George Bennet }	ditto	
Thomas Timpson }	ditto	-2-33
William Dukes	ditto	-1-7
Thomas Morris }	ditto	1-0-0
William Carter }	ditto	
Thomas Rowley	ditto	-1-28
William Williamson	ditto	205-1-20
ditto	ditto	-3-36
Oldington		
William Baker	ditto	231-0-9
Watkin Williams	Edward Ridley	2-0-28
T. Whitmore Esq	T. Whitmore Esq	6-1-34
Rindleford		
Thomas Billingsley	T. Billingsley	- - -
John Stedman	Wm. Hardwick	- 42-1-39
Nathaniel Rhodes	J. whitmore esq	- 5-1-35
William Smethyman	Wm. Smethyman	- - -
Roughton		
John Bell	James Marshall	77-1-21
ditto	John Bell	109-3-1
John Bell	William Stokes	3-2-0
ditto	Thomas Elcock	29-1-17
John Bache	R. Boycott Esq	27-3-25
Edward Pratt	William Stokes	126-3-25
ditto	Lord Shrewsbury	22-0-29
William Stokes	James Marshall	12-0-18
Richard Thomason	William Stokes	2-2-3
Rowley		
Elizabeth Doleman	William Davenport	0-3-11
Thomas Sond Pool	ditto	311-0-34
Sond Farm		
Thomas Sond Pool	Thomas Sond Pool	46-1-12
Stanlow		39-3-0
Thomas Bache	T. Bache	should be interested in
John Bradshaw	ditto	Kingslow
Thomas Devey	Sir R. Pigot	14-0-32
William Stokes	ditto	161-0-8
Stableford		25-0-11
Samuel Dixon	Joshua Scott	
John Jasper	Sir John Jasper	82-3-3
ditto houses etc	ditto	219-3-3
Sir John Jasper	Sir John Jasper	-

Appendix 1

		ARP
Ellis Longden	Mary Taylor	-
Widow Taylor	Widow Taylor	86-2-15
a meadow occupied by	Richard Pool	
Sarah Tedstill	Sarah Tedstill	
a meadow occupied by	William Baker	
Swancott		
John Bache	R. Boycott	73-3-29
Wheel		
Richard Allerton	Mary Congreve	72-0-22
Mary Bromwich	Mary Bromwich	
William Corfield	John Nicholas	
Elizabeth Hill	Elizabeth Hill	
John Nicholas	Alan Pollock Esq	
William Taylor	William Taylor	
Winscot		
William Slater	Thomas Whitmore	150-3-27
ditto	Lord Shrewsbury	9-3-34
Thomas Whitmore Esq	T. Whitmore	2-0-24
Worfield		
Richard Allerton	W. J. Davenport	8-2-31
John Bache	T. Whitmore Esq	7-1-28
Thomas Bache	W. J. Davenport	15-2-2
Timothy Barney	T. Whitmore Esq	1-1-16
Rev. H. Bromwich	Rev H. Bromwich	2-3-9
Elizabeth Clewitt	W. J. Davenport	
William Cooksey	ditto	
John Groom	ditto	
Thomas Haines	ditto	
William Loy	Elizabeth Shaw	
John Nicholas	… Nicholls	1-0-20
William Nicholls	W.J. Davenport	
Luke Nicholls	ditto	
John ?Baker	T. Whitmore	0-1-16
Thomas ?Pritchard	W.J. Davenport	-
Thomas ?Powell	ditto	0-3-24
Thomas Piper	ditto	
John Richards	ditto	
Thomas Richards	ditto	
John Rogers	ditto	
Thomas Rowley	ditto	
Mary Shaw	ditto	
Elizabeth Shaw	Elizabeth Shaw	
William Smith	W.J. Davenport	14-0-38
William Smith	T. Whitmore Esq	5-0-21
Charles Stokes	W.J. Davenport	
George Wheeler	ditto	
Charles Whitehill Esq	ditto	
William Wyer	William Slater	

Appendix 1

Wyken		**ARP**
Richard Merton	T. Smith Esq	31-1-4
John Bache	John Bache	111-0-12
Thomas Billingsley	John Bache	2-1-21
Charles Bowen	A. Pollock Esq	47-2-2

Hilton looking towards the Hilton Bridge with the Black Lion Public House on the right. Date: before the road was straightened in the 1930s.

Appendix 2 - Maps

a. The Lost Township of Ewyke

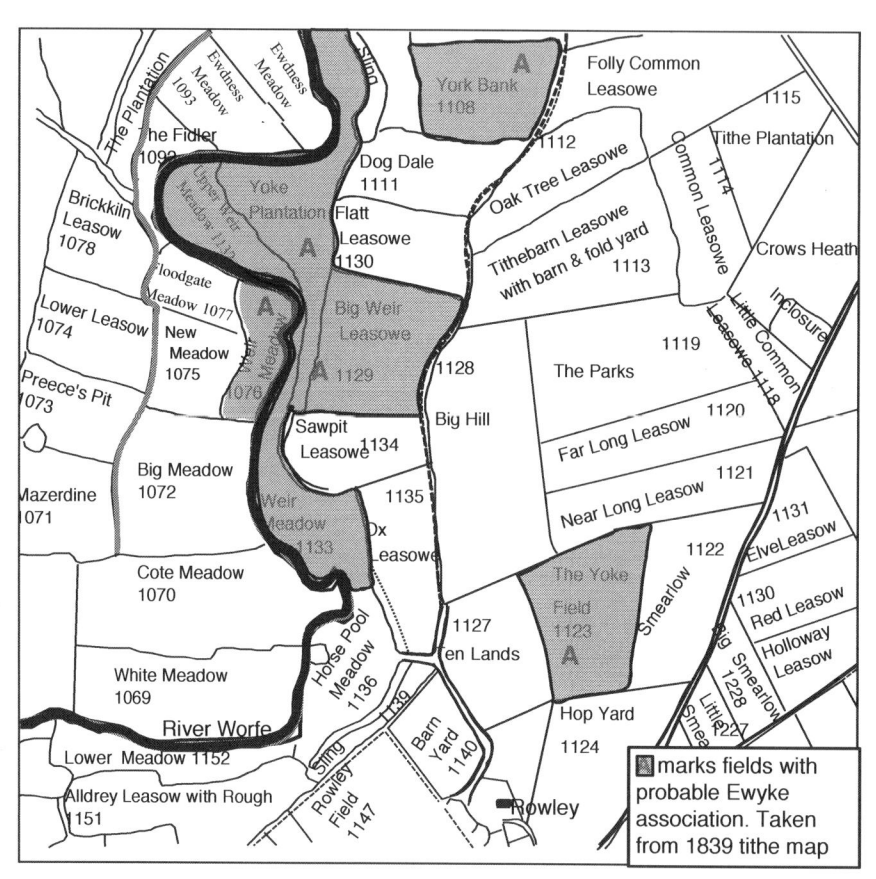

Scale: 6 inches to 1 mile

We know from the manor court rolls that Ewyke had a weir hence the inclusion of fields with a weir connection. Dogdale was also mentioned in association with the township and the footpath running alongside was an ancient track, hitherto much more important than the footpath it is today.

Appendix 2 - Maps

b. The Forest of Morfe 1582
Scale aproximately 3 inches to 1 mile
The villages shown above had common rights in the Forest (National Archives MPB/1/17/1)

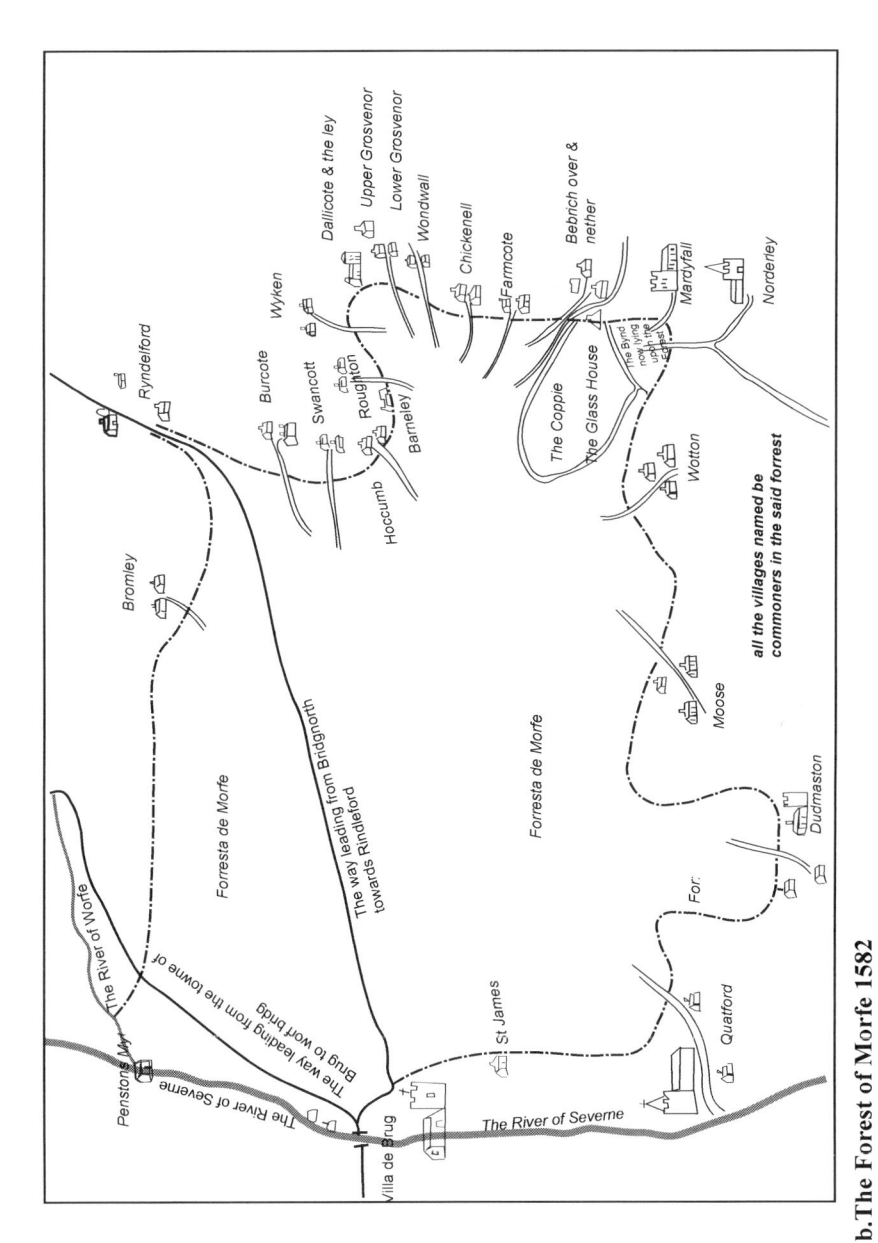

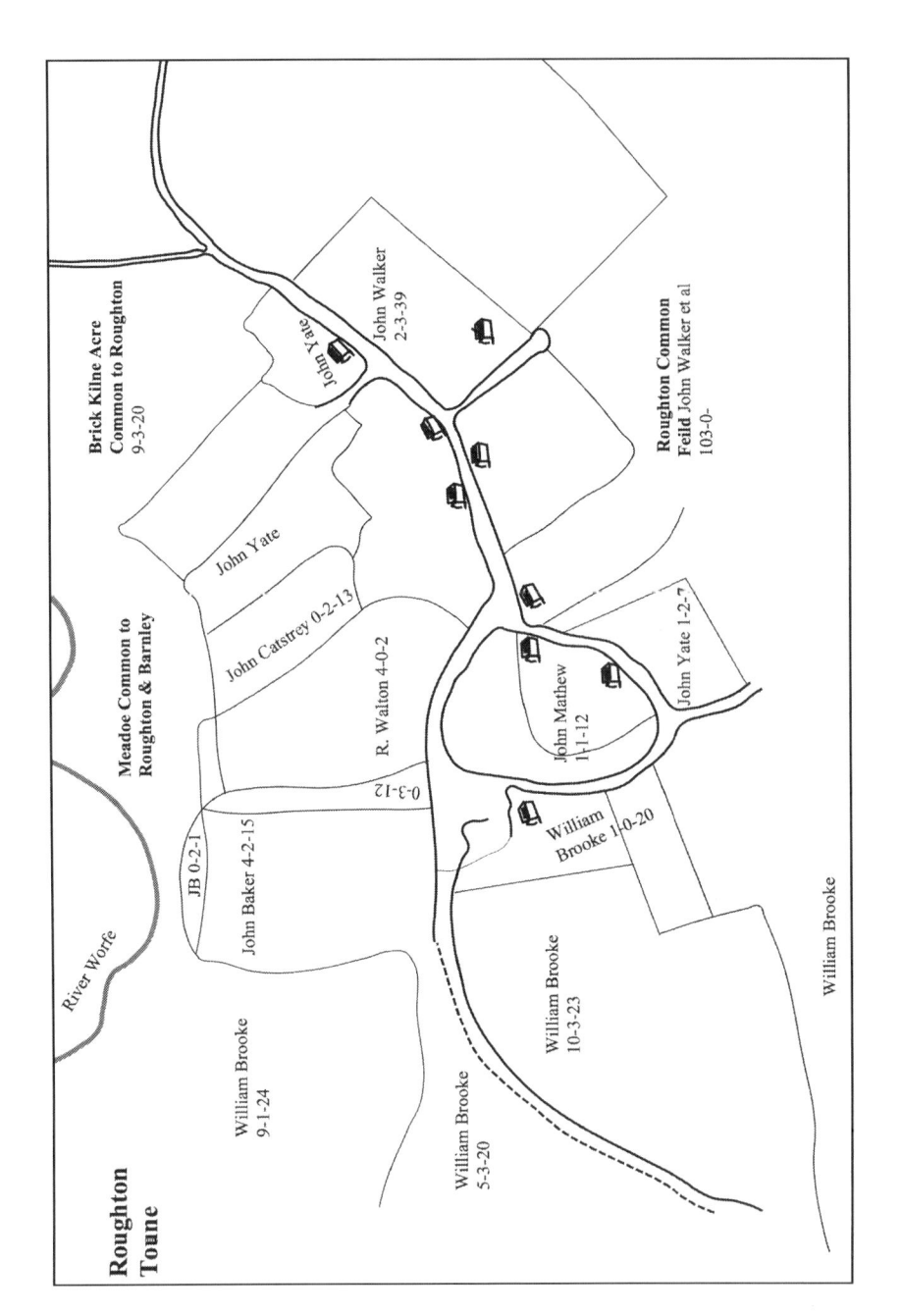

Appendix 2 - Maps

Roughton Toune

River Worfe

William Brooke 9-1-24

William Brooke 5-3-20

JB 0-2-1

John Baker 4-2-15

Meadoe Common to Roughton & Barnley

John Catstrey 0-2-13

John Yate

R. Walton 4-0-2

0-3-12

William Brooke 10-3-23

William Brooke

Brick Kilne Acre Common to Roughton 9-3-20

John Yate

John Walker 2-3-39

John Mathew 1-1-12

John Yate 1-2-7

William Brooke 1-0-20

Roughton Common Feild John Walker et al 103-0-

c. Roughton 1613

Map drawn from the Forest of Morfe Map by Samuel Parsons 1613. 4296/1 (Shropshire Archives)
Scale approximately 1 inch to 100 yards

Appendix 2 - Maps

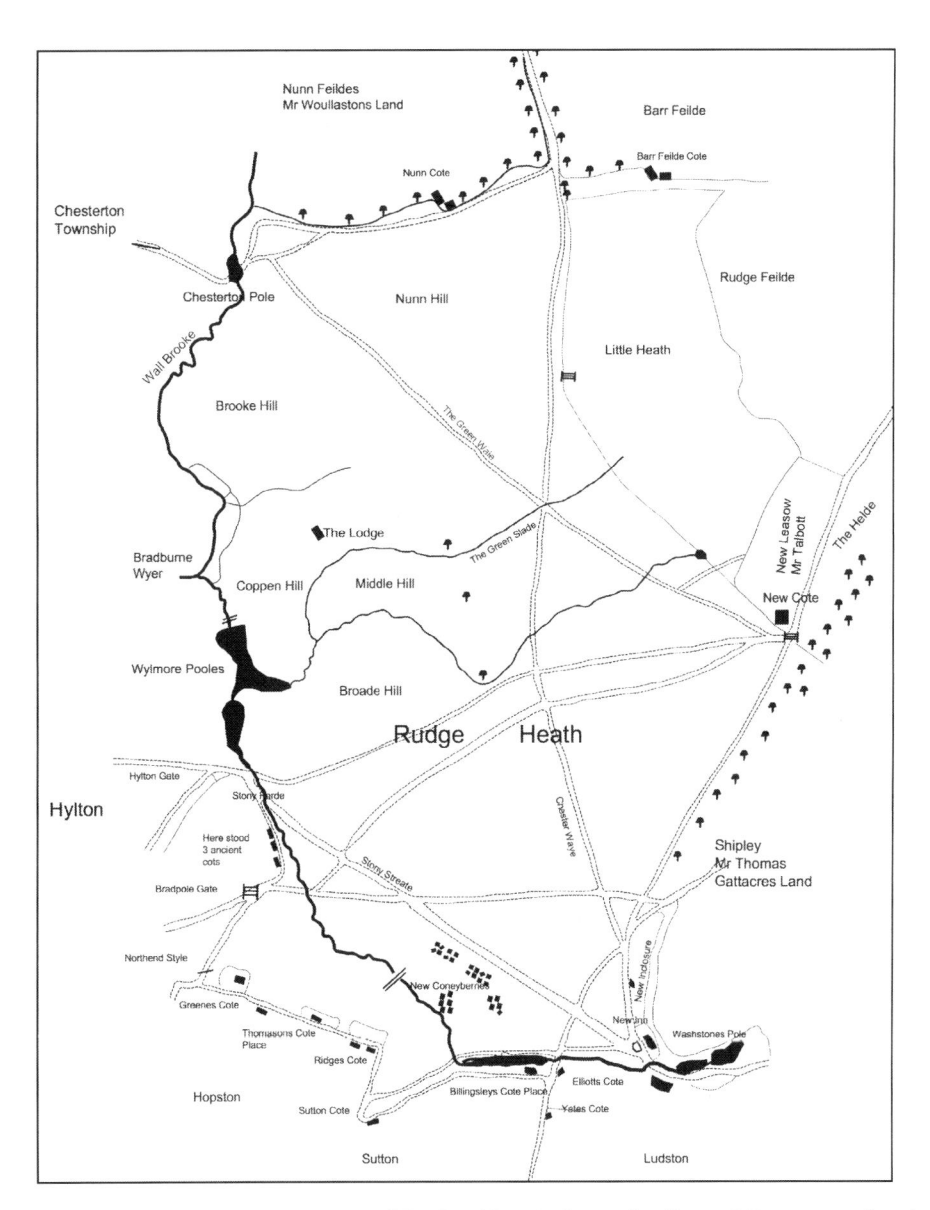

d. Early Seventeenth Century Map of Rudge Heath drawn by Samuel Parsons and endorsed in 1635 by John Denham (5586/13/4 Shropshire Archives). Scale approximately 4 inches to 1 mile

Appendix 2 - Maps

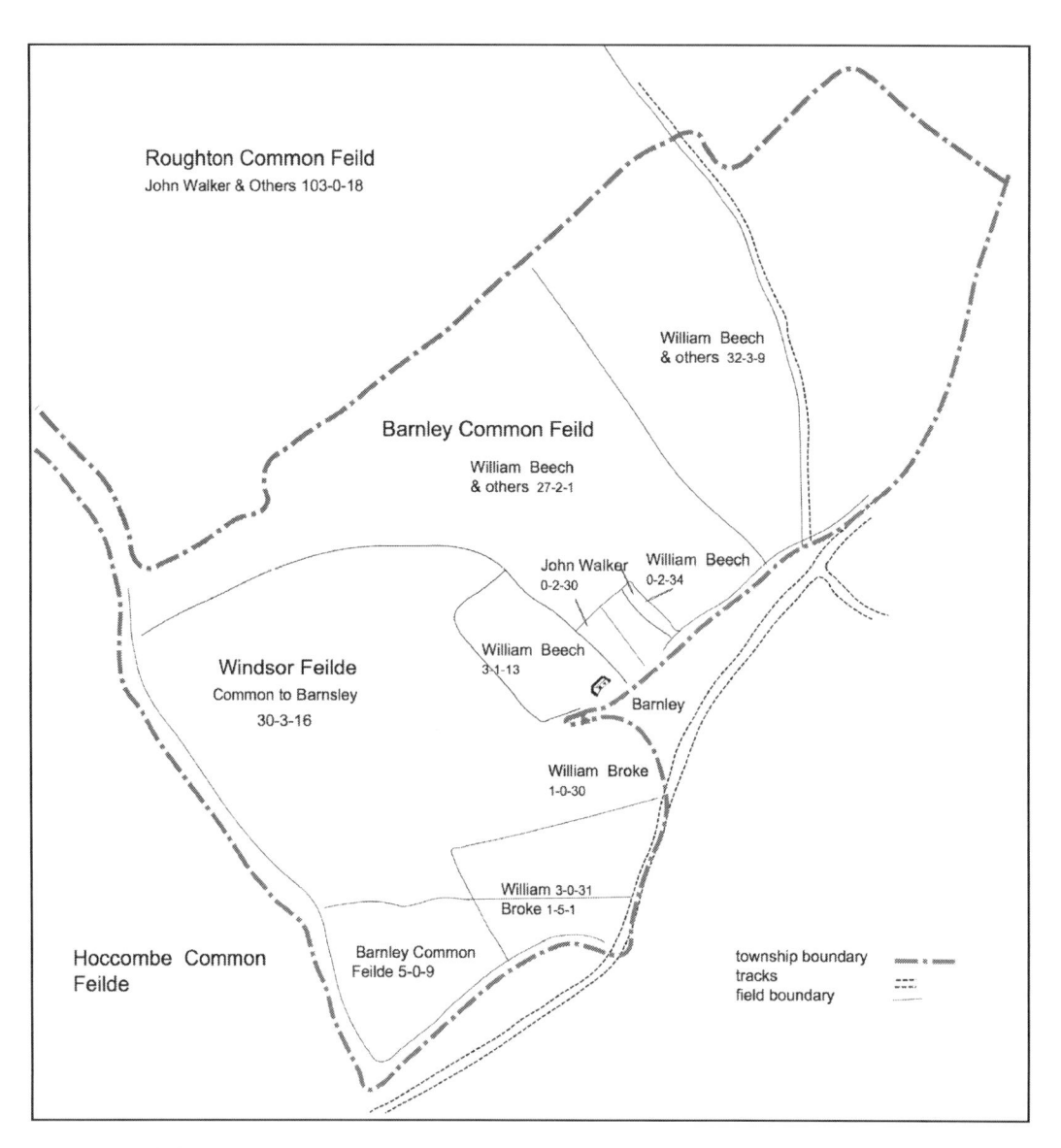

e. Barnley 1613 — Map drawn from the Forest of Morfe Map by Samuel Parsons 1613. 4296/1 (Shropshire Archives). Scale approximately 6 inches to 1 mile

Map labels:
- Roughton Common Feild — John Walker & Others 103-0-18
- William Beech & others 32-3-9
- Barnley Common Feild — William Beech & others 27-2-1
- John Walker 0-2-30
- William Beech 0-2-34
- William Beech 3-1-13
- Barnley
- Windsor Feilde — Common to Barnsley 30-3-16
- William Broke 1-0-30
- William 3-0-31
- Broke 1-5-1
- Hoccombe Common Feilde
- Barnley Common Feilde 5-0-9

Legend:
- township boundary
- tracks
- field boundary

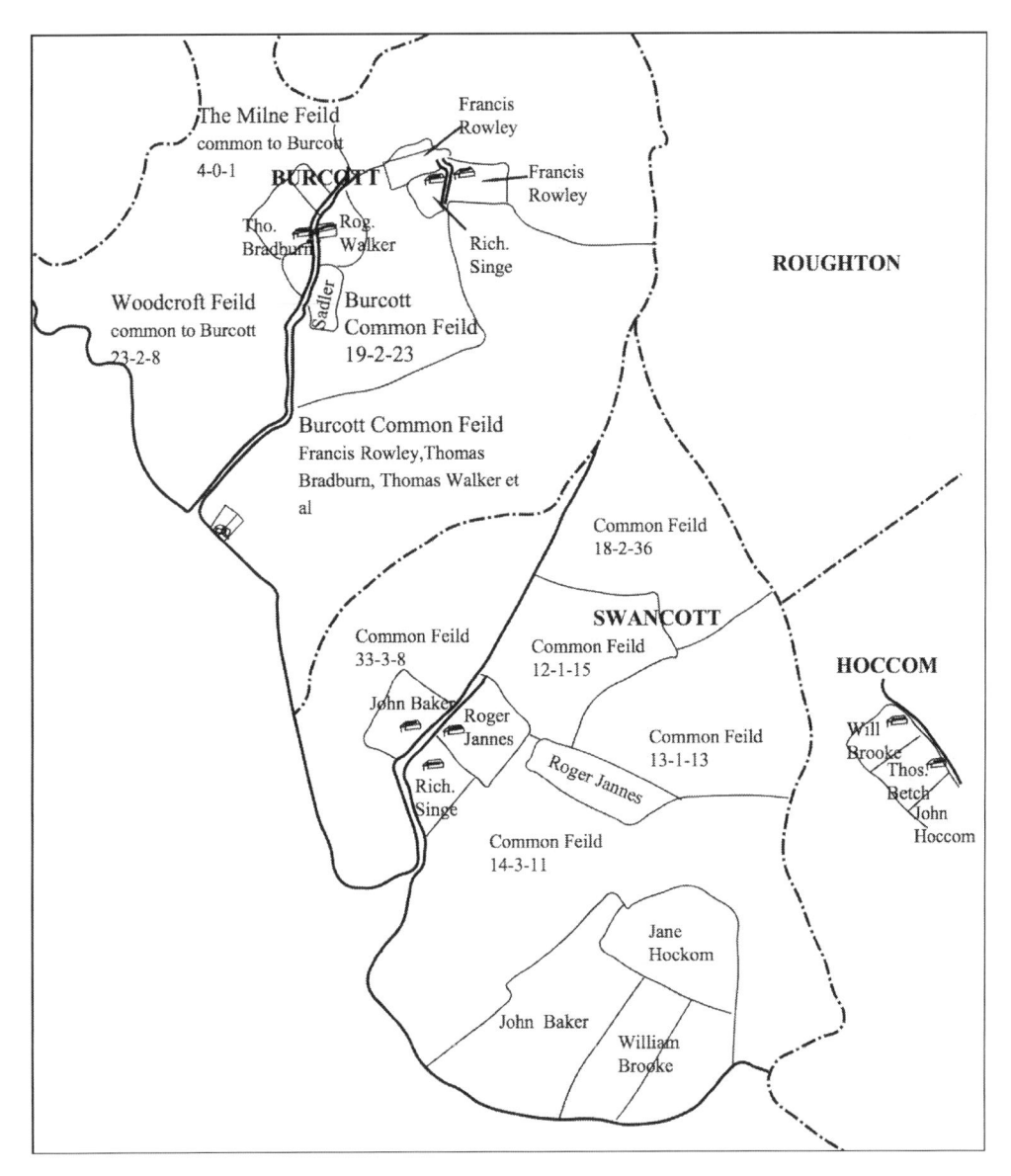

Appendix 2 - Maps

f. Burcott, Swancott & Hoccom 1613

Map drawn from the Forest of Morfe Map by Samuel Parsons 1613. 4296/1 (Shropshire Archives) Scale approximately 6 inches to 1 mile

Appendix 2 - Maps

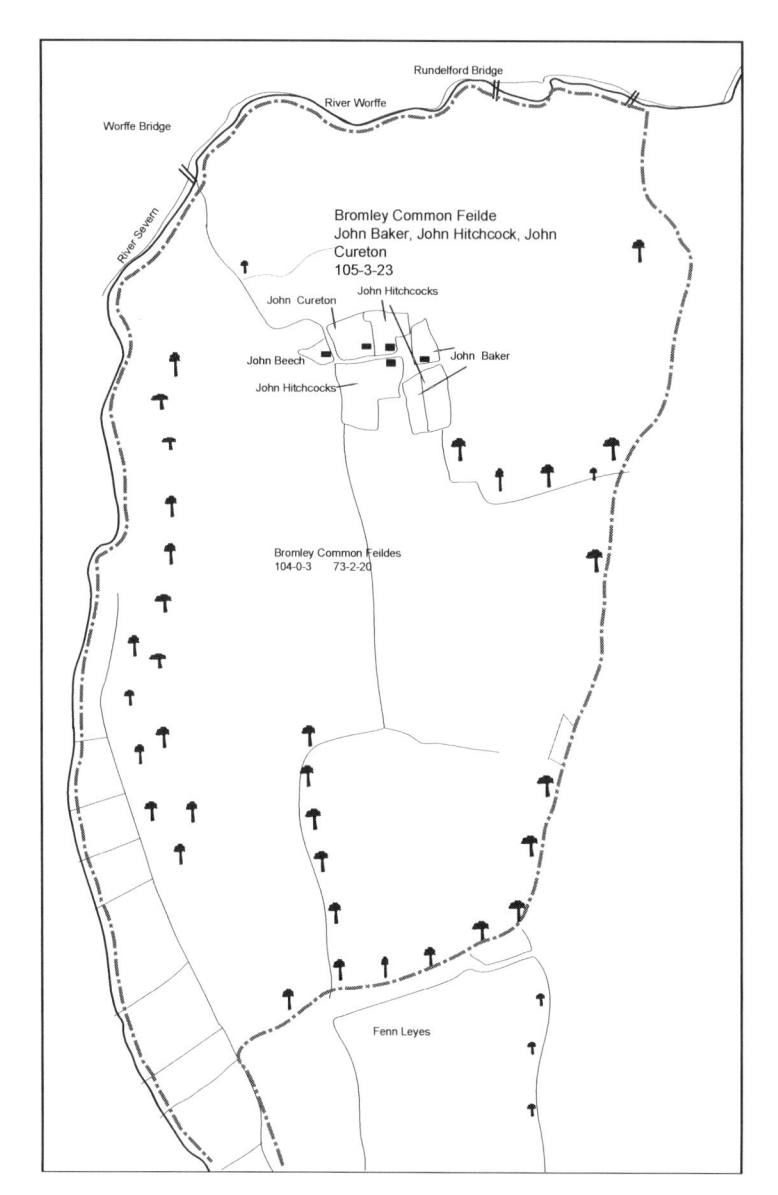

g. Bromley 1613   Map drawn from the Forest of Morfe Map by Samuel Parsons 1613. 4296/1 (Shropshire Archives). Scale approximately 4.5 inches to 1 mile

Appendix 2 - Maps

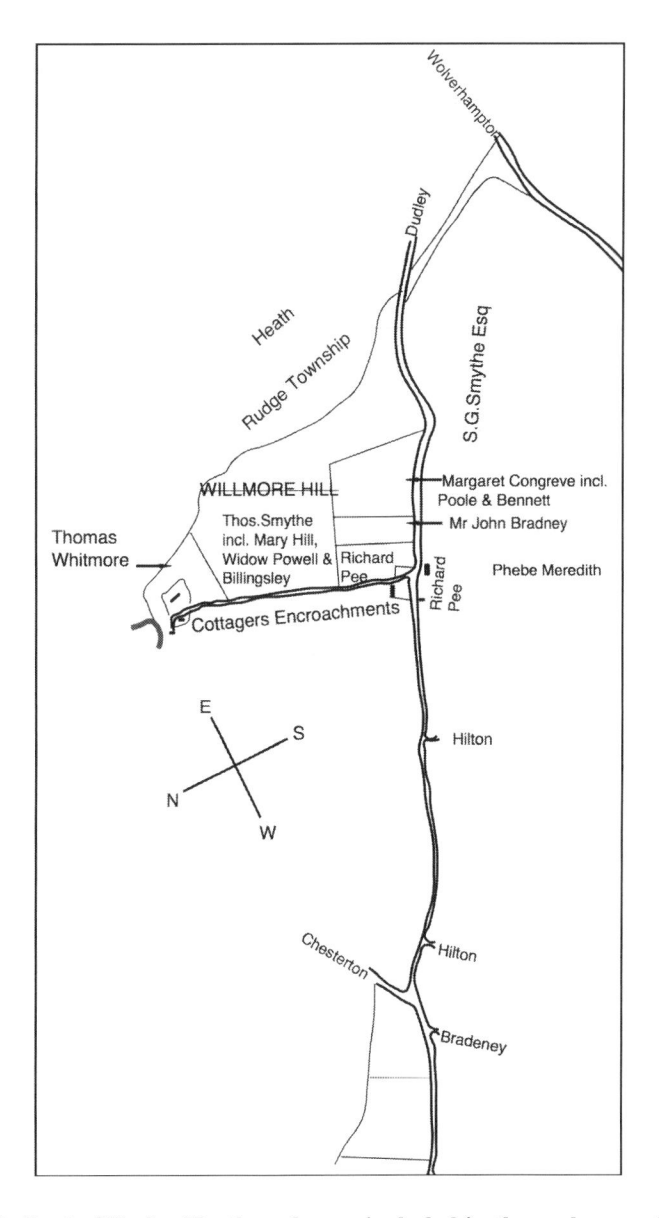

h. Part of Rudge Heath enclosure included in the enclosure of Crows Heath. Cottagers encroachments are at Littlegain. P314/T/1/1 (Shropshire Archives) Scale: aproximately 4.5 inches to 1 mile

Appendix 2 - Maps

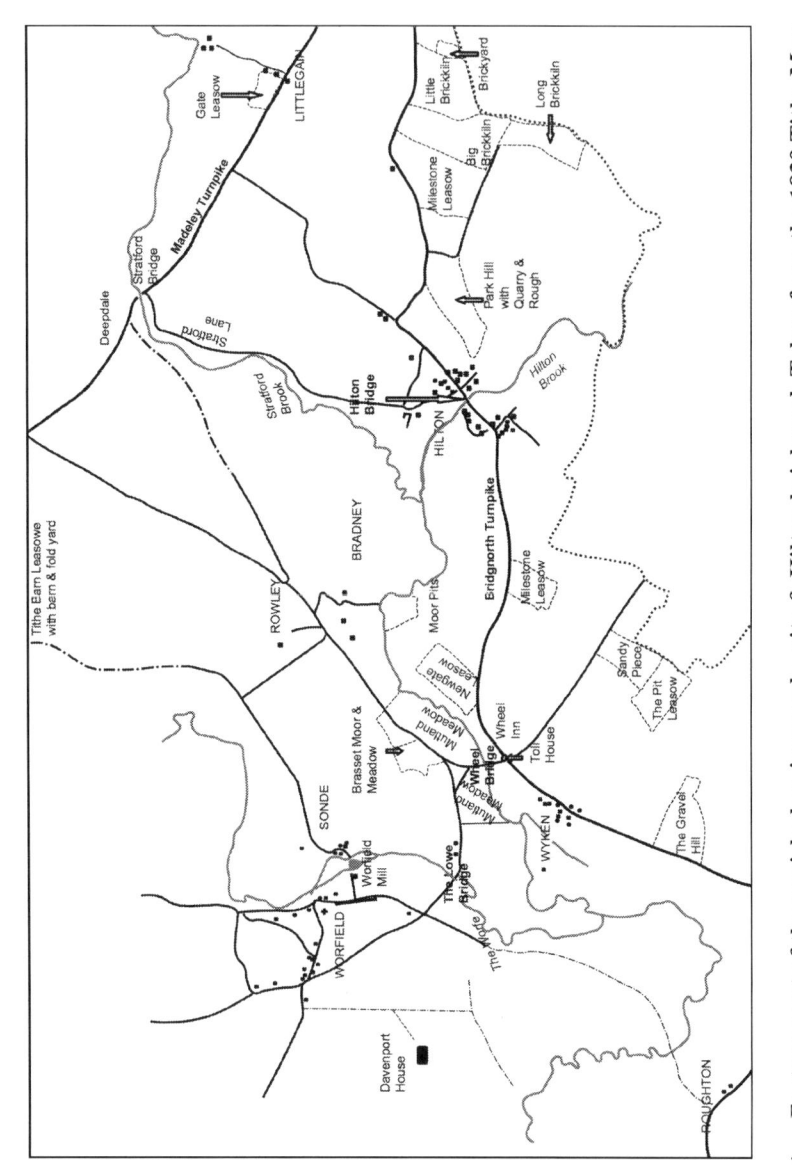

i. **Eastern part of the parish showing roads, pits & Hilton brickyard. Taken from the 1839 Tithe Map**
Scale approximately 2 inches to 1 mile

Appendix 2 - Maps

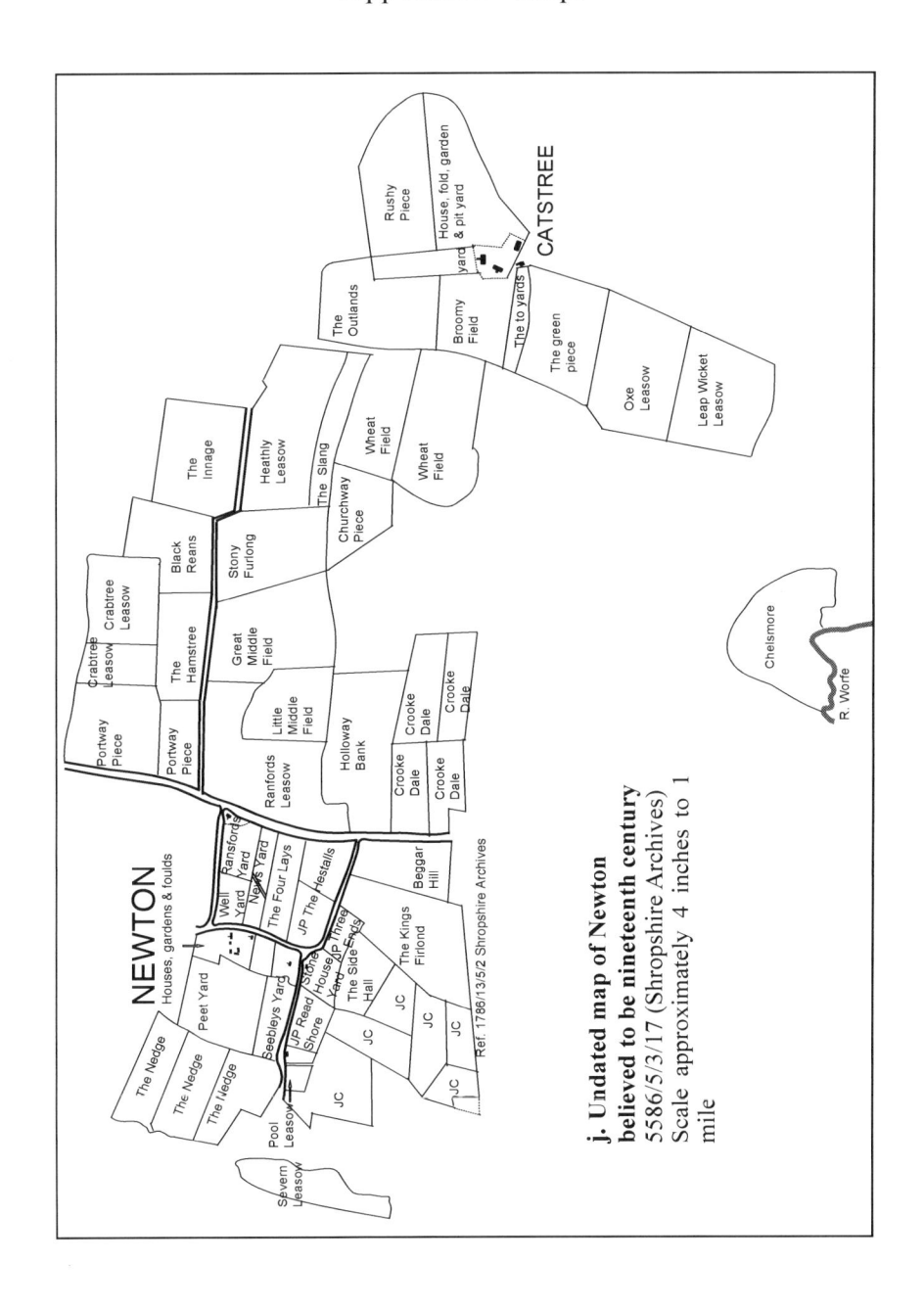

j. Undated map of Newton believed to be nineteenth century 5586/5/3/17 (Shropshire Archives) Scale approximately 4 inches to 1 mile

Index

Ackleton 18,82,92,108,144,147,148,159,160,161,170,173 179
Ackleton Malthouse 53,170,173,180
Acton Round 37
Adams, Bob 154,158
Adams, Richard 103
Adlaston 31
Advowson 24,43,80,88
Aelfgar, Earl 18
Aethelflaed 12,31
Agister 30
Agricultural revolution 79,80,81,102
Albrighton 74,75,159
Alden, Thomas 51
Allenbroke 167
Allscott 14,26,81,84,86,88,95,97,100,107,101,115,151
Allscott Churchyard Field 26
Allscott Farm 151
Allscott Pit 115
Almshouse 25,42
Allscroft Harris 98,99
Amnestre 88
Alvescote 21
Alvescote, Robert of 21
Alveley 18,148
Anglo Saxon Chronicles 11
Anson, Mary 111
Apley 53,86,87,88,97,104,108,130,136,144,147,171
Apprentices 111,123
Archery 54
Armour 56
ARP 162
Ashford Carbonel 37
Askew, William 131

Assarting 22,31
Asterhull 21,105,133
Astley Abbotts 53,92,119,181
Aston Moors 99
Aston, Thomas 47
Athelstan 31
Athelardstone 31
Auden, Elizabeth 111
Bach/Bache, John 59,92,93,96
Bache, Thomas 84,85,93,94,96,133
Badger 18,57,58,117,144,170,179
Badger Mill 43,104,179
Badger Pool 108,179
Badlesmere, Bartholomew de 44
Baker, Jeremiah 107
Baker, John 95
Baker, John of Bromley 41
Baker, Joseph 111
Baker, Richard 109
Baker, Roger 41
Baker's Cottage 46,177
Bakewell, Robert 80
Bamfylde Moore Carew 112
Barbor, John 73
Barker 51,62,63,178
Barker, of Calverhall 44
Barker, of Hallon 44,51
Barker, Alice 44,62,63
Barker, Edward 96
Barker, George 50,62
Barker, John of Aston 50
Barker, Maria 93
Barker, Richard 47,51
Barker, Thomas 50
Barker, William 62,72,79,93
Barker's Land 62,73,98
Barkley, Thomas 41

Index

Barndeley 21
Barney, John 79,94,96
Barney, Joseph 96
Barney, Richard 75
Barney, Theophilus 122,136,137
Barnfield, Thomas 118
Barnsley 82,198
Barnsley Green 82,95
Barrett 98
Barret, Frances 122
Barrett, George 111
Barrett, Humphrey 50,51
Barrett, John 67
Barrett, Margaret 74
Barrett, Mary 53,97
Barrett, Nathaniel 73
Barret, Robert 57,81,82,122
Barret, Thomas 51,97
Barry, Roger 76
Baseley, Isabel 141
Batch, The 134,137,177
Beauchamp, Elizabeth 38
Beauchamp, William 21,34,38
Beddowes, Widow 81,82
Beech, John 56,73
Beech, Thomas 73
Bees 41
Beetlestone, Widow 111
Beggar Hill 97
Beggars 65,76
Bell, Thomas 82,95
Bell, William 95
Belleme, Robert de 18,38
Bellet, George 54
Bennit, Widow 109
Bentley 20
Bergavenny, Henry 38,88,97
Bergavenny, John, Lord 38

Bergavenny, Katherine 97
Berkeley, Thomas 56,175,180
Best, John 57
Betterton, Thomas 48
Bienvillers au Bois 145
Billingsley 98
Billingsley, John 111
Billingsley, Margaret 41
Billingsley, Mary 96
Billingsley, Richard 93,94,96
Billingsley, Thomas 96
Billingsley, William 57
Bind, The 64
Bishop, Ernie 168
Bishop, T. 150
Bishop, Walter 142,143
Bishton, Ann 109
Bishton Dole 98
Bishton, Julian 111
Bishton, Thomas 111
Bitterley 37
Black Death 21
Blacksmith 27,28,29,139,141,156,157
Blakeman, John 79
Blakemon, Richard 42
Blandings Castle 144
Boroughcote 21
Blount, Thomas le 19,38
Blundell, Alfred 129
Blunt, Widow 111
Boer War 139,142,143
Bolton, Guy 144
Bomford, T. H. R. 150
Booth, Widow 111
Botley family 156,173
Boucher, A. E. 150
Boundaries 20,21
Bowen, Edward Humphrey 148

205

Index

Bowen, John 148
Bowen, William 56
Bowman, John 76
Boycott 81,114
Boycott, Thomas 107
Bradburn, Mr 96
Bradburne, James 96
Bradburne, John 93,94
Bradburn, Mary 9
Bradburne, Thomas 56
Bradeney/Bradney 20,34,51,96
Bradley, General 158
Bradney, Ann 68
Bradney Farm 77
Bradney, John 81
Bradney, Jone 68
Bradney, Joseph, 81
Bradney, Richard 51,73,82
Bradney/ Bradeney, Stephen 73
Bradney, Thomas 56
Bradney, William 51,68
Bradney Lane 96
Brass Band, Worfield 152
Breeze, Chippine 159,161
Brettell Lane 153
Brewing 41
Brickyards 90
Bridge Meadow 105
Bridgen, William 88,97
Bridgnorth 29,30,53,54,55,56,57,80,84,87
Bridgnorth Castle 53,54
Bridgnorth Races 131
Bridgnorth Station 143,147
Brierley 66
Brierley Charity 122
Brimstree 11
Bristol 61
Broad Bridge 50,82,96,99,117,118

Broadbent, C.F. 122,129
Broadhurst, Captain 58
Broadhurst, Elizabeth 92
Broadhurst, Griffith 92
Broadhurst, Thomas 92
Brockton Court 108
Brodburne, John 111
Bromley 21,26,81,8295,176,177,200
Bromley, Charles 62,63,70
Bromley, E. 48,64,69,74
Bromley, F. 62,64,69,70,71,72
Bromley, G. 44,45,62,63,74,75
Bromley Hill 30
Bromley, Jane 44,45,62,63,64,69,70,71,72,73
Bromley, Joyce 62,69
Bromley, Robert of 31
Bromley, Thomas 44,62,64,74
Bromley Meadow 98
Bromwich. Rev Henry 10,81,92
Bronze Age 4
Broke, Agnes atte 21
Brooke, Mr 67
Brooke, John 56
Brooke, Thomas 58
Brooke, William 48,73
Brown, James 51
Brown, John 51
Brown, W. J. 150
Buck, Bill 168
Bucknall, Roger 42
Buildwas Abbey 24
Bullerges Yard 98
Bulocke, Amy 42
Bulocke, William 42
Burcote/Burcot/Burcott 4,16,24,81, 112,178,199
Burcote Lane 112
Burcote Mill 107,178

206

Index

Burford 37
Burrows, Jack 170
Burton Abbey 24
Burton, Jane 111
Bury Lands/Buryland 12,51
Butcher, John 96
Butcher, William 84
Cacti 168
Caldecote, John 48
Caldecote, Richard 30
Calo, Richard 50
Calverhall 44
Calverhall, William de 44
Camp Davenport 158
Candles 41,42
Cardington 76
Carne, James 166
Carpet Factory, Bridgnorth 107
Carrots 81
Cartwright, Mary 111
Castell, Henry 51
Castle Hill 13
Catstree/Catstrey 11,18,21,88,97,99
Catstree/Catstrey, Roger 42,50,51
Cave Holloway 118,119
Caves 15
Chamberlaine's Yard 51
Chamberleyne, William 31
Chantry 41,42,43,121,122
Chantry Lands 50,51
Chapple, P. H. 150
Chardin, Daniel 88
Chardin, Mary Louise 88
Charter 19,34
Chemehill 51
Chennai 88
Chester, Annie 148
Chests 28,29,37

Chesterton 5,6,7,8,20,81,93,96,174
Chesterton Chapel/Church 26,37,43,174
Chesterton Green 96
Chesterton Mill 103
Chesterton Mill Farm 103
Chesterton, Roger of 21
Chesterton Street 96
Child, Ann 111
China Bank 179
Chirle/Churle 36,105
Chirleford/Churleford 36,105,133
Christison 168
Christy, F. 150
Chudleton, Thomas 43
Church Avenue 158
Church, Restoration of 128,129
Churchill 168
Church Stretton 19
Chyknell 141
Civil War 52,53,54,55,56,57,58,59,60,61,78
Clare, John 101
Clark, William 55
Clarke, E. C. 150
Clarke's Bakery 170
Claverley 18,55,66,76,84,114,148
Clemson, Thomas 80
Clewett, Widow 111
Cliffe, Thomas 48
Clinton, William de 19,38
Cloth Seal 68
Clout, Thomas 93
Cluet, John 96
Cockram, John 111
Colet, Thomas 21
Colley, John 110
Colley, Mr 92
Colley, Richard 79,93
Collis, John 53

Index

Colyns, John 47
Colynson 44
Common 22,82ff
Common rights 22,29,82
Compton 152
Compton Mill 80
Concealed objects 91
Condover 19,37
Constables 54,55,56,57,58,59,60,75,76
Cooke, H. 150
Corbett, F. H. 145,150,175
Corbett, Helen 145,148
Corbett, Sibell 144ff,179
Corbett, Richard Cecil 143
Corbett, Susan Horatio 143
Corbrigge, Andrew de 31
Corn Laws 108
Corn Mill 103,104,105,106,107
Cornes, William 148
Cornovii 5
Corvehill, William 41
Cotton, George 75
Cotton, Mary 74
Cound 2,37
Court house 24,122
Coventry 67
Cowel, Richard 103
Cox, William 95
Cranage 26
Cranmere 90,91,98,130,149
Cranmere Brickyard 117
Cranmere Heath 84
Cranmore Field 82
Cressett, Captain 58
Cricket Club 152,168
Crime 22,29,66,75,76,141
Crompe, Captain 58
Crompe, William 47

Cromwell, Oliver 52,61,78
Crooe, Captain 58
Crotal Bell 91
Crowe 168
Crowmore Heath 96
Crows Heath 84,85,201
Crucifixes 130
Cruck House 77
Crudgington, Frances 97
Crudgington, John 97
Crudgington, Thomas 97
Crudgington, Rebecca 80
Cuerton, Richard de 31
Cumberland 76
Cunliffe 147
Cunliffe, Miss 161
Curran, Henry 108
Customs of the Manor 21,22,23,34,35,36
Dalicote 170
Danes 11
Dartmouth, Lord 147
Davenport, Barbara 88
Davenport, Edmund Henry 129,141
Davenport, Edmund Sherrington 84
Davenport, Edward 84
Davenport, Henry 62,80,88,89,97,98
Davenport Camp 158
Davenport House 87,89,90
Davenport, Jane 62,63,69,70,71,72,73
Davenport, Margaret 141,146,147
Davenport, Marguerite 141
Davenport, Mary Lucy 88
Davenport Park 89,158
Davenport, Sharington 88
Davenport, Talbot, Neville, Fawcett 143
Davenport, W. S. 122
Davenport, William 45,62,63,64,69,70,71,72,73,129

Index

Davenport, William Yelverton 84
Davey, Gordon 168
Davies, Harry 156
Davies, William 95
Dawkeyn de Oken 13
Day/Dey, Richard 62,63
Day/Dey, William 44,62,73
Deforestation 29,46,47
Demesne 13,19,21,22,34
Detton, Captain 58
Devey, Thomas 84,96
Diamond Hill 143
Dickens, Charles 101
Disease, Livestock 79
Dog Inn 1,78
Dogdale 99
Dole Sunday 141
Doors, picture 28ff
Doughty 111
Dovecotes 81
Dowman, Mr 146
Dragoons 59
Duckwell, Giles 102
Dudley, Lord 46
Dunkirk, Battle 161,166
Dunstall Park 153
East India Company 88
Echoeshill 115
Education 121,122,123,124,125,126,127
Edwards, Benjamin 111
Edwards, Richard 96
Eggington 98
Egyptians 65,75
Eighth Army 167
Eileshall 37
El Alamein 167
Elcock, Elizabeth 130
Elcock, S. T. 150

Elcock, W. 150
Elcock, William 48
Eldrington, Mary 97
Eldrington, Robert 97
Ellesmere, Lord Thomas 72
Elms, The 149
Ely, William 96
Emigration 108
Enclosures 5,64,78,79,90,95,96
Enclosures, Parliamentary 82,83,84,85
Encroachments 82,95,96
Endowments 42,43
Ethelflaed 12
Eudenas 21
Eudenas, Richard of 21
Eudenas, Roger of 21
Evacuees 161
Evans, Miss 161
Evans, Mrs 161
Evans, William 80
Evers, M. E. 123
Ewdness 11,18,52,56,88,90,146,180,181
Ewyke/Ewke 11,18,21,51,98,99,194
Ewyke/Ewke Lane 82,96
Ewyke/Ewke Mill 98,102
Ewyke/Ewke Wear 99
Ewyke, Thomas of 21
Extent of Manor 33
Eykyn, Mrs 147
Eykyn, Richard 129
Factory, The 107,110,178
Farhills Gate 99
Farmer, William 80,108,109
Farming 23,80,81,82,83,137
Fee, Mrs 161
Felt 97
Felton, Elizabeth 42
Felton, John 65,76

Index

Felton, Mary 109
Felton, Richard 42
Felton, Sarah 111
Fenn Gate 109,176
Fenn Lane 82,95
Fennhill 31
Ferrets 31
Ferry 118,180
Fincher 158
Fincher, William 142
Fire 76
First Aid 147
First World War 147,148,149,150,163
Fisher, John 38
Fishing 23,81
Fitz Williams, Captain 108
Flax 23,79,86
Flax oven 82,95
Flower show 152
Fleming, Isabel 48
Fletcher 98
Flint 4,5
Floods 117,118
Folley/Folly, The 109
Food Riots 80
Football 146,152
Fort St George 88
Foster, Mary 9
Foster, W. H. 147
Fox Inn 131
Foxcroft, Samuel 38
Foxall, John 73
Foxall, William 51
Fowkes, John 69,73
Fowler, Hannah 111
Fowler, Sarah 111
Freeman 75
Freewoman, Alice 66

Frichart, Edward 58
Friendly Societies 152
Frodgesley, John 66
Fryer 149
Fulling mill 80,102,103
Garbett, Thomas 121
Gardiner, W. 150
Gaskell, Mrs 101
Gatacre Hill 114
Gatacre, Humphrey 30
Gatacre, Robert 30
Gate Leasow 114
Geddes, Jane 27,28
Gelling, Margaret 11
George 48
Gerbod, William 30
Gerrard, Katherine 76
Gerrard, Richard 76
Gibbons, Mr 131
Gifford, General 168
Gifford, Humphrey 69
Gill, G. 150
Gipsies 112
Gittos, Widow 109
Glover, Thomas 50
Godiva, Lady 14,23
Gold, John 51
Good, Henry 130
Gort, Lord 166
Gotley, Miss 123
Gould, John 73,102
Gould, Simon 102
Grammar School 1ff,124ff,142, 143,175
Grange 26
Grange, Hilton 26
Granger/Grainger, John 73,96
Grant, Eleanor 76
Gravel Pits 82,114ff

210

Index

Gravenor, William 79
Great Dole 98
Great Western Railway 153
Green, Agnes 51
Green, G. 37
Green, Thomas 84
Green, William 82
Greenford 24
Greensforge 9
Grey, Edward 30
Grey, Reginald of Ruthyn 38
Griffiths, Bill 156
Groome, John 48,66
Groom, Robert 96
Groom, William 95
Guest, Elizabeth 109
Gunpowder Plot 52
Gyfford, Peter 62,63
Gyldon, Thomas 68
Gypsies 65,112
Gylis, William 48
Hacklett 98
Hakins, Rebecca 75
Hakins, Thomas 56
Halesowen 24,89
Halfmeadow 98,115
Hall, Elizabeth 111
Hall, Sarah 124
Hallam, B. 141
Hallon 12 13,14,18,24,45,51,62 88ff,96,99,121,157,175,176,178
Hallon Castle 12,13,14,176
Hallon More 99
Hallonsford 12,176
Hallons Yard 98
Hamilton-Russell, Eustace S. 157
Hancox, James 122
Hand, Margaret 111

Harley, R. 150
Hardwicke, Richard 95
Hardwicke, William 10,12,13,14,16, 18,44,100,101,176
Hardwicke's Mill 107
Harley, Thomas 51
Harness Pendant 32
Harper, Widow 111
Harries, Thomas 95
Harrieys 98
Harris Meadow 98
Harris, Widow 111
Hartlebrough 76
Hartlebury 20,88,90,91,117,152,156
Hartlebury Brickyard 117
Haslewood, Dorothy 97
Haslewood, Francis 97
Haslewood, Richard 97
Haslewood, Thomas 84
Haslewood, William 50
Hastings, Ada 19,24
Hastings, Henry 19,38
Hastings, John 19,38
Hastings, Julian 19,38
Hatton, Francis 66
Hatton, Richard 66
Hatton, Roger 66
Hawkers 112
Hay, Colonel 53
Hayes Bank 53,54
Hayncs, Thomas 109
Hayward, John 48
Head 80
Head, Charles 118
Hedges, cutting of 23
Helga's Cafe 158
Hemp 23,79,86
Hermitage 31,92,115

211

Index

Hewitt, W. 148
Heynes, John 96
Heyns, William 47
Hiberno-Norse 10
Higford 75
Higgins, Widow 111
Higgs, William 111
Highley 28,37
Hill, Mary 111
Hill, Roger 30
Hillforts 5,6,7,8
Hilton 20,79,81,82,86,90, 91,96,117,131,142
Hilton Brickyard 117,202
Hilton Bridge 118
Hilton Brook 118
Hilton Green 82,96
Hinckes, Theodosia 39
Hirons, Tommy 156
Hitchcocke(s) John 41,42,47, 51,73,93
Hitchcocks, William 51
Hobbins 20,146,158
Hoccom, Mary 111
Hoccum, William 68
Hodgmans Meadow 96
Hodgkins, James 112
Hokcombe/Hoccum 21,90,95,199
Holdgate 37
Holland, Job 112
Hollow Way 51
Home Guard 162
Hoord, John 47
Hoorde, Thomas 30,87
Hopes, the 92
Hoppett, Isaac 124
Hopstone 84
Horse Racing 131
Hoskins, W. G. 3
Hwicce 11

Hoskins, W.G. 3
Hue and cry 67
Hunter's Bridge 118,119
Hunting 29,47,82,140
Huntingdon, Earl of 19,38
Hwicce 11
Ice Age 4
Ilkley 5
Industrial Revolution 101,102
Inventory 93,94,95
Iron Age 5f,6,7,8
Ironwork, decorative 27,28,29,37
Ivory, Barbara 88
Jannes, William 47
Jasper, Elizabeth 84
Jasper, John 84
Jellico, Joseph 96
John Groome's Orphanage 161
Jones, Abraham 68
Jones, Ann 68
Jones, Captain 88
Jones, Daniel 148
Jones, Edith 13
Jones, Edward 56
Jones, J. 150
Jones, J. T. 150
Jones, Moses 96
Jones, Roger 13
Jones, William 68
Jugmetrot, John 56
Jymetrot, Alice 68
Kentish Tracery 26,175
King, Ann 53
King, William 53
Kingslow 20,21,96,149
Kingslow Common 84
Kingslow, William de 21
Kinnersley, Mr 64

Index

Kyngeslowe, Roger de 103
Lacon, Francis 80
Lacon, Sir Francis 67
Lacon, Sir Thomas 44
Lake Lapworth 4
Lambert, Jack 163
Lamp Meadow 42
Lampas Gate 42
Land Army 161
Langford, H. 150
Langton, Bishop 24
Laszlo, Philip de 164
Law, Elizabeth 110
Lawley, Elizabeth 111
Lea, Richard 178
Lead Token 49
Lee, Humphrey 30
Lee, Miss 161
Lee, Mr 57
Leese, Sir Oliver 163,164,165,166,167,168,169
Leicester-Warren, Cuthbert 165
Leicester-Warren, Hilda 165
Leicester-Warren, John 165
Leicester-Warren, Margaret 163,164,165,166, 167,168,
Leighton, Sir Edward 70
Leighton, Joyce 62
Leofric, Earl 14, 18,23
Leveson, Walter 69,73
Lewis, Benjamin 123
Lewis, J. 150
Lewis, Widow 111
Library, Worfield 124
Lichfield 24,25,80
Lichfield Consistory Court 81
Lilshull Hill 59
Lime 86
Lion 170

Little Chapel Leasow 26
Little Meadow 98
Littleford 82
Littleford, Richard 95
Littlegain 3,6,7,114,201
Lloyd, Edith 123
Lloyd, Fred 123
Lloyd, H. G. 150
Lloyd, John 80
Lloyd, Lewis 75
Lloyd, PC 112
Lloyd, William 122
Lloyd-Acton, C. 150
Lloyd & Parker Charity 122, 124,138
Locke, Beaufoy 112
Locke, Elijah 112
Locke, Unity 112
Lockett, H. 150
Lollsticks/Lollysticks 44,51,97
Lollysticke Land 73
Lomas, William 142
London 76
Lords of the Manor 38
L'Oste Brown 148
Lovell, James 112
Lovell, Major 112
Lowe, The 20,50,115
Lowe Bridge 115
Lowe, Thomas 66,115
Lower Hall 25,37,43,51,80,88,104, 165,175
Loy, Edward 111
Ludstone Hall 87
Lye, Sir John 40,51,121
Lythall, Humphrey 68
Macadam 114
Macmichael, Joseph 107
Macmichael, William 107

Index

Macnamara, Conner 114
Madeley, Isaac 95
Madras 88
Malvern, St Mary's Church 23
Mapp, Jeremiah 142,143
Mapp, Mrs 161
Mapp, William 162
Marrall, John 73,76
Martindale, C. 123
Marshall, James 84
Maslin 79
Mason, Mary 143
Masserdine 14,176
Massey, John 95
Massie's Land 51
Matilda 13
Mattocks, Thomas 110
Maynard, Robert 66
McClellan, William 111
Meare Bank 115
Meer/Mere Pit 115
Mere Pool 178
Meredith 108
Meredith, Alfred 141
Meredith, Charles 142
Meredith, Richard 110
Metes and bounds of the Manor 20
Memory Belt 10
Men's Club 146
Mesolithic 4
Metes and bounds 19,38
Migration 65,76
Mill Close 104
Mill Croft 98
Mill Parocke 105
Millingchamp, Hester 103
Mills 81,82,102ff
Mills, Thomas 96

Millens, William 56
Monks 23
Montgomery, Bernard 167
Montgomery, Hugh de 18, 24
Montgomery, Roger de 18,24
Moore, Rebecca 39
More MP 108
Morfe 82,95
Morfe Common 84
Morfe, Forest of 17,29ff,36, 46ff,64,82,86,195
Moore, Stanley 157,167
Morris, A. E. 150
Morris, J. H. 150
Morris, Thomas 130
Morrison, Mrs 146,147
Mortgage of the Manor 97
Morville Church 131
Morville door 28,37
Mothers Union 152
Mountbatten, 167,168
Moyelyss 98
Muncorn 79
Munslow 37
Murphy, N. T. P. 144
Muster 55
Mutland Green 82,96
Mutlands Meadow 99
Napoleonic Wars 108
Napoleonic Wars, Prisoners of 130
National School 121ff
Neale, Henry 112
Neale, Mr 161
Nedge, the 97
Neolithic 4,5
Nevill, Sir Henry 38
Nevill, Sir Thomas 97
Neville 38

Index

Neville, Edward 38
Neville, Sir George 38
Neville, Sir Thomas 97
New, Robert 13
Newe, John 73
Newe, William 58
Newport 64
Newton 21,26,88,95,118ff,181,203
Newton Chapel 26
Newton, John 73,76
Newton Meadow 98
Newton, William 57
Nicholas 92
Nicholas, E. P. 123
Nicholas, Elizabeth 110
Nicholl, Thomas 48
Nicholls, William 110
Nock, John 81
Norfolk, John, Duke of 38
Norton 76,143,148
Nun Brook 6,9,174
Ohara, James 114
Old Club Room 124,146,175
Old Forest Lodge 30,141
Oil Mill 105
Old Heath 59
Old House 53,60,143
Old Lodge 30,114,141
Old Lodge Farm 141
Old Vicarage ,175
Oldfield, James 95
Oldington 11,18,21,92,180
Omnibus 153
Onions, J. H. 150
Organ 41
Ormerod, Mr 123
Oscott Meadow 98
Oswestry 6,11,53

Oulton, Sister 151
Ouseley 100
Pace, T. 150
Packhorse bridge 106
Painter, John 110
Painter, Susan 111
Painter, Thomas 111
Palmer, William 58
Papal Bull 24,32
Paper mill 103
Park, Mr Justice 130
Parker, H. F. 162
Parker, Joseph 96
Parker, Thomas 122
Parkhill 99
Parsons, John 79
Parsons, Samuel 64
Parton, Mary 143
Passport 75
Pateman 111
Pattens 91
Pattingham 149,152
Patton, General 159
Pemberton, Henry 80
Pendlestone Mill 36
Pendrill, William 60
Penny, Edward I silver 32
Pepperhill 43
Perie 98
Perkins, Lennie 161
Pernum, John 58
Perry, John 51
Perry, William 51,57
Perry and Phillips 143
Perton 80,98
Phillips, Thomas 103
Phillips, Joseph 111
Picture Doors 26ff,38,175

215

Index

Pigeons 81
Piggott, Robert 84
Pillingshall 98
Pinches, Thomas 112
Piper 108
Piper, Joshua, 93
Piper, Samuel 69,73
Piper, Widow 111
Pit alignments 5
Plague 76
Plate Meadow 99
Pooler, Mary 111
Poor 65ff,75,76,109ff
Portable Antiquities Scheme 3
Potatoes 81
Potter, Humphrey 42
Pound 14,174,176
Powell, William 114
Poyner, Andrew 96
Pratt, Edward 82
Pratt, William 112
Pratt, Jonas 96
Preice 98
Price, H. 150
Price, Jane 111
Price, W. N. 150
Prisoners, Scottish 60
Prisoners of War 159,161
Prize fighting 152
Pugh, E. 150
Pugh, John 61
Pugh, Molly 115
Puleston, Susannah 74
Pumping Station 171
Pursehouse, W. 150
Purton 180
Pytt, Thomas 42,50
Quarries 114ff

Quatford 11,24,76,84
Quartering 56ff
Quatt 30,50,157
Quoits 146,152
Rabbit Run 116
Rabbits 31,152
Racecourse 146
RAF Bridgnorth 157,158,181
Railways 118, 152,153
Randall, John 101
Rape, oil seed 82,105
Raworth, Robert 88
Raynold 47
Recreation Room 146ff
Rectors 36,37
Rectory 24,25,37,80
Red Cross 147,161
Reformation 40ff
Reformers 108
Regarders 30,47,48
Richards, James 96
Richards, John 96
Ridley Elizabeth 84
Ridley, George 162
Ridley, Samuel 84
Ridley, William 95
Rindleford 21,79,95,115,176
Rindleford Mill 82,105ff,176,178
Roads 9,82,112ff
Roads, Nathaniel 96
Robinson, Charles 109
Robinson, Elizabeth 110
Robinson, John 157
Robinson, Mrs 165
Rochelle, Catherine 148
Rochelle, Jack 170
Rofe, John 79
Rogers, E. 150

Index

Rogers, Thomas 111
Rogers, Widow 111
Romans 9
Roman Brooch 16
Roman Coin 16
Romsall, Agnes 102
Rookery Cottages 173
Roughton 9,21,31,82,84,86,90,105, 124ff,196
Roughton Chapel 26,43
Roughton Grammar School 124ff
Roundabout Farm 131,141
Rowley 10,18,21,96,99,102
Rowley, Anne 89
Rowley, Elizabeth 92
Rowley Farm 89
Rowley, Francis 52
Rowley, John 53,92
Rowley, Richard 53
Rowley, Roger 42,52,53,73,104
Rowley, Samuel 131
Rowley/Rowlowe, Stephen 51,56
Rowley, Thomas 58
Rowley, Widow 111
Rowley, William 52,95
Rowley Ford 99
Rowley House 53
Rowley Mill 98,102
Rowlowe, Thomas de 13
Rowlowe, William de 102
Rudge ,174,197
Rudge Heath 84,197,201
Rupert, Prince 53
Rushbury 37
Russell Close 158
Ryll, William atte 31
Sadler, John 57
Sadler/Sadyllar, Nicholas 50

Sadler/Saddler, Richard 129
Sadler, Thomas 73
Sadler, William 97
St James Hospital 48
St James Priory 48
St John's Ambulance 147
St Peter's Church 14,24ff,42ff, 128ff, 174,175
St Peter's Well 15,66,176
Salt 6
Sandy Valley 114
Sargeant, J. S. 150
Sargeant, R.T. 150
Saxon Period 10ff
Sceatta 10
School 121
Scott, Joseph 84
Seal 32
Sedley, Elizabeth 38
Sedley, William 38
Seedhouse, Arthur 148,156,157
Seedhouse, Henry 156,157
Seedhouse, Iain 157
Seedhouse, Mike 156, 157
Selions 22,79
Severn Hall 53
Shalcrosse, Anne 89
Shalcrosse, John 89
Shalcrosse, Richard 89
Shaw, Thomas 96
Shenstone, William 89
Sherriffhales 74
Sherwood 109,110
Sheynton 122
Shifnal 54,59,74
Shipley 24
Shooting buttes 54
Shrewsbury 58ff
Silvington 37

Index

Simon de Montfort 19
Slater, Thomas 96
Slater, William 92
Slim, Lieutenant General 167
Smallpox 92
Smethyman,/Smithyman Rowland 82
Smith, Francis 89
Smith, George 38,91
Smith, John 96
Smith, Roger 26
Smith Stokes, Michael 131
Smith, William 89
Smythe/Smith 44,81
Smyth, William 56
Sonde 20,50,54,96
Sond, William 50
Sotherne, Hugh 48,64
South Sea Bubble 89
Southwell, Hannah, 111
Sowdley/Soudley 96
Sowdley Common 84
Sowdley/Soudley Pit 115
Sowdley Wood 178
Spindle Whorl 49
Spinning 107,177
Spring Valley 114
Stableford 9,92,96,115,143ff,179
Stableford Bridge 117
Stanlowe 21,92,96
Stanlowe, John of 22
Stanmore 21,157
Stanmore Country Park 158
Stanmore Grove 90,112,157
Stanmore Industrial Estate 158,181
Stanton Lacy 76
Stanton Long 37
Stapleford 21,179
Starkey, E. H. 150

Staunton, George 66
Stiche, Widow 58
Stinton, Mr 171
Stinton, Mrs 161
Stocks 65ff
Stockhall 66
Stockins 99
Stockton 143
Stokes, Miss 29
Stone picking 115
Stratford 11
Strays 23
Sundial 170
Sutton Maddock 24
Swancote 4,9,21,81,86,88,199
Swanimote court 29ff
Tabley 158,164
Taft, Fred 153
Taft, Harry 154
Taillour, Stephen the 31
Taillour, Thomas the 31
Talbot, Elizabeth 88
Talbot, Sir John 43,175
Talbott 37,80
Talbott Cottages 180
Tantram, Charles 123
Tarrant, Charles 123
Tarrant, Henry 156
Tasley 84
Taylor, Frank 32,44,49,67,68,91,130
Taylor, John 162
Taylor, Joseph 95
Taylor, Mary 84
Taylor, Richard 38,84
Taylor, Robert 51
Taylor, Samuel 111
Taylor, Thomas 66,122
Taylor, William 109,162

Index

Teague, E. 150
Telford, Thomas 117
Tennis Club 152
Tettenhall 152
Thatcher, Alfred 142
Thatcher, Heather 123
Therne, John 47
Theyne, John 102
Thomas, S. 150
Thomason, Samuel 95
Tithe disputes 80ff
Tithes 37,43ff,80ff
Titterstone Clee 6
Toft, the 66
Token, Lead 49
Toll gate 114
Toll house 112,113,114
Tooth, Maria 111
Town Meadow 121
Towner, Thomas 141
Townshend, Thomas 80,81
Toye 115
Tracy 108
Trainers 60
Tucke, William 48
Tull, Jethro 80
Turner, Frank 152,153
Turner R. 150
Turner, Rebecca 153
Turner, Rev. T. W. 124,125,126,127
Turnips 80,81,82, 86
Turnock, John 123
Turnpike 112,113,114,115,116,117
Tyror, Thomas 57
Underhill, Roger 47
Underhill/, Undrell, Thomas 30,51
VAD Hospital 147148,149,150, 161
Vagrants 64,65,66,112

Valentine, Mary 111
Vallance, Joan 66
Vane, John 73
Vaughan, Benjamin 92
Vaughan, Mary 92
Vaughan, Thomas 92
Vernon 57
Vicarage, endowments of 37
Vicarage 25,175,176
Vicars 36
Vickers, Valentine 84,130
Viroconium 9
Voluntary Aid, Scheme 147,148
Wadlow, Harry 142
Wainwright, Mrs 170
Wainwright, R. H. 150
Walford, Grace 97
Walford, Roger 97
Walker's land 98
Walker, John 73,79
Walker, Roger 21,51,105
Walker, Samuel 95
Walker, Susan 66
Walker, William 95
Wall Brook 9
Wall, F. 150
Wallen 96
Walls 5,6,7,8,174
Walston 15,50,121,176
Walton, Roger 68
Walton, Thomas 92
Wannerton, Alice 62
Wannerton, Jane 44,62,63
Wannerton, John 44,62,63
WARAG 158
War Memorial 151
Warter's land 98
Warter, Eleanor 66

Index

Warter, Elizabeth 92
Warter, Jerome 66
Warter, John 73
Warter, Samuel 92
Warter, Thomas 92
Warter, William 88
Wash Leather Mill 105
Weaver, Johanna 66
Webb, John 119
Weights 67
Weirs 81
Welsby, T. 150
Weld, Sir John 38,97
Wells, Richard 91
Wem 53
Wermotts 73,97
Wesley, Wellesley 141
Weston Under Redcastle 6
Wheel Bridge 117
Wheel Inn/Wheel at Worfield 1,113,131
Wheelwright 156
Whipping 75,76
Whipping Post 65,75,76
Whitbroke, William 96
White, Richard 84
White/wheat Furlong 99,176
Whitmore 52
Whitmore, Mary 38
Whitmore, Sir George 38,97
Whitmore, Sir William 38,52,82,87,88,97,104
Whitmore, T. 53,84,108,118
Whitmore, Thomas Charlton 38
Whittimere 87
Whorwood 44
Wilcox, Bill 154
Wilcox, George Wilcox, 154
Wilcox, John Whitefoot 154
Wilcox, Mrs 158

Wilde, William 112
Williams, Fitz 108
Williams, John 82
Williams, Mrs 115
Willmore Hill 96,201
Willoughby, Mr 123
Wilson, Mrs W. O. 148
Wilson, Prudence 110
Wilson, Richard Sidney 149,173
Winnescote/Winscote 68,92,95,181
Winscote Hills 118
Winter's Place 51
Winter's Yard 98
Wystanesiner 31
Wodehouse, Eleanor 143
Wodehouse, Ernest, Armine 143,144
Wodehouse,, Henry E. 143
Wodehouse, P. G. 143,144,145,179
Woghbrokesheth 36
Wolpheresford 12, 18
Wolrich, Dorothy 48
Wolrich, Margaret 74,75
Wolriche, Humphrey 30,47
Wolrych, Thomas 64
Wolstone 15,20
Wolverhampton 56,80
Women's Institute 152
Wood, Samuel 117
Wood, William 90,91
Woodcroft 97
Woodward 30
Woolley, Thomas 66,73,122
Worcester, Battle of 60
Worfe Bridge 114
Worfelden 11
Worfield 1,17,21,50,88,92,175,176,177
Worfield, Roger de 23
Worfield Charter 19,34

220

Index

Worfield Church 23,24,25,26,121,128,131
Worfield Gardens 168
Worfield Grammar School 124,125,126,127
Worfield Library 124
Worfield Manor 17,18,19,20,21,22,23,88,97
Worfield Mill 104,165
Worfield Parish 17
Worfield School 121,122,123,124
Worfield United Charity 124
Worfield VAD 147,148,149
Worfield Yard 96,99
Worfruna Garage 154
Workhouse 109,110,171
World War 1 147,148,149,150,151,163
Worrall 92
Worrall, Thomas 95
Worthington, Michael 120
Wotton, John 30
Woundale 141
Wrekin 6
Wrenic fitz Meuric 19
Wright, widow 95
Wrottesley, Joyce 62,69,70,71,72,73
Wrottesley, Walter 62,69,70,71,72,73
Wrottesley Hall 62
Wulfhere 14
Wulstan 23
Wulfric Spot 12,24
Wyken 1,11,18,21,80,88, 105,115, 154,155,173
Wyken Bridge 115
Wyken Farm 141,151
Wyken Garage 154,155,158
Wyken Green 54
Wyken Mill 80,105
Wyken, Rectory of 80
Wynneswanstone, John de 13
Wynneswanstone, Alice 13

Wystansiner, Edith of 31
Yate, John 73,183
Yate, Thomas atte 21
Yates, W. E. 149,150
Yeat, Hugh 66,74
Yeat, Mary 66,74
Yeekin, Jane 68
Yeekin, Richard 68
Yeldon's Yard 51
Young, Captain 57